WRITING ON THE SOCIAL NETWORK

WRITING ON THE SOCIAL NETWORK

Digital Literacy Practices in Social Media's First Decade

AMBER M. BUCK

UTAH STATE UNIVERSITY PRESS
Logan

Published by Utah State University Press
An imprint of University Press of Colorado
1580 North Logan Street, Suite 660
PMB 39883
Denver, Colorado 80203-1942

 The University Press of Colorado is a proud member of
the Association of University Presses.

The University Press of Colorado is a cooperative publishing enterprise supported,
in part, by Adams State University, Colorado State University, Fort Lewis College,
Metropolitan State University of Denver, University of Alaska Fairbanks, University
of Colorado, University of Denver, University of Northern Colorado, University of
Wyoming, Utah State University, and Western Colorado University.

∞ This paper meets the requirements of the ANSI/NISO Z39.48-1992 (Permanence of
Paper).

ISBN: 978-1-64642-401-6 (paperback)
ISBN: 978-1-64642-402-3 (ebook)
ISBN: 978-1-64642-403-0 (hardcover)
https://doi.org/10.7330/9781646424023

Library of Congress Cataloging-in-Publication Data

Names: Buck, Amber M., 1980– author.
Title: Writing on the social network : digital literacy practices in social media's first
    decade / Amber M. Buck.
Description: Logan : Utah State University Press, [2023] | Includes bibliographical refer-
    ences and index.
Identifiers: LCCN 2023009768 (print) | LCCN 2023009769 (ebook) | ISBN
    9781646424016 (paperback) | ISBN 9781646424030 (hardcover) | ISBN 9781646424023
    (ebook)
Subjects: LCSH: English language—Rhetoric—Study and teaching. | English
    language—Rhetoric—Computer-assisted instruction. | Online social networks—Social
    aspects—Longitudinal studies. | Multimedia communications—Social
    aspects—Longitudinal studies. | Computer literacy—Social aspects.
Classification: LCC PE1404 .B7785 2023 (print) | LCC PE1404 (ebook) | DDC
    808/.0420285—dc23/eng/20230417
LC record available at https://lccn.loc.gov/2023009768
LC ebook record available at https://lccn.loc.gov/2023009769

Cover photo: Diego Cervo/iStock

To my parents and grandparents.
I would not be where I am without you.

CONTENTS

Acknowledgments   ix

Introduction: Studying the First Decade of Social Media   3

1. Digital Literacies on Social Media Platforms   21

2. Studying Social Media Platforms   47

3. Negotiating Audience Across Platforms   72

4. Managing Data and Interfaces   113

5. Managing Identity in Professional Spaces   149

6. Beyond Social Media's First Decade   172

Notes   193
References   195
Index   205

ACKNOWLEDGMENTS

As a longitudinal project, this book has existed in many different iterations, and this research has spanned a decade, three states and three different institutions. From its beginnings at the University of Illinois at Urbana–Champaign, I would like to thank first and foremost my dissertation committee who helped shape this project: Gail E. Hawisher, Paul Prior, Spencer Schaffner, and Lisa Nakamura. Their insights on writing research, writing technologies, and social media were invaluable and shaped this project in its early stages. Gail Hawisher was the perfect dissertation chair, asking questions that allowed me to explore these issues deeper and always offering a supportive word when I doubted the project. In so many ways, this work owes its foundation to the Center for Writing Studies at the University of Illinois and its faculty, students, staff, and alumni.

The research contained in this book was generously supported through grants of both funds and time by the Center for Writing Studies, Department of English, and College of Liberal Arts & Sciences at the University of Illinois; the College of Staten Island at the City University of New York; and the Department of English and the College of Arts & Sciences at the University of Alabama. George Thompson's advice on academic publishing, gentle encouragement, and insights about this project were also invaluable. Special thanks also to Allison Mollenkamp for research assistance and analysis of this project's later stages at the University of Alabama.

I would also like to thank the team at Utah State University Press/ University Press of Colorado, especially Rachael Leavy for the attention and care she gave to this project, her editorial suggestions, and her patience and generosity as this book slowly progressed through many, many drafts. Thanks also to the Editorial Board of the University Press of Colorado for its crucial feedback and support. I will be forever grateful for the sharp insights and suggestions of the anonymous peer reviewers of this project, who provided essential feedback that shaped this work. Almost all of the work at Utah State happened during a global pandemic, and I'm grateful for the entire publication team, the Editorial Board, and the peer reviewers for keeping this project going during extraordinary times.

Many, many people supported this project in less tangible but even more important ways. First, thank you to my family: my parents Tammy Brubaker and Kenneth Buck for their unwavering support of my education that made most of this work possible. My sister Amanda Livingston was always ready with a listening ear and a word of encouragement. Theo Plothe watched me write many drafts of the various versions of this project and always reminded me not to take myself too seriously. The CWS community at Illinois provided support and early feedback on this work, especially Hannah Bellwoar, Christa Olson, Samantha Looker, Patrick Berry, Martha Webber, Cory Holding, Andrea Olinger, Heather Blain Vorhies, and Lauren Marshall Bowen. In Tuscaloosa, friends who are essentially family helped sustain me through this project's later stages: Cindy Tekobbe, KellyAnn Griffiths, Madison Parks, and Chris Cowles. Through shared meals, shared projects, and welcome distractions, they were always ready to celebrate a small milestone or help through a setback. Thanks especially to Cindy Tekobbe for the supportive feedback, coffee, and company during many, many writing sessions.

I also want to acknowledge the coffee shop spaces in which I wrote drafts of the words contained here: the Urbana Free Library and Caffe Paradiso in Urbana, Illinois; several Starbucks cafes in Manhattan, but especially the location at 5th Avenue and 35th Street next to the CUNY Grad Center; the 24-hour Au Bon Pain at Union Station in Washington, DC; and UPerk and Monarch Espresso Bar in Tuscaloosa, Alabama.

And finally, I am especially grateful to the research participants who devoted their time and whose writing and online activity shaped this research project. Their generosity and their willingness to share their online lives with me made this work possible.

WRITING ON THE SOCIAL NETWORK

Introduction

STUDYING THE FIRST DECADE OF SOCIAL MEDIA

From 2004 until 2016, social network platforms grew from niche spaces online where individuals of similar interests would gather to massive platforms that connect billions of users. Under development through a variety of forms and incarnations throughout the early 2000s, with influences from sites like SixDegrees, Asian Avenue, BlackPlanet, and MiGente (boyd & Ellison, 2007), the impact of these websites on American society and culture became extraordinarily visible in 2010, which can be considered the year the social network site became part of mainstream American culture. While early sites Myspace and Friendster were on the decline, the most popular social network site, Facebook, gained 500,000,000 followers in July of 2010. Twitter, a newer social network site especially popular with journalists and celebrities, had an average of 65,000 tweets per week, culminating in record traffic to the site during the 2010 World Cup. Much of the attention paid to social network sites, aside from the focus on Twitter connected to political movements, emphasized Facebook. In April, David Kirkpatrick published *The Facebook Effect*, a thorough history of the company. Aaron Sorkin's film *The Social Network*, also about the founding of Facebook based primarily on Ben Mezrich's 2009 book, *The Accidental Billionaires*, was nominated for eight Academy Awards and won three for Best Original Screenplay, Best Editing, and Best Original Score. *Time* also named Facebook founder Mark Zuckerberg as 2010 Person of the Year, "for connecting more than half a billion people and mapping the social relations among them, for creating a new system of exchanging information and for changing how we live our lives" (Grossman, 2010).

Not all of this attention was positive, however. A backlash to changes in the way privacy settings were configured in December 2009 grew to a breaking point in the spring of 2010. This situation was caused by Facebook's announcement of its new Connect feature on April 21, 2010, that allowed a single sign-on for Facebook and sites across the web,

https://doi.org/10.7330/9781646424023.c000

which drew not only media criticism and public panic, but also separate complaints filed by Senator Charles Schumer and the Electronic Privacy Information Center to the Federal Trade Commission. In addition, Henry Joost and Ariel Schulman's documentary *Catfish*, released shortly before Sorkin's film, also commented on anxiety over the nature of identity representation and authenticity on Facebook and similar sites. Jaron Lanier published his book, *You Are Not a Gadget*, in resistance to what he saw as an increased reliance on social network sites for communication, and Nicholas Carr wrote *The Shallows*, a larger look at the impact of the internet on cognitive ability and attention.

If 2010 was the year that brought social network sites into the American national consciousness in a sustained way, 2016 demonstrated the long-term social and political consequences of those platforms. Invigorated by the #GamerGate controversy,[1] far-right extremists partnered with Russian-backed hackers, fake-news creators, and Twitter bots to bombard American social media users with disinformation about the 2016 presidential election campaign and its candidates. In February 2018, Special Counsel Robert Mueller indicted 13 Russian nationals and three companies for interfering with the 2016 presidential election, primarily by impersonating Americans and American organizations on social media platforms in order to sow discord and support the candidacy of Donald Trump.

News from a whistleblower of the political data company Cambridge Analytica in early 2018 also brought fresh scrutiny to Facebook's data privacy practices before, during, and after 2016, leading to Facebook founder Mark Zuckerberg's testimony in April of 2018 in front of the Senate Commerce and Judiciary committees. The impact of the Cambridge Analytica revelations and Facebook's data policies with their company partners continue to be felt throughout the industry. Facebook's role in Rohingya refugee crisis, political violence in the Philippines, and its public relations response to ongoing crises draw almost constant criticism as of this writing. Former Facebook data scientist and whistleblower Frances Haugen also brought up many similar concerns through both confidential documents and congressional testimony in 2021.

Along with the presidential election, prominent feminist writers and public figures faced increased harassment on social network sites, including Twitter, leading to a sustained harassment campaign of actress Leslie Jones by right-wing blogger and provocateur Milo Yiannopolos. Lindy West, a prominent feminist blogger and writer, also publicly left Twitter because it was "unusable for anyone but trolls, robots, and dictators" (West, 2017). The publicly traded social network site Twitter celebrated its 10th birthday amid business problems over stagnated usage numbers and a public rumor that Disney had backed out of a purchase offer over Twitter's inability to reduce harassment on the site (Sherman & Frier, 2016).

These incidents and ongoing revelations about the impact of increased surveillance and the use of user data on social media platforms like Facebook have led to increased popular press speculation about social media's future. Despite concerns about misinformation and harassment on social network platforms, however, they also continued to grow. The Pew Internet and American Life project found that in 2016, 79% of all online adults used Facebook, while Twitter reached 24% of all online American adults, with similar numbers for Pinterest (31%), Instagram (32%), and LinkedIn (29%) (Greenwood et al., 2016). Facebook reported 1,150,000,000 active mobile users in December of 2016 (Zephoria, 2016), and Snap, the parent company of Snapchat, continued to expand in preparation for its first public offering, with active daily users of Snapchat exceeding Twitter for the first time. The year 2016 demonstrated that the long-term implications of social network sites could be impactful on public and private lives, yet the sites themselves continued be integrated into more and more aspects of American life, moving from spaces for identity representation and communication to platforms with influence on politics and civic discourse.

The ways that social media has entered into the public consciousness and established itself within the larger media landscape throughout this time period demonstrate the importance of studying social media platforms and their influence on communication, individual literacy and identity practices, and even civic life. From 2006 to 2016, individuals collectively grappled with living lives at least partially online, where personal relationships and civic discourse play out on social platforms. Living a "literate life in the information age" (Selfe & Hawisher, 2004) increasingly means learning to present oneself and one's ideas to a multitude of audiences as well as navigating complex issues of privacy and the management of one's online data. Internet users take advantage of easier ways to share content: engaging in short textual interactions with friends through social media, uploading video to YouTube or images to Instagram, and managing a variety of social events and groups through different kinds of social software. Not only do these literate activities take place on networked computers but they occur on social media platforms stored on commercial websites; content is syndicated in 100 different places, blurring boundaries between work and leisure, friends and strangers, public and private, and online and offline. And these online activities are, in fact, writing. As Regina Duthely (2018) argues in her article about hip hop and digital writing, "As we curate our Twitter timelines, try to get the best shot for our Instagram photos, and try to capture funny moments for Snapchat, we are composing" (p. 359).

José van Dijck (2013) has argued that social media platforms and the activities in which individuals participated on these services evolved together. While many social media sites began as general places to communicate with friends and contacts and share creative content, through their development, these services perpetuated and reinforced certain habits and ways of being among their users. "Friending," "following," and "liking" are now specific rhetorical acts, recorded within social media platforms. As van Dijck described, checking in on friends, sharing vacation photos, and scribbling notes used to be private, ephemeral acts. Through social media, though, these activities are now "formalized inscriptions" (p. 7), tracked and traced, logged in databases for posterity and sometimes shared in more public ways to wider online audiences. The endless parade of popular press stories reporting the latest individual fired for online transgressions and the public service announcements warning teens to think before uploading pictures demonstrate that the new boundaries are not yet settled. Our definitions of authorship, audience, and participation change with these communication practices, creating crucial questions for language, literacy, rhetoric, and education.

PURPOSE OF THIS BOOK

The advent and growth of social network sites has also meant a growth in academic research on social media in a variety of fields. Writing researchers, for example, have noted the prominence of writing in digital environments in the work they do outside of the classroom. Andrea Lunsford et al. (2013) followed undergraduate students for 4 years of college through the Stanford Study of Writing. They found that not only are students writing more, but they are also effective in crafting and communicating specific messages to specific audiences. As Lunsford and her colleagues found in their study, 38% of the writing that the student participants completed happened outside of the classroom, and most of this writing happened online. Similarly, a study by Jeff Grabill, Bill Hart-Davidson, and their colleagues in the Writing in Digital Environments research group found that first-year college students engage in digital writing most frequently, primarily on mobile phones, social network sites, and email. The study found that this type of writing is ubiquitous, noting the centrality of digital media in students' writing outside of the classroom (Grabill, 2010). At the end of the first decade of social media, Stephanie Vie (2018) reported that social media platforms had "changed writing," giving writers more choices "thanks to the broadened reach, greater rhetorical velocity, and wider and more varied audiences prevalent in social media" (p. 122), and that writing had changed university classrooms as well.

Indeed, the changes in the way information is presented and accessed on the internet in the past decade have altered the nature of writing, participation, and learning in online spaces. A study from Pew Research Center's Internet and American Life Project in 2010 found young adults (ages 18–29) to be the most active in managing their identities and data online; the report claimed that reputation management had "become a defining feature of online life for many internet users, especially the young" (Madden & Smith, 2010). As those young adults continued to grow alongside social media platforms, their role in the personal and professional lives of individuals of all ages expanded. While social media integrated itself into individuals' daily lives, the events I mentioned above from 2016 demonstrated that they also had a great deal of impact in social and political events. From the Iranian protests in 2009 and the Arab Spring to the 2014 protests in Ferguson, Missouri that expanded the #BlackLivesMatter movement, social media platforms have also been used to influence public discourse. The use of social media for protest and organizing, for spreading disinformation, and for weaponized harassment campaigns have also impacted world events. What information an individual shares online, with whom, as well as what information is deemed credible and accurate are some of the most important questions for writing, rhetoric, and citizenry.

Writing on the Social Network takes a historical look at what I am labeling as the first decade of social media, roughly from 2006 to 2016. I argue that the events discussed above provide an opportunity to look back on the first decade of social media use in order to consider user experiences and digital literacy practices that developed on these sites. Studies of user practices on social media have inevitably focused on short periods of time, a few days or weeks, and have provided excellent snapshots of use within that time period (DeLuca, 2015; Ellison et al. 2014; Marwick, 2008; Marwick & boyd, 2011, 2014; Walls, 2017). These studies have been crucial to considering the ways individuals negotiate specific aspects of different social media sites, yet Facebook in 2007 was not the same site as Facebook in 2018.

To that end, *Writing on the Social Network* uses a longitudinal approach for studying digital literacy practices on social network sites. This project reports on qualitative case studies I conducted between 2010 and 2016, both pivotal years in social media history, through which I examined the literate activity that individuals engaged in on social media. Through this research, I explore how the literate activity I observed on social network sites coalesced around three areas crucial for writing in digital environments: (a) a heightened awareness of audience and an ability to tailor messages to specific audiences; (b) an understanding of how personal data is collected and circulated in online spaces as well as ways to subvert that data collection; and (c) a means through which to utilize the first two skills for self-promotion and self-presentation in both personal and professional settings.

I contend that social media platforms represent important locations where the different influences on writing discussed by literacy scholars become visible, laying bare the influence of social, economic, and structural forces that shape literacy practices. A close study of the rich literate practices that individuals have engaged in on social network sites over the first decade of their use allows us to better understand the roles these sites play in shaping current digital literacy practices over time. This introduction defines some key terms used throughout this book, provides an overview of social media in its first decade, and outlines the remaining chapters.

DEFINING SOCIAL MEDIA

As social media research has developed, the terms used for social media sites have also changed. "Social media" can be seen as an umbrella term that refers to internet-based sites and services that have characteristics Tim O'Reilly (2005) called "Web 2.0": services with many-to-many communication configurations where individuals can share content they create and connect with other users on the site. José van Dijck (2013) divided social media sites into four categories: *social network sites* (SNSs) that emphasize interpersonal content, including Facebook and Twitter; *user-generated content* (UGC) services like YouTube and Flickr; *trading and marketing sites* (TMSs) such as eBay and Groupon; and finally, *play and game sites* (PGS), including social games like FarmVille (p. 8).

danah boyd and Nicole Ellison (2007) used the term "social network sites," which they defined as "web-based services that allow individuals to (1) construct a public or semi-public profile within a bounded system, (2) articulate a list of other users with whom they share a connection, and (3) view and traverse their list of connections and those made by others within the system" (para. 4). boyd and Ellison updated their definition in 2013 to include the increased importance of the news feed feature of social network sites:

> A social network site is a *networked communication platform* in which participants (1) have *uniquely identifiable profiles* that consist of user-supplied content, content provided by other users, and/or system-provided data; (2) can *publicly articulate connections* that can be viewed and traversed by others; and (3) can consume, produce, and/or interact with *streams of user-generated content* provided by their connections on the site. (p. 151)

The key features of what boyd and Ellison describe as "social network sites" allow individual users to create profiles, connect with other users through friending and following, and view and explore content uploaded by other users, usually in an aggregated stream like a news feed or timeline. While the term "social media" can apply to a large amount of web content and online communities, from blogging platforms like WordPress, web forums like Reddit, and fan fiction services like Archive of Our Own, social network sites have a narrower focus, but still include a range of sites, from popular services like Facebook and Twitter to sites focused on video content like YouTube, and more niche social network sites like Goodreads, where users share and review book they've read, and Ravelry, a social network site for knitters. boyd and Ellison's definition includes sites that van Dijck (2013) categorized under UGC; while the primary goal of these sites is to share content, they do have social network site elements as well, including profile pages and ways to follow other users' content. The boundaries between them blur a great deal.

In recent years, the term "platform studies" has emerged through which to study social media as well. José van Dijck's (2013) book provided a consideration of social media sites at the level of policy and financial considerations and used the term "platform" to study the impact of these internet companies and services at multiple levels. José van Dijck and Tomas Poell (2016) defined platforms as "online sites that facilitate and organize data streams, economic interactions, and social exchanges between users" (2). Similarly, Dustin Edwards and Bridget Gelms (2018) described platform studies as "the infrastructural layer of computing, a meeting point of hardware, software, and culture." For Edwards and Gelms, platforms are "moving assemblages" of technologies, financial systems, and social and cultural systems.

Writing in 2021, I find the current, and arguably most precise, term for these services is "social media platform." The word "platform" acknowledges the combined assemblage of technologies, companies, policies, and users, and it also understands the fact that many users access these services not from a web page, but from a mobile app or similar device. Yet at the time I conducted this research, boyd and Ellison's 2007, and later their updated 2013, definition of "social network site" was the most precise term to describe the sites I was studying and the services my research participants were using, sites that included a profile, the ability to friend or follow others, and, in most cases, a news feed of updates. I therefore use the term "social media platform" when discussing the social media sites and companies as entities in their current configuration, but I also use the term "social network site" in the context of specific literacy practices of the people I describe here in this book. I use "social *network* sites" rather than the other popular term, "social *networking* sites." boyd and Ellison argue that these services are primarily used to maintain already established relationships, rather than relationship initiation. Hence, "social network site" is a more appropriate term than "social networking site." The literacy practices I emphasize here are primarily from social network sites that fall under van Dijck's more narrow definition, but I also examined practices on sites that fall within van Dijck's category of UGC sites, like YouTube and Flickr, yet meet the qualifications for boyd and Ellison's "social network site" definition.

THE FIRST DECADE OF SOCIAL MEDIA

For this project, I define the first decade of social media as roughly spanning from 2006 to 2016. danah boyd and Nicole Ellison (2007) identify online communities like SixDegrees.com, LiveJournal, BlackPlanet,[2] and MiGente as precursors to social network sites, as online communities centered around specific identities that allowed users to create profiles and connect with friends. Friendster, launched in 2002, is considered by many to be the first social network site, and Myspace was founded in 2003, with Facebook following in 2004 (boyd & Ellison, 2007). Twitter was launched in 2006, which was also the year Facebook introduced its news feed feature, which substantially changed user experience on the site; in September of 2006, Facebook also opened its service beyond users with a .edu email address to anyone over the age of 13. See figure 0.1 for a brief timeline of this first decade of social media.

Alice Marwick (2013) traced the history of social media platforms, and Web 2.0 as a whole, to the technolibertarian ethos of Northern California and Silicon Valley in a way that blended counterculture activism with business culture. Social media can be traced to a number of different influences from this specific time and place, from zines, e-zines,

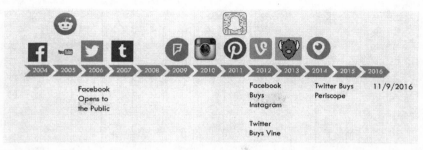

Figure 0.1. The First Decade of Social Media.

and hacker culture to Usenet groups, personal homepages, and finally, blogs. Marwick pointed to Tim O'Reilly's "Web 2.0" conference in 2004 as instrumental in coining the term and branding these new internet companies as different from those that drove the first .com boom and bust of 1997 to 2000, emphasizing "collective intelligence" and "the web as platform" approaches (pp. 63–64). Indeed, many of the first social media sites were launched in that post-bust era, including Friendster in 2002, Myspace and LinkedIn in 2003, and Flickr and Digg in 2004. José van Dijck (2013) notes that Web 2.0 turned websites and online platforms from "offering channels for networked communication to becoming interactive, two-way vehicles for networked sociality" (p. 5). The crowd-sourced orientation of Web 2.0 services was embraced both by the technology industry and the popular press. *Time* named "you" its Person of the Year for 2006, described by journalist Lev Grossman as a gesture to the popularity of social media platforms, and the crowdsourcing and user-generated content practices of Web 2.0. The year 2006, then, represents the year that social network services became a genre unto themselves that had wide adoption within the mainstream United States.

By 2010, Marwick noted, early enthusiasm over the idea of social media startups and the power of crowdsourcing had faded as the term "Web 2.0" gave way to the broader, catchall term "social media," as well as the dominance of more established companies like Facebook. As noted in the introduction of this chapter, Mark Zuckerberg replaced "you" as *Time*'s Person of the Year in 2010, an acknowledgment of the maturation and establishment of social media and its consolidation into an ever-smaller number of established platforms with large user bases. This consolidation continued over the next several years, as many smaller social media platforms folded, and others were bought out by larger services, such as Facebook's purchase of Instagram in 2012 and of WhatsApp in 2014.

Scholars and technology critics have always touted social media's potential for collective organization and social change, from crowdsourcing (Shirky, 2008) to protest through the Arab Spring (Tufekci, 2017). By 2014, two events in the United States demonstrated its impact on social movements and public discourse. First, the protests against police brutality in Ferguson, Missouri, that grew into the #BlackLivesMatter movement were organized, expanded, and discussed on platforms like Twitter, which was central for documenting events in Ferguson and raising awareness about police brutality (Freelon et al., 2016; Tynes, et al., 2016). Also in 2014, the online harassment campaign #GamerGate demonstrated how coordinated efforts across platforms could also fuel online harassment (Trice & Potts, 2018). Both events took social media platforms from tools for personal identity representation to tools for mobilization that impacted American civic and public life.

I mark the end of the first decade of social media on November 9, 2016. The day after the 2016 presidential election in the United States represents a change in the way that the mainstream press covered and considered social media platforms. While internet scholars, digital rhetoricians, privacy advocates, and other experts have long raised concerns about the impact of social media platforms on society and culture, this event demonstrated in a large way how online activities can impact offline global and political events. The impact of political polarization, data modeling, surveillance, and disinformation and misinformation campaigns, as noted in the introduction of this chapter, grew throughout the decade and have forced many social media users, as well as elected representatives, to question social media's role in our lives. While it is currently unclear if social media companies will face greater regulation, there is no other date than November 9, 2016, that represents a more definitive shift in mainstream public attitudes about social media platforms. While many of the innovations and changes that social media platforms have taken up since 2016 had been building before this point, the year 2016 represents a tipping point for many of these changes as well.

STUDYING SOCIAL MEDIA PLATFORMS

Scholarship on social media expanded during the first decade of social media from studies of individual user practices to a more global view of the impact of social network sites, considering their impact on politics and civic discourse, activism, relationships, and media industries. As van Dijick (2013) has described, social media platforms are assemblages, "both techno-cultural constructs and socioeconomic structures" (p. 28). There are six distinct elements that make up these platforms, van Dijck suggested: the technology itself, users, content, business models, governance, and ownership. These six elements cover the software design, the individuals who use the platforms and upload content, as well as what van Dijck terms to be the socioeconomic structures involved as a system of production: who owns the platforms, who manages their use, and how the platforms generate revenue as businesses.

Rhetoric and composition, and the subfield of computers and writing specifically, has a long history of investigating technologies for writing and writing instruction, not only at the level of user experience, but also of policy and infrastructure. From Cynthia L. Selfe's landmark 1999 text *Technology and Literacy in the Twenty-First Century: The Importance of Paying Attention* to Adam Banks's 2005 groundbreaking book *Race, Rhetoric, and Technology: Searching for Higher Ground*, and Heidi McKee's 2011 *Computers and Composition* article on surveillance and data collection policies of internet companies, writing researchers have studied the technologies, technology policy, and individual user practices that have influenced literacy practices. Within rhetoric and composition, I argue that it is most productive to consider social network sites as an assemblage of three different elements: technology, policy, and users. By assemblage, I mean a unified entity that contains people, texts, and technologies. Jodie Nicotra (2016) describes "assemblage thinking" as a perspective that shows nonhumans, material objects, and individuals within a mutually constitutive system: "All actions come not as products of deliberate human decisions, but from a heterogeneous, distributed agency of many actants, both human and nonhuman" (p. 187). André Brock (2020) argues that in studying technologies, scholars need to consider an assemblage that includes: (a) the artifact itself; (b) the cultural practices surrounding it; and (c) the "technocultural beliefs about the artifact as evinced by its users" (p. 8). Viewing social media platforms from this perspective allows us as scholars to acknowledge the distinct elements that collectively create social media platforms. Here I briefly describe approaches to social media research in writing studies that examine technologies and polices before turning to user practices.

Technologies

The first way that writing studies and internet scholars study social media platforms is through the perspective of technological design and infrastructure. Each social media platform is, of course, based in computer code that represents the very materiality of the social network site. Kristin Arola (2010, 2017) and Colin Lankshear and Michele Knobel (2008) have analyzed the design and interface of social media platforms and profiles, demonstrating how the design itself allows for and restricts identity representation and expression in different ways. The element of social media platforms that have received some of the greatest attention is the algorithmically organized news feed. Rather than presenting updates in a chronological fashion, most social network platforms weigh certain updates over others, governed by proprietary algorithms that take into account user behavior, preferences, and time spent on the site. As Jessica Reyman (2017) and Estee Beck (2015, 2017) have argued, these algorithms are not value-neutral and they present the social media users with information designed to keep them on the site. Algorithms are increasingly "mediators of online communication and information" (Reyman, 2017, p. 114) that along with the design of the platforms themselves have a great deal of impact on how writers use social media platforms, how they represent themselves, and how they connect with others through these services. While not solely focused on social media platforms, Safiya Noble (2018) and Ruha Benjamin (2019) have also demonstrated the means through which algorithms and other technologies on digital platforms also reinforce racism and white supremacy.

Policies

Social network site technologies and interfaces do not just determine specific responses from users. Social media scholarship from writing and rhetoric scholars also considers the role of platform policies in shaping activity and user experiences. Along with content and moderation policies, these sites' terms of service also dictate what they can and cannot do with user data, an issue of recent concern in the Cambridge Analytica case. The policy issue that has received the most attention in academia involves privacy concerns. McKee (2011) drew attention to web companies' data collection policies, and Estee Beck (2015) also noted the importance of considering internet surveillance for writing and rhetoric scholars, as online advertising companies have built what she described as an "invisible digital identity." Jessica Reyman (2013) argued that the metadata users generate on social media platforms falls into a gray area; while connected to the content that users write and upload on social media platforms, it is "treated as unclaimed property free for the taking" (p. 513) by social media companies. Estee Beck and Les Hutchinson (2020) also take up these questions in their edited collection *Privacy*

Matters, arguing that expanding digital surveillance systems represent an important area of study for writing researchers and instructors. Edwards and Gelms's (2018) special issue of *Present Tense* on the rhetoric of platforms also does crucial work in considering social media platforms both at the level of technology and policy in order to examine the influence of different platforms, including Grindr (Faris, 2018), Twitter (Trice & Potts, 2018), and YikYak (West & Pope, 2018). By studying social media at the level of policy, scholars are able to examine the role these platforms' policies—including data collection, privacy settings, and content moderation—have on users' experiences.

User Practices

While it is crucial for writing studies' scholars to study both social network site technologies as well as the companies' policies, these two elements do not wholly control what happens on social media platforms. User practices themselves are also crucial and represent the focus of this book. Social network sites are often critiqued for providing too much structure over communication and creative expression online (Arola, 2010, 2017). It is important, however, to avoid viewing social network sites through a technologically determinist lens. Social network site users write, connect with others, and express their identities and opinions on services that provide restrictive constraints at times, from categories on a profile page to 140-character tweets. These individuals also use creative practices in order to work against the constraints of these sites in order to suit their own aims. As van Dijck (2013) has argued, many practices on social media platforms have evolved alongside changes to the platforms themselves, not as a result of those changes. Much more research is needed on specific user practices in order to understand how individual users work within and against these constraints in order to communicate and connect with others on social media platforms.

While research on user practices in social media is growing within rhetoric and composition, most research comes from other fields, namely communication, media studies, and what might broadly be considered internet studies. danah boyd's (2014) book *It's Complicated: The Social Lives of Networked Teens* is the most visible of these studies, in which she interviewed youth on their use of Myspace, theorizing the concept of "networked publics" in which these young adults operate. Along with an interface analysis of Twitter, André Brock (2012, 2020) also described the user practices of African American Twitter users that constitute the cultural space known as Black Twitter. Alice Marwick (2013) detailed the user practices of individuals she described as "microcelebrities," and a great deal of research on teens using digital platforms (Debatin et al., 2009; Greenhow & Robelia, 2009; Livingstone, 2008). Recent work has also focused on more specific topics, including how user practices on social media intersect and interact with activism (Tufekci, 2017) and visual culture (Rettberg, 2014; Tiidenberg, 2018). Catherine Knight Steele (2016, 2018) has studied Black blogging and internet communities, and Jenny Korn (2016) has examined racial identity representation in Facebook Groups.

Among writing researchers, Bronwyn Williams's (2009) book *Shimmering Literacies* provided an early look at the ways that students used social network sites and reported on research gathered from interviews with 18-to-19-year-old college students on their use of popular culture material in their online writing activities, including social network sites. Studies of hashtags on Twitter are common in order to examine the popular and contemporary conversations around a particular topic. LaToya Sawyer (2017) examined a number of different social media spaces, including closed Facebook groups and YouTube vlogs, to examine Black women's discourse and literacy practices on social media in ways that allowed them to assert rhetorical agency. Caroline Dadas (2017) analyzed conversations around #yesallwomen and #bringbackourgirls to examine how hashtag activism connects to other activist rhetorical practices, Bill Wolff (2015) studied Bruce Springsteen fans' tweets, and Liza Potts (2013) considered social media for disaster response. While these studies sometimes focus on the practice of tweeting itself, some also consider the online discussion around a particular topic instead. Other larger studies of user practices include Stephanie Vie's (2008) early *Computers and Composition* article that surveyed writing students and instructors on their attitudes toward social network sites in the writing classroom. Her work has continued to survey these two groups on their perceptions of privacy and surveillance on social network sites (Vie, 2015), as well as following up on that initial research to discuss university faculty's continued and changing experiences on social media (Vie, 2018). Discrete studies of individual users' practices on social media are also a common area of investigation for writing studies scholars, including work by Bronwyn Williams (2017), Brian McNely (2015), and Douglas Walls (2017). Elaine Richardson and Alice Ragland (2018) have examined memes and hashtags of the #BlackLivesMatter movement that cross social media platforms into offline spaces. As Pamela Takayoshi (2018) has argued, however, writing studies as a field needs a great deal more close studies of composition processes, including digital writing processes.

A significant portion of scholarship within the field of rhetoric and composition on social media considers the use of social media platforms for pedagogical purposes. Erin Frost (2011) provided an account of her students' use of Facebook for a class project; Elizabeth Buck (2015) also discussed the ways that composition instructors can capitalize on the rhetorical knowledge students already have about social network sites. Ryan Shepherd (2015, 2016) studied the use of Facebook in first-year writing classrooms and gender differences in the Facebook profiles of first-year writing students. Similarly, Lilian Mina (2017) and Michael Faris (2017) have provided close studies of social media use in different writing classrooms. Louis Maraj (2020) also analyzes hashtagging as "digital counter/public commonplaces" (p. 46) and employing hashtag-composing practices in the classroom can decenter "hegemonic ways of reading/writing" (p. 47). David Coad (2017) also focused on the issue of graduate student professionalization and social media in his study of graduate students using Twitter at academic conferences. While considering the impact and potential role of social media practices for the teaching of writing is important, it is crucial to first understand how social media users integrate these sites within their daily literacy practices outside of the classroom.

Along with the need for more close studies of situated literacy practices that Takayoshi notes, there is also a need for writing studies researchers to consider social media on longer time scales. While close and discrete studies of social media use can help us better understand how individual writers use networked, digital tools for connection and self-expression, it is important to consider that these practices are integrated within specific digital platforms that have changed greatly over time. Features change, news feed algorithms are adjusted by developers, and social conventions for appropriate social media use shift with different platforms and practices. Yet there are very few longitudinal studies of social media use. Cory Bullinger and Stephanie Vie (2017) note the need to not only balance pedagogical accounts of social media with those that consider more self-sponsored writing practices, but also to step back and consider that use over time. Bullinger and Vie interviewed ex-social media users and non-users in order to consider why individuals have abstained or stepped back from social media platforms. Stacey Pigg (2016) also examined a Twitter user's navigation of changes on the platform over a 2-year period, noting how literacy practices on social media platforms are always in flux.

In addition, it's important to consider users' experiences on social media across different platforms. Many studies within writing studies as well as in internet studies writ large focus on one platform. According to the Pew Internet and American Life project, the average adult has profiles on more than one social network site, and many users synchronize certain kinds of content across different sites, from Twitter to Facebook, for example, or they use a site like Tumblr to contain media from a number of the different sites on which they participate (Lenhart et al., 2010). To trace literate activity, then, writing researchers need to follow users across a number of different social media platforms to consider how their practices change across sites as well as over time.

To that end, *Writing on the Social Network* extends this inquiry by examining digital literacy practices on social network sites over a 6-year period. Using case studies of users' social media practices, I identify several challenges these writers encountered in managing audiences and sharing content, and I consider the strategies these writers developed in responding to these challenges as literacy practices. This research began with a core group of seven research participants in 2010–2011, four of whom I interviewed again in 2016. In order to expand the project in terms of individual experiences and represented demographics, I conducted additional interviews with eight research participants in 2014 and 2016. Despite these additional participants, as a project based in case studies, I must note that the results of this research are limited to these participants and not generalizable beyond this group. Each writer profiled in this project found different ways to direct content to different audience groups, manage data shared on the platform, and represent themselves for professional audiences. Yet these individuals' experiences exist as "telling cases," (Sheridan et al., 2000), and the experiences detailed in this book are reflective of many others during the first decade of social media. I argue in this project that looking back on the first decade of social network sites through these specific stories and experiences can provide us with insight and perspective in considering literacy skills necessary for social media's second decade.

OUTLINE OF CHAPTERS

This introduction provided an overview of the first decade of social media, as well as an overview of the study of social media platforms within the field of rhetoric and composition. Chapter 1 describes this study's approach to studying literacy practices on social media platforms. This study takes a sociomaterial approach to literacy practices, considering the ways that users integrate social media platforms within their daily literate activity, and how they work with and against the technologies of social media platforms to share information and represent their identities. This chapter outlines three different areas of concern for social media users during its first decade (audience, data, and professional identities), the topics that will constitute most of the organization of this book. Finally, chapter 1 provides a summary of the strategies the writers in this study developed to manage their own social media use.

In chapter 2, I examine methodological considerations for studying digital literacy practices on social media, and I propose an ethnographic and longitudinal case study methodology for studying social media platforms that combines methods of data collection from different sources. Using social media as a site for writing research brings up unique ethical challenges in the collection and representation of data from these sources. In this chapter, I describe specific ethical concerns I faced through this research as well as more general questions that other social media researchers might confront in conducting social media, considering the data of research participants, and representing that data.

Chapter 3 introduces one of the three primary challenges that the writers profiled in this book encountered when using social media platforms: managing multiple audience groups. Social network sites flatten different audiences into one friend or followers list, a phenomenon Alice Marwick and danah boyd (2011) call "context collapse." Along with managing messages shared with general and specific audiences, social media users also had to consider how that content might circulate outside of its intended audience. This chapter details how the research participants in this study managed multiple audiences within and across different social network platforms and shaped content for those specific audiences.

In chapter 4, I detail the second issue social media users encountered: managing their own data with different groups and with the social network sites themselves. This chapter illustrates the ways that individuals navigate social media platforms as assemblages, managing site infrastructure, different hardware and software tools, privacy settings, and data in order to share information and restrict it to specific audiences. Each individual combined different technologies and tools in order to fit these specific social media platforms within their own daily literacy practices. While some research participants self-censored what they posted, other individuals utilized omissions and even false information to protect their privacy and personal data. The participants' experiences discussed in this chapter describe the literacy practices used by my research participants in managing technologies, data, and policies.

Chapter 5 considers the third category of literacy practices and challenges I examine in this book: self-presentation and self-promotion. I detail trajectories of my research participants' social media use over time, and how that role shifted as these individuals moved from positions as students in undergraduate and graduate programs to professionals in their chosen fields. I combine this work with descriptions of pedagogical interventions from my teaching that asked students to consider their professional digital identities and to build digital portfolios that presented these identities for professional audiences beyond the university. Using social media professionally brings challenges for individuals at all levels and can also create what Alice Marwick (2013) has described as "safe for work" selves. Yet there are opportunities for self-expression, self-promotion, and connection. This topic is one area, I argue, where teachers of digital and professional writing can intervene in teaching students to be strategic and savvy communicators.

In the final chapter, I summarize this longitudinal case study research and discuss its implications for our understanding of literate activity connected to social media platforms and the representation of identity on these sites. Through the literacy practices I identify and discuss in this book, we can reflect on the first decade of social media platforms and look ahead to social media's second decade. Examining the social, technological, and structural factors that influence digital literacy practices in online environments is crucial in understanding the impact of these sites on writing practices and literate activity going forward. This chapter also considers concerns for writing researchers and scholars in social media's second decade. The growth of social media platforms over the past decade, their professionalization and monetization, as well as their impact on global sociopolitical events, have implications for the ways that individuals use social media and the ways that writing researchers study these platforms as well.

1

DIGITAL LITERACIES ON SOCIAL MEDIA PLATFORMS

As soon as he woke up in the morning, Ronnie,[1] an undergraduate student at a large, Midwestern research university in 2011, sent a tweet from his phone, which let his roommates know he was awake. Rather than leaving a paper note for them in the kitchen, Ronnie visited their private group page on Facebook. On his walk to class in the morning, Ronnie took a picture of some graffiti in front of a local restaurant and sent it to Twitter. Unwinding before orchestra rehearsal on an unseasonably warm day, Ronnie and his roommates blared music from the roof of their apartment building, and he filmed a 12-second video of a squirt gun fight and posted it to Facebook and Twitter. He ended his evening studying in the library on campus, listening to music through the website last.fm, which recorded his music preferences and shared them with his friends. While he often worked alone, Ronnie was always connected to friends on campus and across the country through social media, his mobile phone, and his desktop computer. For millions of internet users like Ronnie, throughout the first decade of social media, everyday literate activity took place in networked digital environments, shaping individuals' literacy experiences and online and offline lives. Writers with access to a digital device inscribed their actions and thoughts on social media platforms, sharing their information through networks and creating data for those companies to monetize.

Here I emphasize the kinds of practices that Ronnie and other social media users like him engaged in as literacy practices; practices that required them to not only gain fluency in the technologies and genres needed to participate in social network sites, but also to integrate social media activities and habits into their larger writing lives. As noted in the introduction, social media platforms are online spaces where writing happens, where individuals connect with others, and where people live a portion of their lives. Through this book, I examine situated digital literacy practices over both time and space in order to understand the ways that social media platforms are integrated within individuals' writing

https://doi.org/10.7330/9781646424023.c001

lives. This project explores how these situated digital literacy practices are integrated within individuals' everyday literacy practices, and how writers are influenced by the technologies they use to represent their identities online. Social media platforms, as assemblages, represent an important location where the different influences on writing discussed by literacy scholars become visible, laying bare the influence of social, economic, and structural forces that shape literacy development in the 21st century. A close study of the literacy practices that individuals engage on social media allows us to better understand the roles they play in shaping current digital literacy practices.

In studying the writing that individuals do in these online environments, I focus on two elements for analysis: literate activity and literacy practices. I direct my attention to the literate activity that individuals engage in across social media platforms, using Paul Prior's (1998) definition as "not located *in* acts of reading and writing, but *as* cultural forms of life saturated with textuality, that is strongly motivated and mediated by texts" (p. 51). The actions that individuals take on social media platforms represent rich literate activity that is integrated within their daily lives. Through a study of this literate activity, we can consider the literacy practices that writers employ in managing their social media use. Paul Prior and Julie Hengst (2010) note that "practices are marked by repeatability and recognizability," defined by Bourdieu as "habitus" (p. 11).

By studying literate activity, then, I identify several key literacy practices, as a type of habitus, that these case study participants engaged in on social media. While Street and other scholars in new literacy studies examine literacy events, specific moments and activities that involve literacy, they use those moments to identify and study literacy practices, which "refers to both behaviour and the social and cultural conceptualizations that give meaning to the uses of reading and/or writing. Literacy practices incorporate not only literacy events, but also folk models of those occasions and the ideological models that underpin them" (Street, 1995, p. 2). This project identifies specific literacy practices these writers engage in on social network sites. I am not working here to identify particular literacy "skills," or even successful strategies, but instead to provide descriptions of "cultural forms of life" (Prior, 1998, p. 51), descriptions of how the individuals I spoke to managed the challenges that social media platforms presented and found ways to integrate them within their larger writing, social, and professional lives. Therefore, *situated digital literacy practices*, as I define them, refer to established literacy activities connected to computer technologies that are also embedded in individuals' everyday experiences.

Examining digital literacy practices on social media presents a few epistemological and methodological challenges. The first is the fleeting and distributed nature of literate activity on social media platforms. Unlike extended writing sessions that someone might engage in with a word processing program or other digital tool, activity on social media platforms is often short and distributed across multiple devices. While an individual might spend an hour scrolling through one's Facebook news feed and make a few comments on friends' posts, that is writing that is both difficult to capture and ephemeral, distributed across multiple platforms and devices.

It is also possible to view the writing that individuals are engaged in on social media platforms as little more than form completion and box clicking. Over social media's first decade, outlined in the introduction of this text, constructing a social media profile has become more restrictive, reduced to uploading an image, writing a short description, and clicking a few choices in predetermined boxes. As Kristin Arola (2010) has argued, the popularity and expansion of social media platforms has led to less emphasis on web design, including html coding and visual design in web development. There are other kinds of literate activity happening on social media platforms, however. Rather than time spent designing a layout and writing content for a profile page, literate activity on social media is distributed across time and in different places on the digital platform. Rather than composing a well-designed profile page, social media users instead write carefully constructed status updates that use language strategically, including through hashtags and in concert with images. They also comment on the posts of other users, and these short texts are not archived on their own profile pages. Recent trends in social media composing, including stylized text on Facebook, Instagram, and Snapchat, duet videos on TikTok, and long, threaded posts on Twitter, provide examples of the creative ways in which individuals compose in digital spaces. Social media users are always rewriting and reconstructing their identities and profiles through each status update and image upload.

This chapter, then, provides an exploration of the theoretical perspectives in which this research is rooted and further defines and explains concepts central to the remaining chapters. I first summarize work on digital literacies and describe sociomaterial approaches to literacy before outlining three specific areas of activity that I've identified as important in the first decade of social media. As social media platforms developed and writers learned how to reach people through these tools, express themselves, and share information, the individuals

I describe in this study had to grapple with three challenges: reaching specific audiences, managing and monitoring their own data, and representing themselves in professional spaces. Examining how these writers approached these challenges can provide us with insights into literacy practices on social media platforms over its first decade that can also help us inform the second.

SITUATED STUDIES OF LITERACY

When discussing literacy practices on social media platforms, it is important to note that I am examining literacy practices on social network sites not to identify skills that internet users need to manage social media platforms effectively but instead as descriptions of reading and writing practices that are embedded within other cultural and social practices. This approach to literacy research comes from new literacy studies (NLS), a particular orientation toward the study of literacy that emphasizes its use within particular practices and social contexts, including the work of David Barton, Mary Hamilton, Brian Street, Roz Ivanič, and James Gee. Brian Street (1984, 1995), for example, viewed literacy through an ideological model as opposed to a skills-based autonomous model. NLS scholars understand literacy as a social practice, embedded in specific social contexts and imbued with cultural meaning. Street (1984) defined literacy as a "shorthand for the social practices and conceptions of reading and writing" (p. 1). Literacy, then, can only be viewed as multiple and cannot be separated from the specific ideological, political, and cultural practices through which it is learned and used.

In the inaugural issue of *Literacy in Composition Studies*, Bruce Horner (2013) drew a direct line from NLS and Street's ideological model to the study of academic literacies taken up by the field of composition studies. While Horner noted that frameworks for studying literacy that use the autonomous model are still pervasive, Horner, Vieira (2013), and Street (2013) himself use their contributions to this issue to trace connections between the work of NLS and examinations of literacy practices centered within composition studies. Patrick Thomas and Pamela Takayoshi (2016) argued that within the field, academic literacy practices have by far been the most studied, with an examination of literacy practices in individuals' private lives and even in workplaces given less attention. While I make some connections later in the book to the pedagogical implications of this project, I approached this research as a means through which to understand the ways that individuals integrate social media within their personal lives rather than their academic experiences specifically. All of the participants in this study were either undergraduate or graduate students at the time of the initial data collection, but I was most interested in considering extracurricular literacies outside of the classroom as well as their intersection with academic literacies.

DIGITAL LITERACIES

While many NLS scholars did not study the impact of writing technologies on literacy practices, Colin Lankshear and Michele Knobel (2008) have extended the NLS concept of literacy to digital environments. They argued that while NLS has a tradition of studying literacy in context, and also studying self-sponsored or unofficial literacies, they contended that most work in NLS did not consider "new literacy" practices, particularly digital literacies. Similarly, Annette Vee (2017) noted that while NLS scholars pointed to and included the materialities of literacy, as well as different technologies, their focus on "situated literacies" most often emphasized the social rather than the material. Lankshear and Knobel used NLS as a starting point for their own work in defining and studying digital literacies, and Ilana Synder did the same in her 2002 edited collection *Silicon Literacies*, which defined literacy practices and pedagogies for digital environments.

Wysocki and Johnson-Eilola (1999), however, critiqued the extension of the term literacy beyond print texts to other forms of modes and competencies because of the historical ties to the concept of literacy as a discrete skill. Wysocki and Johnson-Eilola (1999), Brandt (2001), Kress (2003), and Vee (2017) have noted the ways that campaigns to assist individuals in gaining literacy have always been imbued with ideology, and literacy programs have also been used to uphold systems of power, including religion, colonialism, and capitalism. While I am mindful of these critiques, and the complicated histories that a term like literacy invokes, it is still a productive term within writing studies and more specifically computers and writing, especially when defined similarly to Wysocki and Johnson-Eilola's description "not as a monolithic term but as a cloud of sometimes contradictory nexus points among different positions. Literacy can be seen as not a skill but a process of situating and resituating representations in social spaces" (p. 367).

Cynthia Selfe and Gail Hawisher (2004) have argued that naming these particular abilities literacies, such as "technological, digital, electronic, as well as the all-encompassing literacies of technology," demonstrates "the enormous importance they hold for functioning in today's literate world" (p. 1). Annette Vee (2017) has also drawn attention to the rhetorical power in naming a particular skill or practice a literacy. Vee noted, for example, that calling computer coding a literacy positioned it as something valuable that should be taught widely as important to the future of "students, workers, and citizens" (p. 51). Adam Banks (2006) and Vee (2017) have also separately traced state and institutionally sponsored literacy programs from the post-war period to the present in order to examine the ways that calls for computer skills and programming literacy were entwined with other literacy programs. Digital literacy can also be described in much the same way, and digital literacy or digital literacies are discussed throughout education and information studies as important skills that young people should acquire in the 21st century for the reasons that Vee identifies for coding literacy: "individual empowerment, learning new ways to think, citizenship and collective progress, and employability and economic concerns" (p. 76). As Banks notes, many of these digital literacy programs were tied to larger systems of educational resources, providing more meaningful and successful programs in better-resourced school systems. Banks described the ways that programs focused on computer literacy and digital literacy also map onto systems of inequality, where under resourced schools serving marginalized student populations focus on "skill/drill/kill" (p. 19) language programs rather than critical or transformative literacies.

The concept of digital literacy, or digital literacies, has a complex and fragmented history. As Bruce Horner (2013) noted, there is a tendency to approach "new" literacies connected to technology and incorporate them within the frameworks of an autonomous literacy model (a skills-based framework), rather than to study them from an ideological one, in Street's (1984) definition, embedded in cultural practices. Indeed, many definitions of "digital literacy" lean toward the functional. Lankshear and Knobel (2008) argued that it is important to separate the various uses of digital literacy into two different categories, one that considers literacy as conceptual, and another that considers skills-based definitions. David Bawden (2008) also chronicled the history of the term, attributing the origin of conceptual definitions of digital literacy to Paul Gilster, whose 1997 book was the first to call the ability to understand and use information from digital sources "digital literacy." The competencies outlined by Gilster included internet searching, hypertext navigation, knowledge assembly, and content evaluation.

As Bawden noted, confusion around the term "digital literacy" has persisted, with many using it to refer to skills-based definitions, while others have used terms like "e-literacy," "electronic literacy," and "information literacy" with meanings quite similar to Gilster's definition for digital literacy. The term "digital literacies" also relates to the New London Group's (Cazden et al., 1996) discussion of multiliteracies, which argued for an expansion of conceptions of literacy beyond linguistic modes to include others as well: audio, visual, spatial, and gestural. While these different modes, or what the New London Group called "design elements," were not solely digital, they had a newfound importance within conceptions of literacy because of some of the changes brought about in part by digital technologies.

Stuart Selber (2004) further expanded on these concepts and described digital literacies as three distinct tiers: functional literacy, critical literacy, and rhetorical literacy. Selber's tiers of digital literacy moved the concept beyond a functional skill to one that incorporated critical and rhetorical awareness, but his discussion of digital literacy still considered it as a skill to be gained rather than a kind of cultural practice. Selfe and Hawisher (2004) approached digital literacies more descriptively, as one of many influences on an individual's literacy practices. Computer technologies, they argue, are situated within "the larger contexts of the historic, political, economic, and ideological movements" (p. 6) and the important role of this context—"how particular historical periods, cultural miles, and material conditions affected people's acquisition of the literacies of technology" (p. 7). Selfe and Hawisher described digital technologies as part of a larger literacy ecology, building from Marilyn Cooper's (1986) ecological view of literacy that viewed writers as engaged in a series of "social constituted systems" (p. 367).

Specifically for Selfe and Hawisher (2004), ecologies are a dominant metaphor for understanding technologically mediated writing practices. Specific technologies, their interfaces, and their infrastructures represent systems that have an influence on writers and their writing experiences. Technologies form part of "the cultural ecology of literacy" (p. 5), and together, these different factors (personal, educational, historical, social, cultural, political, economic, and technological) become the material conditions through which individuals' literacy practices are situated. In their 2012 book, Berry, Hawisher, and Selfe build on this earlier definition and use the term "cultural ecologies of literacy" as a means to describe "the intimate relationship between literacy practices and values; educational practices and values; social formations of race, class, and gender; political and economic trends and events; family practices and experiences; and material conditions—among many other factors." Digital literacies in particular, they argue, can only be understood when situated within "a particular historical period a particular cultural milieu, and a specific cluster of material conditions." Collin

Brooke (2009) noted that technological ecologies as connected to literacy are not stable either and advocated for an attention to an "ecology of practice" that considered the technological interfaces through which literate activity takes place. Louis Maraj (2020) also examines online and offline literacy events through deep rhetorical ecologies in order to examine their power dynamics, specifically racial power dynamics. Ecological models of literacy acknowledge the reciprocal relationship between individual writers and these systems, as they mutually influence each other.

While it is important to address the range of influences that make up an ecology of literacy, Carmen Kynard (2013) argued that studies of literacy within rhetoric and composition have too often seen race as just one of many influences, in a kind of benign multiculturalism (p. 64). As she noted, "we have not done so from the perspectives of interrogating deep political and ideological shifts that have left structured inequalities and violence firmly in place, especially in reference to, but not solely based on, race" (p. 64). While an ecological model of literacy, including digital literacy, might place a writer within specific cultural and material systems, not all of the influences that constitute an individual's literacy practices hold equal weight. Indeed, Selfe and Hawisher (2004) concluded that "race, ethnicity, and class too often assume key roles" in the acquisition of digital literacy skills (p. 216).

In terms of digital literacy specifically, Lankshear and Knobel (2008) took the idea of digital literacy Bawden described and integrated it within Street's ideological model. "Digital literacy" then became "digital literacies," acknowledging the multiple nature of literacy in digital contexts. Lankshear and Knobel (2008) defined digital literacies as "a shorthand for the myriad social practices and conceptions of engaging in meaning making mediated by texts that are produced, received, distributed, exchanged, etc., via digital codification" (p. 5). As Annette Vee (2017) has pointed out, Street's approach to literacy acknowledged that "communication was not fully determined by its technologies" (p. 103). In emphasizing digital and computational literacies, Lankshear and Knobel and Vee draw attention to the material aspects of literacies that NLS scholars have emphasized less. Referencing other scholars who examine the material practices of literacy, such as Deborah Brandt, Niko Besnier, Christina Haas, Kate Vieira, and Tim Laquintano—and I would add Eileen Lagman here as well—Vee described these approaches this way:

> For these researchers, literacies circulate in technologies such as pens, papers, and dictionaries; in symbolic systems such as English, alphabets, and genres; and in networks such as workplaces, families, schools, and the

global post. Literacies are plural, multidimensional, heavily inflected by orality, acquired along with value systems, as well as intertwined with the technologies in which they are enacted. (p. 104)

Sociomaterial approaches to literacy, as Vee argued, allow literacy researchers to consider the social and cultural influences on literacy as well as the technologies through which they are enacted. Annette Harris Powell (2007) argues that it is the collective of these sociomaterial literacy practices, and their accumulation over time, that continues to shape one's future literacy practices, a concept she discussed primarily through access to digital technologies.

Adam Banks (2006, 2011) has also examined not only the barriers to access of digital technologies that are embedded within structures of inequality that map onto racial difference, but also the ways that use of digital technology are embedded in race and culture. He has analyzed the ways that digital literacy programs and government initiatives often exacerbated inequalities and contributed to a digital divide. Yet issues of race and technology should not be seen strictly through a deficit model. Banks (2011) also identified and analyzed the importance of African American rhetorical traditions in digital and multimodal literacy practices, using the figure of the griot and the DJ to center the cultural practices of remix for 21st-century literacies. He identified inventive cultural practices that exist at the intersection of race and technology, centered on "technology use, production, and design" (p. 14) through the concept of remix. Through the cultural practices and literacies that Banks examined, he demonstrated the ways that African American rhetorical and cultural traditions work in concert with oral, print, and digital traditions. Maraj (2020) also pointed toward hashtagging as a "marginalized literacy" that creates rhetorical commonplaces and develops relational meaning (p. 60). While he did not call these practices literacy practices, André Brock (2020) also argued for the centrality of Black cultural practices in developing internet culture itself.

Les Hutchinson Campos and Maria Novotny (2018, 2021) pointed to a tradition in rhetoric and composition—and specifically in computers and writing—of critiquing technologies and their usage through an approach they described as "critical digital literacies." Critical digital literacies, in their description, involve

critical methods of inquiry that (1) identify ethical concerns or issues within a technological infrastructure, (2) understand the rhetorical implications of these concerns or issues for how they impact people (users and non-users), and (3) respond with a range of tactics that promote more

ethical outcomes for use of these technologies. (Hutchinson Campos &
Novotny, 2021, p. 1)

The critical digital literacy tradition continued Selfe's (1999) call to
pay attention to digital technologies and their influence in the work of
writing and rhetoric scholars and teachers. Hutchinson and Novotny
(2019) traced this tradition through work that examines and critiques
social media platforms (Vie, 2008), surveillance technologies and social
media platforms (Beck, 2015), algorithmic audiences (Gallagher, 2017),
and larger, physical data infrastructures (Edwards, 2020b). This tradition
enacted Selber's definition of critical literacy into a critique and inter-
vention into digital technologies and the role they play in writers' lives.
While this approach to technology is practiced by scholars within the
field of computers and writing, Hutchinson and Novotny (2018) noted
that this critical digital literacy approach can also be used by students to
approach a wide range of technologies.

I see these orientations toward digital literacy as falling within a sociomaterial approach to literacy, as described above. This sociomaterial
approach also allows me to consider literacy practices on social media
platforms as embedded in, and intertwined with social, cultural, and
technological systems. In their 2012 book, Berry, Hawisher, and Selfe
noted that their participants "shared a complex, nuanced, and culturally situated understanding of technology's affordances and limitations,
which they employed to make decisions about the rhetorical and material
appropriateness of various technologies both within the digital landscape
and outside of it." In studying digital literacy practices on social media, I
aim to describe and understand the processes through which individuals
navigated and utilized these technologies for their own aims.

While Selfe and Hawisher took a life histories approach to studying digital literacy ecologies, this project takes a closer view of literate
activity in order to examine literacy practices on social media platforms
specifically. Like Roozen and Erickson's (2017) work, I tie individuals'
literacy practices to longer trajectories, but my analysis examines more
recent composing processes and texts, within sociomaterial contexts.
As noted earlier, I use the term *situated digital literacies* to emphasize the
materialist and embedded nature of digital literacy practices.

Thomas and Takayoshi (2016) noted critiques of New Literacy Studies
perspectives and methodologies in providing a limited view of local and
situated literacy practices in context. They positioned their work and the
Literacy in Practice edited collection as an example of ways to study literacy practices in context, across different trajectories and domains, and

embedded within other systems of activity that "emphasizes the ongo-ing, socially situated ways people do things with writing" (p. 13). As they argued, situated studies of literacy practices allow "the accumulation of moments within local practices, that, taken together, provide insight into the functions of literacy as a constructive force in contemporary culture" (p. 13). As I noted in the previous section, these considerations also involve the material conditions and systems of which that literate activity takes place. In taking a sociomaterial approach to literacy here, I can examine literacy practices on social media platforms as dispersed and embedded in these material systems as well.

My analysis in the following chapters considers the texts that the indi-vidual writers I studied posted and shared on social media platforms, but it also examines the material aspects of their literacy practices: the tools they used and technical strategies through which they shared these updates with specific audiences. These literacy practices, then, involved word choice and design features as well as choice of platform, genre, and format. While these literacy practices were in part more functional technological literacies, they were rhetorical literacies as well, deeply connected to the communities these writers were a part of and informed by the genre conventions used by those communities. Writing on social media platforms involved crafting updates, navigating technical struc-tures, and using all aspects of what we might consider sociocultural and material literacies.

SOCIAL MEDIA CONTEXTS AND CHALLENGES

I noted in the previous section that studying social media platforms provides significant challenges for writing researchers, but they also pose challenging situations for their users. As social media platforms developed over the course of the past decade, social media users had to learn to negotiate new sociomaterial contexts and situations, contexts that were constantly changing. Internet genres change frequently, and on social media, writers constantly need to learn new conventions and affordances through which to communicate with other users.

I argue that we can consider these literacy practices through two broad approaches, and each writer I describe in the following pages used these two tactics to manage each of the three challenges I describe here. The first approach we might think of as proactive approaches and invention strategies. These are ways that writers actively worked to represent them-selves on social media platforms, created a particular image or view of themselves, and connected with others around that image. The second approach we might think of as defensive and revision strategies: ways that writers responded to or anticipated critique, or blocked information from certain audiences. Some writers incorporated critique into their future social media posts, edited posts after initial publication, or used privacy settings and other strategies to keep information to smaller audiences. Recent scholarship in digital rhetoric has considered the ways that digital content circulates and is repurposed through networks (Dieterle et al., 2019; Gries, 2015; Gries & Brooke, 2018), but individual writers themselves are also constantly revising previously written and future texts based on online feedback. Individuals use both of these strategies in writing and sharing content in digital environments. They learn about social media genres and practices based on work shared by other writers. They also revisit their own content and revise according to group and platform conventions, as well as direct and indirect responses to their posts. Each of the writers I profile through this project engaged in both invention and revision strategies in managing their information in digital environments.

As social media platforms developed over the course of the past decade, social media users had to learn how to negotiate new sociomaterial contexts and situations, contexts that were constantly changing. Genres of content on the internet in general change frequently, and on social media, writers need to constantly learn new conventions and affordances through which to communicate with other users. These situated digital literacy practices, as I've noted earlier in the chapter, are shaped by these writers' identities, literacy histories, social and cultural contexts, and technologies. In the last section of this chapter, I summarize the three largest challenges I observed through the course of this research. Each of the writers I spoke to for this project developed their own approaches in order to navigate these situations, and their strategies for doing so are the primary focus of this project. The core challenges social media presented, and the literacy practices these individual writers developed in response, represent the core of chapters 3, 4, and 5, but I present a summary here below.

UNDERSTANDING AND NAVIGATING AUDIENCES

Writing for an audience on the internet can always be challenging, but it is especially so for social media users, where slippage between one's actual audience and intended audience can be quite severe. Each writer I profile in this text first had to come up with solutions to issues of audience. There are two concepts at play here in considering audience on the internet: *context collapse* and *rhetorical velocity*.

Context Collapse

Social network sites flatten audience behind what Alice Marwick and danah boyd (2011) have called *context collapse*, where sites collapse different social networks and histories of friends, family, coworkers, and acquaintances within the same category of "friend" or "follower." As the endless parade of popular press stories of individuals fired or reprimanded for displaying information on Facebook and other sites throughout the decade can attest, many social media users face challenges in distributing content to so many different audience groups. Some individuals use groups to restrict content to certain people, others self-censor information, and some place certain kinds of content on certain sites, while reserving other content for other social network sites.

As I noted in the previous section, writers use both technical tools and rhetorical strategies to address messages to specific audiences, which happens through every tweet and every message sent. Marwick and boyd (2011) noted that one's personal network of connections influences this process, as writers interact with others and respond to the messages and interests of their own personal networks. The challenge for social network site users, as Marwick and boyd discussed, is context collapse: "The requirement to present a verifiable, singular identity makes it impossible to differ self-presentation strategies, creating tension as diverse groups of people flock to social network sites" (p. 9). On some sites, such as Facebook, a user can restrict updates to "friends," an overarching group containing all connections on the site, or to smaller groups. On Twitter, one's account can either be set to public or private. With a public account, tweets are public by default, which means that an individual's audience on the site includes one's Twitter "followers," but also includes internet users in general.

In addressing an audience, Walter Ong (1975) emphasized the writer's role in imagining that group of people the writer is addressing. As Andrea Lunsford and Lisa Ede (1984) have argued, there is an important interplay between identifying a real audience of individuals that a writer is communicating with (*audience addressed*) and constructing the text in such a way that imagines an ideal audience (*audience invoked*). Both concepts of audience must be considered in the larger rhetorical situation a writer is addressing. Catherine Knight Steele (2016, 2018) has described the ways that African American bloggers build alternative publics specifically for Black audiences in online spaces through both language use and technological affordances.

Marwick and boyd (2011) also noted the importance of the audience invoked for social network site users:

> While Facebook or Twitter users don't know exactly who comprises their *audience addressed*, they have a mental picture of who they're writing or speaking to—the *audience invoked*. Much like writers, social media participants imagine an audience and tailor their online writing to match. (p. 15)

Similarly, John Gallagher (2018) considered audience in online contexts to be a "developmental" process (p. 35). In considering how one blogger responded to feedback on her posts, Gallagher suggested that a writer's audience invoked adjusts through feedback, often online through comments. He argued, "An online writer's perception of audience, if that writer considers comments, can develop after initial delivery and while a text circulates" (p. 44). With frequent and almost immediate feedback to their texts, writers in digital environments also frequently adjust their concept of audience and adjust their content in response.

André Brock (2020) argued that context collapse, as Marwick and boyd defined it, is a concern of whiteness and white identity construction. While Marwick and boyd described the difficulty of identity representation on social media platforms that combine audiences, Brock argued that Black internet users are always addressing more than one audience at a time. They also have the experience of having their own individual identities erased into one racial category through stereotyping. He argued:

> Individualist identities are constrained by the informational scale necessary for the success of SNS; thus these identities could be understood as collapsing under the coercive instrumentality of self-presentation afforded by social media profiles. But individualism is a perk that white folk have long reserved for themselves and denied to others—that is, Marwick and boyd overlook another manner in which context collapse could be better understood: as stereotype. (Brock, 2020, p. 24)

Marwick and boyd (2011) argued that context collapse constrains and flattens identities through this audience problem. Brock compared this flattening to the ways that white supremacy and dominant culture have constrained and dehumanized historically marginalized people, especially Black people. In naming context collapse to be a new process created by social media platforms, Marwick and boyd overlooked the ways institutional and cultural constraints on identity have always taken place through racism and racial stereotypes. My discussion of context collapse focuses on the flattening of audiences, not on the subsequent flattening of identities that Brock points to as an issue here. Brock also pointed out that Black internet users have significant experience speaking to more than one audience at once, an object of study for many African American rhetorical scholars as well (Smitherman, 1986; Young, 2009). Not having to consider more than one audience for one's writing—online or offline—is indeed a privileged position.

Depending on their own subject position and lived experience, some participants in this study were more skilled at addressing multiple audiences at once than others. Each participant in this project thought a great deal about how to solve the audience problem of context collapse, from restricting messages, to using linguistic and context cues about one's intended audience, to segregating different audience groups by platform.

Rhetorical Velocity

While addressing messages for a specific audience group within one's friends or followers list can be a challenge, it is even more difficult to anticipate how social media content might circulate beyond one's own friends or followers list. For writers whose content goes viral, issues arise not from connections within one's own group but through responses from those who spread the information beyond the initial audience group.

This second audience slippage is called "rhetorical velocity," defined by Jim Ridolfo and Danielle DeVoss as "a conscious rhetorical concern for distance, travel, speed, and time, pertaining specifically to theorizing instances of strategic appropriation by a third party" (Ridolfo & DeVoss, 2009). This term describes a situation in which "composers anticipate and strategize future third-party remixing of their compositions as part of a larger and complex rhetorical strategy that plays out across physical and digital spaces" (Ridolfo & DeVoss, 2009). Composing with rhetorical velocity in mind requires an understanding of delivery in digital spaces, and in how content circulates in different contexts. Ridolfo and DeVoss also noted the importance of understanding the speed of digital composition, composing texts that can be easily taken up, appropriated, and circulated with different audiences and in different ways. For example, composers might ask themselves: "If I release the video in this format, could the video be used in this way, and would it be worth their time to do this? And would it be supportive of my objectives for them to do that?" (Ridolfo & DeVoss, 2009). These choices include considerations of language, media, format, colors, and other elements in ways that optimize a text for further circulation and use by different audiences.

As Ridolfo and DeVoss discussed, however, rhetorical velocity is about anticipating and optimizing this future circulation and an attention to designing texts strategically to allow for and encourage that future appropriation by new audiences. In a social media context, that circulation is often unintended and often unwelcome. While Laurie Gries (2015) traced the digital afterlife of the Obama Shepard Fairey image, she called her object of study more of a "runaway object" that was transformed by different media composers for different aims. For many social media cases, particularly those Ronson (2015) described as public shaming, the result often reflects back on the author of the original content.

Navigating audience can be particularly difficult in online environments. In many cases, however, social network site users know the exact people they are reaching through a friend list on Facebook, but even this list is not exact. The number of users that one interacts with on the site is, in most cases, considerably smaller, as some site users update more than others and some rarely participate. For sites like Twitter, individuals have a specific list of followers they are reaching through the site, but most Twitter users keep their updates public, which means that anyone visiting their profile pages can see their updates, even internet users who do not have Twitter accounts, and any user can retweet another user's comments to their own followers.

It is this practice of copying and circulating that a writer cannot control. While a comment or update may be written, or an image or video shared, in a specific rhetorical situation for a specific group of people, given the ease of circulating information online, that information often does not remain in its original rhetorical context. Negotiating these situations can also be challenging for social media users.

STRATEGIES TO REACH AND MANAGE AUDIENCES

Chapter 3 details the specific literacy practices of the writers I spoke to for this project, as well as their strategies for managing issues of audience. I provide a short summary of these strategies below, in order to provide a collective view of how these writers in particular managed some of these concerns in the first decade of social media.

Proactive Strategies

Composing on social media platforms involves writing and posting short updates, sometimes through different media, but it also involves developing and crafting profiles. A well-crafted profile was especially important early in the first decade of social media, where profile pages themselves played a more central role, and the options for composing and sharing information allowed for more choices, design and otherwise, as noted by Kristin Arola (2010, 2017), danah boyd (2011), and John Gallagher (2020). The writers I studied used their profile writing and creation to manage audience in two ways:

- **Split audience through different social media accounts:** Several of the writers I studied created different accounts on the same platform, using distinct usernames, profile pictures, and status updates to address a specific audience, usually centered around a particular part of their identity or a specific interest.

- **Split audience through different social media platforms:** Another common audience-management strategy throughout the first decade of social media was to shape audience by friend and follower choices and then share content accordingly. As many of the writers discuss in chapter 3, they used Twitter (and later Instagram) with a smaller group of closer friends, while Facebook included updates from multiple and more diverse groups. While writers made choices about who to friend and follow on these platforms, their choices were also guided by social norms, like in friending family or coworkers. The audience and the platform, then, shaped the kind of content they shared on the site.

Defensive Strategies

Along with proactive invention strategies, writers also used defensive strategies in restricting their content on social media platforms. Defensive strategies included posting content, but in private channels or restricted from certain audiences, self-censoring content entirely, or anticipating potential negative feedback in posting specific content.

- **Restricting content for specific audience groups:** While most of the writers I studied here described proactively creating profiles to reach specific audiences, they also restricted audience in specific ways by adjusting privacy settings, sharing content in private groups, and restricting audience through other technical means. These approaches anticipated potential issues based on either context collapse or unintended wider content circulation, and users defensively restricted content as a result.

- **Self-censoring information:** Each participant in this study also decided not to share certain information on social media, either anticipating concerns or criticism from certain audiences, or reacting in response to specific comments. One participant did not post many photos on Facebook in order to "avoid drama," while other writers adjusted future content based on comments and concerns from parents, professors, coworkers, and friends. In these cases, feedback from past audiences or anticipated feedback from future audiences shaped individuals' writing and information sharing.

MANAGING DATA AND TECHNOLOGIES

Managing audience was an issue of primary concern for each of the social media users I spoke to over the first decade of social media use, especially because audience concerns were most visible and immediate, sometimes involving instant feedback. A friend might comment on a Facebook post who was not part of the initial intended audience and take the conversation in a different direction. A tweet shared within a relatively small community might be retweeted beyond this group. In her discussion of doxxing as a rhetorical strategy, Les Hutchinson (2018) has described the ways that releasing personal information on social media became an online harassment strategy by the end of the first decade of social media. Managing and controlling one's information in online environments, then, is important. This study's participants were also concerned with the ways their data was visible, both to people and to the platforms themselves. The second challenge these individuals encountered was navigating the entire assemblage of the social media platform (technology, policy, and other users) and managing the data they generated.

As discussed in the introduction, writing and rhetoric scholars (Brock, 2020; Cagle, 2019; Edwards & Gelms, 2018; Gries, 2015) have begun to study social media platforms as assemblages, and this is a concept I use here as well, as social media combines not only websites and people but distributed systems of technologies, companies, policies, and other users. While we cannot easily separate social media activity from its consequences in offline life, neither can we distinguish the influences of different parts of the social media assemblage from each other. Jodi Nicotra (2016) described assemblages as "complex, dynamic entanglements of material and discursive factors that produce specific kinds of relations and effects." In her discussion of "strangershots," a genre of photography in which individuals take photos of others in public and upload them to online platforms, Lauren Cagle (2019) noted that this particular genre relies on the complex relationships between all of these human and nonhuman actors: "The genre of strangershots only exists as a combination of human and non-human elements: photographers, mobile cameras, social media, wireless internet, subjects of photos" (p. 71). As Dustin Edwards and Bridget Gelms (2018) described, social media platforms are "moving assemblages with computational, economic, social, and other dimensions" that contain "people, technologies, discourses, materialities, financial decisions, community practices, and more that shape the possibilities for social, civic, and political exchanges."

While this project focuses on the practices of individual users, it is important to consider how individuals navigate these systems. In deciding how much information to share on social media platforms and in using these services to stay connected with people from different aspects of their lives, social media users had to make decisions about the technologies they used to compose on social media platforms, and they often developed idiosyncratic ways of combining different types of hardware, software, and strategic rhetorical practices to achieve their aims with these social media services. The research participants in this study developed their own ways of using technology that were embedded within their own literacy practices. Each person I interviewed described the unique ways they integrated social media platforms into their daily lives, the technologies through which they managed and updated their information (from university-owned desktop computers in libraries to laptops, smartphones, and iPods), and the places from which they shared and uploaded content. In documenting both large and small moments in their lives, these individuals navigated assemblages that included computer hardware, software, digital cameras, social media applications, site interfaces, and policies.

The primary means through which the individuals I studied here navigated platform policies was through privacy policies and settings. In an overview of privacy issues on Facebook, David Kirkpatrick (2010) connected privacy concerns on social media with age. "The older you are," he argued, "the more likely you are to find Facebook's exposure of personal information intrusive and excessive" (p. 202). Unlike popular accounts of young adults' lack of concern for privacy on social network sites, however, a decade of research on social media platforms, including work from Kate Raynes-Goldie (2010) and danah boyd and Eszter Hargittai (2010), has found teenagers and young adults to not only be concerned with issues of privacy but to have developed complex practices to manage the amount of information they share with others, including frequently "scrubbing" one's Facebook wall of comments (Raynes-Goldie, 2010), changing privacy settings (boyd & Hargittai, 2010), and deactivating accounts every time the user logged off, therefore hiding their information and records of interactions with friends (boyd & Marwick, 2011). According to Pew Research, 18-to-29-year-olds represented the age group most concerned with sharing information online during the first decade of social media use, as 74% of them had cleared cookies and browser history, and 71% had deleted or edited something they posted in the past (Rainie & Duggan, 2015). A previous Pew study also found that 71% of 18-to-29-year-olds reported that they had changed the privacy settings on the sites they use (Madden & Smith, 2010).

Discussing the introduction of the Facebook news feed, danah boyd (2008) noted that for many programmers and designers, privacy is an on/off switch; information is either public or it's not (p. 14). For users, however, the issue of privacy is about exposure and control. As boyd (2008) described, privacy "is about the sense of vulnerability that an individual experiences when negotiating data," and social media platforms "alter the previously understood social norms" (p. 14). By making an individual's information visible to either many people (friend connections on a site) or everyone (publicly available), social network sites change the social contexts for information sharing and identity representation. As danah boyd (2008) argued, "Privacy is not simply about controlling access. It's about understanding a social context, having a sense of how our information is passed around by others, and shared accordingly." She noted three different elements of privacy: "A sense of control over information, the context where sharing takes place, and the audience who can gain access" (p. 18). Yet privacy is not only about an individual social media user making decisions based on their own use and context. As Alice Marwick and danah boyd (2014) later argued, it is also networked. An individual's visibility on a specific platform is also determined by one's friends and contacts because a friend can tag someone in photos and grant third-party app developers access to a list of friends.

Beck and Hutchinson Campos (2020) noted the ways that data collection and surveillance by social media platforms are just one piece of a comprehensive and overwhelming surveillance apparatus, involving everything from traffic cameras to grocery store shopping and online course-management systems. In order to successfully represent an online identity and interact with individuals from different audience groups, social network site users need an understanding of where their information is displayed, who can see that information, and who has control over it. Managing one's data and controlling and understanding privacy settings represent important literacy practices for users of social network sites. Like the site designs, privacy settings change frequently over time, and the research participants in this study had to constantly reevaluate and renegotiate their perspectives on privacy and how much they were sharing online. As with their management of different audiences, these individuals developed successful strategies for doing so, each to fit their particular situation and concerns with social media.

Proactive Strategies

The primary means through which individuals proactively managed social media platforms and their own data was by self-selecting the technologies they used and integrating them within their daily literacy practices. As described above, social media platforms are assemblages of technologies, policies, and users, and each individual profiled here found ways to navigate the technologies (both hardware and software) available to them and integrate those technologies within their everyday activities in ways that worked for them.

- **Managing devices:** Social media users accessed these sites from many locations: desktops, laptops, and mobile devices—wherever they had an internet or cellular data connection. The individuals profiled here all utilized these technologies to best fit their own needs and integrated them within their daily lives. Some frequently took photos or videos with smart phones and used third-party applications to share them on their favorite social network sites. Others used different platforms to track their daily activities. Some integrated social media services into their most important life milestones. All of these individuals used these services to integrate hardware, software, platforms, and people in ways that worked for their own lives.

- **Managing distance and space:** Several of the individuals in this study managed social media assemblages in order to traverse boundaries. Some updated their social media accounts frequently while they were traveling in order to reach friends and family back home and to stay connected. Others had contacts living in other parts of the world, and social media platforms made frequent communication easier and cheaper. Some only turned to these platforms when they were in specific locations: libraries, waiting rooms, and trains. In these ways, individuals used social media platforms in ways that helped them traverse some spaces and manage others within their own daily literacy practices.

Defensive Strategies

Managing technologies and data during the first decade of social media often meant defensively protecting one's information. The individuals I interviewed here addressed these challenges by attempting to learn and make sense of the algorithms that automated many mechanisms on social media platforms and protected their own information by managing privacy settings.

- **Understanding black boxes:** Latour (1999) defined blackboxing as "the process that makes the joint production of actors and artifacts entirely opaque" (p. 183). An assemblage, such as a social media platform, can seem like one entity when it is made up of a number of different moving pieces. When one of those pieces does not work as it should, or part of the mechanism changes, its inner workings become visible. Throughout this study, the social media users profiled here often came into contact and conflict with these inner workings, often algorithms, and struggled to manage and make sense of their use. Sometimes these changes involved settings automatically changed in platform redesigns and sometimes these changes involved account deactivation and other issues.

- **Privacy and data management:** The research participants in this project all managed privacy in different ways, and they were all concerned both about the information that they shared with others on these platforms as well as the information the platforms collected about them. Each of these individuals found different ways to manage these situations, from self-censoring information, to frequently adjusting privacy settings, to even sharing false information to subvert data collection methods. Navigating privacy settings and making decisions about the visibility of information were also key literacy practices.

REPRESENTING PROFESSIONAL IDENTITIES

The social network sites that form the core of this research study were primarily oriented around identity and representing identity. For the social media users I spoke to over the course of this project, a fundamental question for them was to determine what aspects of their identity they were sharing with whom, especially as they entered professional spaces and joined professional communities. As noted in the introduction, social media platforms developed from earlier technologies like personal homepages and have oriented most of their activities around identity representation. Identity in itself is often used as a catchall term for diverse categories of an individual's experience.

Kevin Robins (2005) described the concept of identity as "the imagined sameness of a person or of a social group at all times and in all circumstances. . . . Identity may be regarded as a fiction, intended to put an orderly pattern and narrative on the actual complexity and multitudinous nature of both psychological and social worlds" (p. 172). Manuel Castells (2000) has discussed the fragmentation of identity and its separation from traditional roles but also argued that identity is the most important source of meaning in what he described as the "network society." Scholars have struggled to define identity and the balance between individual agency and social influences. Jay Lemke (2008) called attention to the increased reference to identity in scholarship by noting the "theoretical burden" that the term "identity" has to carry when used as the primary concept to describe notions of selfhood and suggested that we need to understand identity in how it functions as a mediating term between sociostructural phenomena and lived, interactional experiences.

Previously considered a stable concept based on an individual's essential characteristics, many now view identity as continually constructed in particular contexts and in interaction with other individuals. Dorothy Holland, William Lachicotte, Debra Skinner and Carole Cain's (1998) conception of identity works at that intersection Lemke described and viewed identity as "specific to practices and activities situated in historically contingent, socially enacted, culturally constructed 'worlds' " (p. 7). While aspects of race, class, ethnicity, and gender, among other social markers, are important in this conception of identity, these categories are in constant negotiation within specific contexts and situations and in negotiation with other individuals (pp. 7–9).

Bakhtin's concept of dialogism is also central to Holland and her colleagues' conception of the authorship of the self. In making meaning, individuals pull language from a variety of other sources, in order to "author the world" (Holland et al., 1998, p. 170). Holland and her colleagues argued that Bakhtin saw the construction of identity in much the same way. We see and represent ourselves through the words of others in a continuous social process: "The meaning that we make of ourselves is, in Bakhtin's terms, 'authoring the self,' and the site at which this authoring occurs is a space defined by the interrelationship of differentiated 'vocal' perspectives on the social world" (p. 173). Literacy, then, is important to the creation of identity. We borrow language from different sources in order to understand ourselves and to present our continuously constructed identity to others.

This idea of "authoring the self" is important when considering constructing online identities, which are represented primarily through text and images, sometimes created by oneself, but often taken from other sources. Other scholars have viewed the idea of individual identity as embedded in particular contexts and have seen identity as based in individual performance within certain social constraints (Butler, 1990; Goffman, 1959). Early scholars of identity on the internet have been influenced by these ideas; Donna Haraway's concept of the cyborg and post-human concepts of identity see the internet as a place where identity, particularly gender identity, is fluid. Scholars like Sherry Turkle (1995) described online identity as disconnected from users' identities in offline spaces, based instead in performance, primarily through text. Others have critiqued this position as a misrepresentation of Butler's

(1990) work on identity performance and provided critiques of this post-human view of identity (e.g., Hayles, 1999; Nakamura, 2002; Paasonen, 2002). Critiques such as Nakamura's, for example, have drawn attention to the ways in which one's online identity is still embedded in, and influenced by, an offline, embodied self. Nakamura's work in particular draws attention to the ways that race and gender function in online spaces, demonstrating that Turkle's (and others') concepts of fluid identity representation online was problematic and incomplete. Adam Banks (2006), Lisa Nakamura (2002, 2008), Nakamura and Chow-White (2013), Catherine Knight Steele (2016), Kristin Arola (2017), André Brock (2020), and other scholars have noted that whiteness has been, and still is, seen as the "default internet identity" (Brock, 2020, p. 7). Design, discourse, and infrastructure choices of social media platforms privilege whiteness in centering the identities and experiences of white users. BIPOC internet users have to navigate these structures and assumptions when using social media platforms and representing themselves in online spaces.

André Brock (2020) used the term "networked online identity" (p. 13) to refer to the ways that Black internet users he studied constructed and negotiated their identities in digital spaces, including social media platforms. A networked online identity, for Brock, includes both a "discursive and informational formulation" (p. 13) of identity, involving technology and culture. Digital identity, particularly racial digital identity, has two components: a social-discursive component and a technological-interface component, which Brock described as a "code-content-hardware" component (p. 21). Identity "creation and maintenance" (p. 19), as Brock defined it, involves interactions with technological infrastructure, digital spaces, and intended and unintended audiences (pp. 19–20). Brock argued that there is a tension between the individual and the social in online identity formulation, and both must be taken into account: "An examination of cultural online performance must incorporate both the intended and unintended audience's technologically and culturally mediated reception of that performance" (p. 20). For Brock, then, identity online is both created and maintained through negotiations with both in-group and out-group audiences and technological components, negotiations that evolve over time.

In her concept of writer identity, Roz Ivanič (1998) identified four categories of identity that interact: (a) an autobiographical self, shaped by prior social and discoursal history; (b) a discoursal self that is conveyed within a particular text; (c) the self as author, which is the self

a writer creates through one's authorial voice; and finally, (d) a subject position, or the possibility for self-hood in sociocultural contexts
(pp. 23–27). Ivanič noted that the author's identity was created by an
interaction between the first three categories and the last one, where
one's identity is created through interaction with a larger community in
text: "Writing is an act of identity in which people align themselves with
socio-culturally shaped possibilities for self-hood, playing their part in
reproduction and challenging dominant practices and discourses, and
the values, beliefs, and interests which they embody" (p. 32). Ivanič was
primarily focused on the writer's persona in academic writing, but as
noted earlier, one of the primary concerns for social media users were
concerns about audience, which also involved concerns of identity. If my
boss or my professors are my Facebook friends, what image do I want to
present of myself, and what information should I be sharing? Identity
representation, then, was an ongoing negotiation of multiple rhetorical situations.

The participants in this study all grappled with ways to represent their
identities as professionals on social media platforms, to join professional
communities, to represent their work, and also to obscure certain elements of their lives from more professional audiences. For some of the
individuals who were undergraduates at the beginning of this project,
they were concerned about hiding photos and other information from
potential employers as they began looking for jobs. For others, social
media platforms provided access to professional networks and ways to
join communities.

Proactive Strategies

Engaging with professional audiences on social media platforms are both
identity and literacy practices. The participants in this study developed
specific content on different social media platforms for potential employers, academic colleagues, and other audiences interested in their professional work. Social media can offer a way to engage with these audiences,
and each individual profiled here found their own way of doing so.

- **Joining professional communities:** Some of the individuals I profile
  here used social media in order to observe how professional communities used the service before representing a professional identity for
  that community and actively joining as well. Professionally oriented
  platforms and communities allowed these undergraduate and graduate students the ability to make connections and represent themselves and their work in digital spaces for professional audiences.

Defensive Strategies

Many internet users, as well as many of the writers in this study, primarily used more defensive strategies for approaching professional audiences. An individual's social media profiles, especially for those who were early adopters, might contain years of notes and late-night musings, photos from parties with friends, silly videos, and memes. As college students, for example, review their social media content over time, they might remove information they find does not present the right image to a professional audience.

- **Censoring information:** For most of the individuals I profile here, representing themselves in professional digital spaces meant removing information, including photos, more personal data, or anything that these writers thought would jeopardize the potential for professional opportunities. Some of these strategies were based on advice from authority figures or peers. Others adjusted settings to hide information from the public or specific audiences. This kind of identity management allowed them to consider the aspects of their identities they wanted to share in more professional spaces.

CONCLUSION

Through this study, I conceptualize digital literacy on social media platforms not as a set of discrete skills that social media users needed to master, but instead as situated digital literacy practices and "cultural forms of life" (Prior, 1998), influenced by sociomaterial contexts, and embedded within these individuals' lived experiences. Navigating audiences, managing data, and representing identities were challenges each of these writers faced in writing and developing content on social media platforms. I have presented an overview here of the primary ways through which the research participants I profile in this project managed these challenges through the first decade of social media. These particular approaches are specific to the individuals I describe through this project, yet they do provide a view of a specific group of people's literacy practices on social media during its first decade. I address each of these issues in depth in the following chapters, but first I turn my attention to methodological challenges for studying social media in chapter 2.

2
STUDYING SOCIAL
MEDIA PLATFORMS

Before describing the specific experiences of this study's participants, I want to pause here to discuss some of the methodological decisions I made in designing and conducting this research, both to ensure transparency as well as to continue a conversation about digital methods within writing studies more broadly. Studying social media presents a number of distinct concerns for writing researchers, from bounding studies, to navigating online/offline boundaries and recruiting participants, and representing those participants and data in written accounts of social media activity. Caroline Dadas (2016) distinguished between studying social media and using social media as a methodology—drawing a line between using social media for data collection of a different topic and studying social media itself. This project uses social media, particularly literacy practices on social media, as the object of study rather than a means to studying a different topic.

The introduction divided research on social media into three broad categories: technology and interfaces, policy, and user practices. While there is growing research within rhetoric and writing studies on social media, there have been fewer conversations within the field on methods for that research, though that conversation is growing. James Porter (2007) argued in the forward to *Digital Writing Research* that studies of digital writing cannot rely on the same methodologies simply translated to digital environments (p. xiii). What are needed instead are research methodologies that, as Porter described it, "account for the local—'local' meaning the technological environments in which writing occurs" (p. xiv). Digital writing research methodologies, Porter argued, "should be viewed . . . as changing the fundamental assumptions about methodology, particularly the humanist assumption that divides the human from the technological" (p. xv). In their introduction to the same volume, McKee and DeVoss noted that as digital technology has radically changed the nature of writing and writing processes, so too has it changed the methods by which we investigate

https://doi.org/10.7330/9781646424023.c002

these processes in workplaces, classrooms, and other contexts. The word "digital" in digital writing research reflects an emphasis not on instrumentalist tools of writing but on "technology-as-cultural-space as well as technology-as-production-space, as a virtual environment in which humans live, not just a medium through which they talk" (Porter, 2007, p. xviii). Methodologies that consider these realities of digital writing environments can best respond to and investigate digital writing practices. Responding to these transformed notions of authorship, process, and collaboration to study the kinds of writing practices that occur on social media platforms requires approaches that understand the situated nature of digital writing within and across digital environments.

WRITING RESEARCH METHODOLOGIES AND SOCIAL MEDIA

Writing researchers have both adapted more traditional writing research methodologies for digital contexts and have also borrowed other methods used in communications and media studies research to study social media. Some scholars have used discourse analysis and visual rhetorical analysis to some conclusions about the ways that social media platforms configure user experiences and even the users themselves (Arola, 2010; Brock, 2020; Deluca, 2015; Faris, 2018; Goodling, 2015; Maraj, 2020; Maranto & Barton, 2010; West & Pope, 2018). While these kinds of studies vary in terms of subject matter, they all use either public posts, the researcher's own information, and/or elements of the interface itself. This research analyzes and interprets different parts of the site design or platform infrastructure in order to draw conclusions about the ways that these platforms configure users and user behavior.

A significant number of studies also take advantage of digital research tools in order to conduct "data scraping" of social media platforms in order to collect larger datasets. These studies are becoming common for studying social media discourse and range from studies of Twitter use at a conference (McNely, 2010), at a Bruce Springsteen conference (Wolff, 2015), among geocachers (McNely 2015), for disaster response (Bowdon, 2014; Adkins, 2017), for activism and public protest (Dadas, 2017; Hayes, 2017), and within particular communities, including those who participated in #GamerGate (Trice & Potts, 2018). These studies generally collect tweets over a set period of time in order to collect discourse *in situ*, as Wolff (2015) described, though not all of these studies use Twitter. Brian McNely's (2015) study, for example, pulled data from Instagram. Nicole Brown (2019) also used topic modeling and scraping of Facebook, combined with autoethnographic data. The tools for collecting these tweets, including Node XL and TAGS, allow research-ers to automate the data collection process and collect all tweets within that timeframe.

Other research within writing studies uses qualitative case study and ethnographic research methods, including interviews, observations, and other small-scale case study methods (Arola, 2017; Cedillo, 2020; Coad, 2017; Penney & Dadas, 2014; Pigg, 2016; Alexander & Hahner, 2017; Potts, 2015; Sawyer, 2017; Williams, 2017). These studies range a great deal in terms of both scope and duration. Yet to varying degrees, these studies combine newer, digital data collection methods with traditional qualitative research methods used by literacy and writing researchers, including methods used for case study and ethnographic research. While some scholars are more interested in examining social media practices at the level of the individual, others choose a small group or network as their unit of analysis and trace social media activity through or across that network in terms of community building or information circulation. These studies, then, sometimes draw conclusions about social media use at the level of the individual; some place social media use in the context of individuals' other literacy practices; and some study their place within specific communities, both online and offline. Studies that examine networks and communities are instead interested in how individuals' social media use works in connection to others. While these studies differ, many researchers who take this approach note the connec-tion between online and offline activity. While this survey of social media research methods is not comprehensive, it demonstrates the ways that writing studies scholars have adopted and adapted research methods from offline studies of literacy practices with newer, digital data collec-tion methods and tools to examine the practices of social media users.

SITUATED STUDIES OF LITERATE ACTIVITY

Brian McNely (2015) argued that social media research methodologies centered on specific digital texts or those that focus on a network as a unit of analysis "may unintentionally obfuscate complex rhetorical literacies that both precede and extend beyond social media participa-tion." As I noted in chapter 1, social media posts take place within larger chains of literate activity that bridge online and offline contexts. McNely described the complex literacy practices of geocachers that involved not only snapping a picture and posting it to Instagram with a particular hashtag, but also using GPS receivers, mobile phones, maps, text mes-sages, emails, and both digital and print note taking. Crafting a tweet or a Facebook post can sometimes be the end result of a longer chain of literate activity that can include many of the technologies that McNely described. These posts can also be the result of prolonged conversations with others, either in person or through messaging applications. Social media users can also craft similar but distinct messages for different platforms to reach more than one audience. In addition, what we think of as a social media platform has also changed. As Douglas Walls (2017) has noted, Facebook is not just a website: "What we mean by 'Facebook' is not tied to a single platform or type of technology but exists in multiple places with similar types of rhetorical performances. Clicking 'Like' on a laptop is similar to pressing 'Like' on a mobile device" (p. 149). Studying literate activity on social media platforms, then, involves multiple tools, contexts, and trajectories of activity.

As McNely argued, though researchers in writing studies have long been interested in studying literate activity that occurs in digital spaces and have utilized different methods through which to do so, these types of literacy practices are still a challenge for researchers to archive and to study both because they can be difficult to capture and because they can examine trajectories of literate activity that are difficult to draw boundaries around. Social media research in writing studies, as I described in the previous section, often includes either the study of content around a particular hashtag disconnected from the content's authors or studies of individuals using a particular platform. This research utilizes methods of other situated studies of literacy practices in order to expand those boundaries slightly to examine literate activity that takes place over longer timescales, across social media platforms, and between online and offline contexts. Studies and methodological approaches upon which this work builds includes Prior's (1998) study of graduate students' academic writing and introduction to disciplinary writing practices, Prior and Shipka's (2003) research on the places in and activities through which academic writing happens, Kevin Roozen's (2009, 2010) work on the self-sponsored writing of undergraduate students and professional writers, Kendall Leon and Stacey Pigg's (2011) study of the writing habits of graduate students, and McNely's (2015) examination of geocachers using Instagram.

Most of this work uses case studies and data collected from multiple sources and across a range of texts in order to provide thick descriptions of literate activity. Roozen's (2009, 2010) work and his more recent book with Joe Erickson (2017), for example, drew connections between case studies to draw larger conclusions about the connection between academic and "extradisciplinary" writing for a number of undergraduates in order to trace texts through a variety of activities and "trajectories of practice" (p. 321). Roozen (2009) argued for "less bounded approaches to writing and literate practice" (p. 321) and situated studies of literacy like his case studies allow for that focus. In order to explore multiple types of writing in multiple settings, Leon and Pigg (2011) similarly collected data through the use of diary logs of writing activity, screen captures of writing sessions, and interviews about these writing sessions. This combination allowed the researchers to view these academic writing activities from a number of different perspectives. In studying social media literacy practices, Sawyer (2017) combined larger scale surveys of Black women internet users with rhetorical analyses of online content and qualitative interviews from survey respondents in order to describe Black women's experiences on social media at both a broader and more detailed scale.

This approach of studying literacy practices through trajectories of activity is an approach that is suited for studying writing on social media platforms and is also particularly needed in social media research. The literate activity that writers engage in on social media platforms is interesting particularly for its occurrence in unofficial spaces, as opposed to academic ones, and its perception as often invisible writing that occurs in short moments throughout a writer's daily experience. Someone writes a comment on a friend's Facebook status, for example, then leaves for class, takes a picture of a sign by the side of the road, and uploads the picture to Instagram, sharing the image with followers. A study of these kinds of literacy practices can help writing researchers to gain an understanding of the distributed nature of literate activity and its connection to digital technologies.

Because the types of studies discussed here rely on multiple methods that attempt to capture the situated nature of literate activity, they are especially appropriate models for the research challenges I described here for social media research. Prior and Hengst (2010) noted in their edited collection on semiotic remediation that all of the studies in their text use the same "methodological toolkit" that combines ethnographic methods of observation and data collection with interpretive analysis (p. 16).

Situated studies of literacy practices can be conducted over long or short periods of time. While Kevin Roozen and Joe Erickson (2017) engaged in multiple interviews with their research participants, the scope of their research projects and information gathered in their interviews covered much longer timescales connected to specific literacy practices of their research participants. Brandt (2001) and Berry et al.

(2012) emphasized life history research and conducted most of their research through interviews that spanned important literacy events of an individual's life. Antonio Byrd's (2020) study of African American adults in a coding bootcamp also took place over several weeks, though his interviews covered much longer literacy histories across the lifespan. Similarly, Eileen Lagman's (2015) study of Filipino care workers occurred through observations and interviews over several months, though the in-depth interviews also covered the participants' longer literacy history.

The original research that forms the basis of this book was initially collected over a 10-month period. That time span was chosen as one that would allow me to observe literate activity over a long enough time period to draw some conclusions about the types of literacy practices in which my research participants were engaged on social media. After this initial 10-month study, I extended this research into a longitudinal project of situated digital literacy practices on social media. In order to gather information about a more diverse set of individuals' experiences, I also conducted additional follow-up studies with new participants in 2013 and 2016.

Considering literacy practices on social media over longer timescales allows writing researchers to consider their continued impact on individuals' writing lives. Facebook in 2007 was not the same site as Facebook today. Since my own initial qualitative research on social media practices in 2010 and 2011, a plethora of new sites and apps have come into popular use, from image-based sites like Instagram and Snapchat to other services, including YikYak, GroupMe, WhatsApp, and TikTok. The social media platforms that have spanned this first decade of social media also have considerably more features now, including trending topics, stories, and others, and social media users have adjusted their practices along with these shifting affordances.

While the individual cases of my research participants cannot be generalized to other situations or other individuals, they represent what Sheridan et al. (2000) called "telling cases" that work "not through empirical generalisation, but by revealing the principles that underlie relationships between specific writing practices, the local events of which they are a part, and the institutional contexts in which they take place" (p. 14). For these researchers, a telling case is more important than a typical case, as it can make theoretical relationships more apparent that were previously obscured and suggest greater connections to theory, as Stake (1995) argued. Mary Sheridan (2009) described telling cases as those "that exceed what generalized theories might expect of them and work against the flattening theoretical appraisals that offer predictable answers" (p. 8). Some of the individuals in this study spend more time on social media than others, but the practices and the situations they confront in using social media platforms make visible the issues that many others confront in their social media use, usually in more subtle ways, when engaging in common activities such as sharing family and vacation photos or making comments on a political issue or event. Studying individuals like those represented here, then, illuminates the stakes for participating in social media spaces, most especially rhetorical questions of authorship, audience, and privacy.

The experiences of the individuals represented in this project also represent historical accounts. As noted in the introduction, this research uses longitudinal case studies combined with shorter, interview-based case studies to examine situated digital literacy practices in what I am calling the first decade of social media (2004–2016). The experiences described here examine literacy practices these participants engaged in on social media from 2010 to 2016.[1] A number of different social media platforms have appeared and disappeared in the time since this data was collected, and even more between my time writing this manuscript and your time reading it. The practices examined and described here are historical ones, yet the literate activity discussed here still points to the larger implications discussed in this study.

ETHICS AND SOCIAL MEDIA RESEARCH

As with digital research methods, research ethics also cannot just be transferred from methods used for print and offline contexts. All internet research, but especially research involving human subjects, requires a careful attention to research ethics, as many of the situations that qualitative researchers of all kinds have developed to manage the ethics of human subjects research—including informed consent, observation, and interview practices—become more challenging online in situations removed from the context of traditional research settings. These concerns are especially pronounced for social media, where activity happens quickly but persists for long periods of time. Given the ways that social media activity is embedded within individuals' daily lives and the networked nature of the site infrastructure, it is especially difficult to bound these kinds of research studies and incredibly easy to study individuals who may not have given their consent for such research. Privacy settings and access to information are often controlled by the individuals a researcher would study within a complicated range of privacy settings that frequently change, and for these reasons, social media research requires a careful consideration of a number of factors in both data collection and reporting on that research.

Issues of consent, levels of access granted to researchers, and the publication of that data are therefore often messy negotiations, ones that should be determined by the researcher and participants in each unique situation. Heidi McKee and James Porter (2009) have advocated for a rhetorical approach to internet research that treats the relationship between researchers and participants as a constantly negotiated rhetorical situation, and "fundamentally a communication situation" (p. 13). This approach, they argued, leads to a focus on situational context, rhetoric, and casuistry, allowing "a practical mechanism for addressing complex issues," (p. 13). They suggested an orientation to ethics in internet research as developed in part by negotiation and discussion with colleagues, as well as the use of heuristics to determine issues such as whether the research requires informed consent. McKee and Porter also noted that ethical issues need to be negotiated at the level of the situation. These are "messy propositions" (p. 22), as they noted, but allow researchers to respond to the unique situation in which they find themselves. McKee and Porter advocated for an approach to participants that is not applied in a dogmatic manner or in ways that make decisions about communities and individual members without their participation that treat them as other: "Ethical decision-making requires attentiveness to people's lives—and to the complexities, differences, and nuances of human experience, including the researcher's own experiences" (p. 27).

In a reflection of her own research methods, Caroline Dadas (2016) also emphasized the messiness of these research considerations and recommended a remixed approach, building on Annette Markham's research, that encourages researchers to blend methods and distinct perspectives as appropriate, to constantly reflect on the use of those methods, and to adjust with the instability of context in so many internet research contexts. In proposing a queer methodology for social media research, Dadas built from queer theory's problematizing of concepts like public and private, as well as the danger of applying "troubling normative attitudes toward research" (p. 70). Her emphasis on the importance of questioning binaries in internet research, including public/private and online/offline, demonstrates the need for social media research methods that are situated and context-specific. She also emphasized the importance of the research process more than its ultimate outcomes; even when the research results do not produce the data hoped for, or research questions are not answered, the process of conducting that research can lead to its own insights.

For their part, the Association of Internet Researchers' (AoIR) ethical guidelines for internet research, to which Heidi McKee and James Porter contributed, emphasize a process and case-based approach that emphasized the importance of researchers making ethical decisions based on their and their participants' circumstances (Franzke et al., 2020). Through their heuristics, they asked internet researchers of all kinds to consider the context, objects of study, privacy expectations, representation, data storage, and harms and risks. The guidelines identified three areas of tension and ongoing concern in internet research: informing participants, collecting and storing data, and protecting the information of participants as well as researchers. While these questions are not settled and are best decided by within the researchers' particular contexts, it is also important for writing researchers to spend more time considering these issues as well. While writing researchers can analyze public discourse on blogs, message boards, and public Twitter and Facebook threads as information publicly published online that does not require consent, the AoIR guidelines warned that such a position might be an oversimplification. If that information is traceable and people might be identified, publishing and analyzing that information might cause that person harm. As writing researchers, I argue, we need to consider not only informed consent processes but also the representation of that published data, how individuals might be identified, and what the consequences might be for their representation in these research projects. While these questions must be decided on a case-by-case basis, it's crucial for writing researchers to consider these questions carefully.

RESEARCHER POSITIONALITY AND ETHICAL DECISIONS

I want to spend a bit of time describing how I worked through some of these concerns as a writing researcher studying social media. I am talking through these considerations here not to present a narrative on the correct way to study social media platforms. I figured out much of these issues as I went along, and not all of my decisions were the right ones. I present a detailed consideration of the ethical concerns I encountered as a way to be transparent about the decisions that I made as a researcher, and to deliberately emphasize a conversation that is often erased or sidelined. Methodological issues are often brushed over in research accounts, and I want to emphasize them here in order to foreground the importance of conversations about method.

First, I have to say something about my own position as a researcher, which informed all of these decisions as well. As noted by Haas Dyson and Genishi (2005), among others, the position of the researcher in qualitative research is central to the research conducted and can never be separated from the conclusions drawn. My own position as a researcher, first as a graduate student and then as an assistant professor, as well as my history as a computer-literate, middle-class, heterosexual white woman who was raised in the Midwest play a role in the participants I was able to recruit, how I interacted with them, and how I interpreted my results. As described in more detail below, I initially recruited participants from a large, Midwestern public university that has a Carnegie classification of "very high research activity." These participants included five white-identifying participants and two Asian and Asian-American participants. While these demographics are generally reflective of the student body at this institution, my ability to recruit students was also certainly shaped by my own identity and who students felt comfortable interacting with. My follow-up studies at a regional public university in the Northeast and at a public flagship institution in the Southeast included a more diverse pool of participants, but they were still majority white, reflecting both the enrollment of these institutions as well as my own identity regarding with whom students might feel more comfortable discussing social interactions and social media identity representations.

Prompted by my own concerns of identity, representation, and privacy on social media, I asked questions of my participants based at least in part on my own online experiences as well as a growing body of scholarly research on the topic. Interested in the social nature of writing and its connection to technology, as discussed earlier in this text, my interpretations of my participants' activities and experiences are inevitably filtered through this perspective. I also had previous connections and relationships with a few of the participants in this study, while others I met through the course of participant recruitment. My interpretations and assumptions factor into my data collection and analysis processes, something I hope I have made explicit throughout the descriptions of these case studies and my results.

Case study-based research projects, like all qualitative research methodologies, involve delicate negotiations between the researcher and the participants. Therefore, in this study, the specific combination of data-collection methods was decided in close consultation with the participants. Some participants allowed me greater access to their social networking profiles than others, with many of my participants friending or following me online, while others preferred to share texts with me only when we met for face-to-face interviews. In addition, I used both online and offline collection methods as well, recording data, as described in more detail below, from Twitter feeds and Facebook profiles and from face-to-face interviews.

In approaching my research participants, I treated each initial conversation about the research as a rhetorical negotiation, but one based in similar beliefs and goals. While some of the information that these individuals shared with me was publicly available online, some of it was not. Some material was personally sensitive information about religion, personal relationships, or beliefs and some of it was just a reposting of links and images this person liked. I worked out a system with each participant to share information that this individual was comfortable with. Most participants gave me full access to their Twitter and Facebook profiles, allowing me to see individual posts, images, and interactions with friends. One participant was happy to talk with me about her social networking site use, but I could only see her profile during interviews, as she wasn't comfortable friending me on either space. A third participant allowed me to friend her, but I relied a great deal on her explanations to gain access to her materials, much of which was written in Korean. While she translated for me during our interviews, at times she skipped a post or update, noting that it was "personal."

Negotiating interactions with participants in online spaces was an issue I anticipated. Research on internet communities has an established tradition of participant observation. McKee and Porter (2009) described a number of different researchers who have studied communities of which they are a part, who announce their presence as researchers and negotiate their participation with the community. This research project was different in two ways: first, I was interested in the online interactions of several discrete individuals, not the dynamics of a community as a whole. Second, social networking sites represent a different kind of community online. Unlike the tight-knit communities organized by common interest studied by the researchers McKee and Porter discussed, most social networking sites function as many different communities, as users primarily connect with those they are connected to in their offline lives (boyd & Ellison, 2007). After informed consent was negotiated in person, then, I observed participants' interactions online as more of an observer than a participant outside of our interviews.

As Amy Bruckman described in McKee and Porter's (2009) text, "Most work on the Internet is semi-published" (p. 81). The line between public and private on the internet is a blurry one, and researchers cannot treat all publicly available information online as public, because participants might not see it with the same level of publicness as the researcher does (McKee & Porter, 2009, p. 78). While writing is publicly accessible online, it may not be as polished as work published in print, and it may not have been written with the same expectations of a large audience. Some young people, for example, may consider their social networking profiles private if their parents do not have access to them (McKee & Porter, 2009). For many researchers, as McKee and Porter discussed, the question is about treating the work as public and published texts, or semiprivate conversations in which a researcher would need informed consent to access. Many of the interactions my research participants were involved in were public, occurring in public Twitter accounts and similar forums, yet some of it was also private, or semiprivate, hidden behind a Facebook password and available only to friends. Many social media platforms allow more private messages and private groups as well, such as private emails through Facebook and direct messages in Twitter. As noted above, the study participants and I negotiated my access to their material through the informed consent processes. In our interviews, we discussed private messages broadly and the situations in which they were used, but I did not look at the individual private messages.

I kept my participants' information confidential, referring to each by a pseudonym, and their screen names and website addresses as pseudonyms as well. I was first concerned that providing these names and screen names would make participants incredibly easy to find, given the nature of digital data and search engines. Not only would their data be easily available, then, but their friends' data would as well. Many of my participants had public Twitter accounts, for example, where they not only posted but also interacted with friends and also retweeted friends' content. While this was publicly available information, I only had informed consent from the participants, not from those they interacted with. By making social media accounts public, then, I would expose not just the research participant, but an entire friend group as well, individuals who were most likely unaware of the research project. For these reasons, I kept my participants' data confidential, not only using pseudonyms but also altering screen shots and other visual data. Textual data is only reproduced here when it was not found through online search engines. At the time of my initial data collection, search engines did not index individual tweets on Twitter. In reproducing data from my participants in my initial publications from the first phase of this study, I ran the text through the Google search engine to verify that this data would not come up in a search engine and identify my participants.

Another aspect of identification lies in the way that information persists online. It is important for social media researchers to responsibly report participants' information and consider the ways that reported data might make them easy to identify. A few years after the initial reporting of this study, Google began indexing tweets, and it became possible to search for the text of specific tweets on Google.[2] While most of the tweets I included in my initial reports of this research are too old to come up in Google searches, I have altered the way I report many of my participants' tweets, including paraphrasing instead of quoting directly. While it can be impossible for researchers to anticipate future changes to social media platforms, being mindful about how one is reproducing individuals' data is important for mitigating the risk of participant identification.

STUDY PARTICIPANTS

Initial 2010 Participants

The initial research for this project took place on the campus of a large, 4-year university in the Midwest with an R1 Carnegie classification of very high research activity, and on the social networks used by the study's participants. While one participant had significant transnational ties and used a social media platform popular in Korea, the rest of this study's participants were based in the United States, and their social media use thus reflects a U.S.-based focus. The four initial undergraduate students were recruited by class visits to an advanced composition course focused on composition through a variety of media, including image, audio, and video. As I was interested in studying writing practices that occurred between a number of different social network sites, I recruited participants from this course, since they are typically active on many social network sites and interested in discussing and analyzing their own practices in these composing spaces. Criteria for participation in this study included a strong presence on social networking sites, as judged by an up-to-date profile and daily participation on a social network site and participation in a writing-intensive course. I measured students' participation levels on social network sites through a preliminary questionnaire distributed to during my classroom visit, which invited interested students to include an email address if they were interested in talking with me further about their social network site use. Two additional undergraduate research participants were recruited through a list of students who had previously taken this course and were initially contacted through email.

The three initial graduate student participants were recruited from invitations to instructors of writing-intensive courses at the university. Two of the graduate student participants were instructors of the multimodal advanced composition course mentioned above, and the third was an instructor in the Academic Writing Program, a two-semester course sequence for first-year students. Both graduate and undergraduate students were chosen to participate in this study in order to examine literacy practices among groups of writers with different concerns and experiences. Follow-up interviews were conducted with four of the seven participants in 2016; two interviews were conducted in person, while two others were conducted online using the video chat application Skype.

I conducted additional follow-up research as part of this project in 2013 and 2016. In 2013, I recruited four undergraduate participants who were the students in a similar upper-level, multimodal writing course at a public 4-year university located in an urban area in the Northeast, this institution is part of the largest urban university system in the United States. In 2016, I also recruited five undergraduate and two additional graduate student participants from among students and instructors of writing courses at a large, public university in the Southeast. The interviews with these students covered the same topics as the interviews with the initial set of participants, but these conversations were one-time interviews rather than a series of conversations over time. The data from these interviews confirmed major themes and trends to those provided by the initial case study participants and provide additional perspectives on situated digital literacy practices.

Regarding the social media platforms themselves, I focused on the sites that my participants used rather than looking for individuals who used specific sites. Each participant had a Facebook account, and 15 of the 18 participants used Twitter. Other sites used by some individuals included Instagram, last.fm, Ravelry, Cyworld, Academia.edu, and other websites considered more niche social media platforms. Each participant was engaged in a variety of other interesting online activities. One person, for example, was an avid blogger; while we discussed this activity, I focused my analysis specifically on the activity he posted on social media instead. In making distinctions between these sites, I used danah boyd and Nicole Ellison's (2007) definition discussed in the introduction:

> A social network site is a *networked communication platform* in which participants (1) have *uniquely identifiable profiles* that consist of user-supplied content, content provided by other users, and/or system-provided data; (2) can *publicly articulate connections* that can be viewed and traversed by

others; and (3) can consume, produce, and/or interact with *streams of user-generated content* provided by their connections on the site.

This definition allowed me to make determinations about which sites I included as part of the study and which ones I excluded.

As noted above, the seven original research participants in this study were all graduate or undergraduate students when the study began, though they had all transitioned into different roles by 2016. While I reached out to all of the participants for follow-up interviews, for logistical reasons in some cases on my part and in some cases on my participants' part, I was able to conduct follow-up interviews with four of the original seven participants. What follows are descriptions of each research participant. Analyses of the literate activity of each participant follows in chapters 3, 4, and 5. The data in these chapters discusses the initial seven case study participants in greater depth, but that data is supported by additional examples and information from the additional 11 interviewees.

Ronnie. An undergraduate math and statistics major and informatics minor of Chinese and European descent, Ronnie grew up in Park Ridge, Illinois, a suburb of Chicago, and was 20 and 21 years old at the time of the initial study. Ronnie played bass in the university orchestra and for local theater productions. In 2016, Ronnie was a software developer enrolled in a master's program for computer science. Ronnie initially had active accounts on the following social network sites: Twitter, Facebook, Blogger, Myspace, Tumblr, Flickr, YouTube, Last.fm, LinkedIn, Academia.edu, PureVolume, Digg, LibraryThing, and Ning, and when we talked again in 2016, he also had an Instagram account and also used GroupMe. Ronnie first used computers in elementary school (fourth grade), primarily for word processing and email. He described his father as an early technological literacy sponsor (Selfe & Hawisher, 2004) who helped him run DOS programs on the family computer. In 2010 and 2011, Ronnie primarily used a Dell laptop for his social media use; he also bought an iPhone during the course of the initial data collection period, through which he also updated social network sites. He noted in 2016 that he still preferred to use social media from a computer, but he used his phone when he had to. Most of the photos he posted on social media were also shared from his phone. Experienced with web design, Ronnie had been blogging for six years at the time of the initial study, having started blogging at the suggestion of a high school English teacher. He began using Facebook in 2006, when the service opened itself up to high school students, primarily to keep in touch with friends who had already graduated. He considered himself an early adopter of many different social network sites; he joined Twitter in 2008, and he reported that he often joined new sites to "claim real estate," that is, reserve his username, on the site in case it became popular later.

Alexis. Alexis was a 22-year-old Korean undergraduate media studies major at the time of the initial data collection period. Alexis was born in South Korea and lived there until she was 8 years old. Her family then moved to Raleigh, North Carolina, and stayed there for 4 years. They returned to Korea for 5 years and then returned to the United States, moving to Illinois, in 2004. By 2016, Alexis had earned a master's degree in media and communications technology. While Alexis's parents had returned to South Korea, she was living in a large city on the East Coast of the United States and was working for an advertising company, specializing in social and mobile marketing and analytics. As an undergraduate, Alexis lived at home rather than on campus, and she had accounts on Facebook, Twitter, Cyworld, YouTube, and WordPress. By 2016, Alexis also had accounts on Instagram and LinkedIn. Alexis first used computers in elementary school and used the family Windows 98 desktop for homework as well as games like solitaire and educational word games. Alexis named her father as an early computer literacy sponsor, although she reported that his computer knowledge used to be better than it was at the time of our conversation. She had two computers at the time of the initial study, a Dell laptop and an Aces netbook. Alexis primarily left the laptop at home and used the netbook for checking email and updating social network sites away from home, as well as for taking notes in class. She joined Facebook in 2008, although she did not use her account very actively until 2009. Alexis also joined Twitter in 2010, while she had been sending updates to the Korean social network site Cyworld for much longer.

Beth. Beth, a white undergraduate earth systems, environment, and society major and an informatics minor, used social network sites less frequently than many of her peers, for both time and privacy reasons. Beth grew up in Oklahoma and moved to Illinois in high school. Beth cited her father as an early literacy sponsor, and he programmed an early counting, animal, and color-matching game she played on the computer. While she used a computer primarily for games at home, by sixth grade Beth was also connecting to the internet to answer daily science questions for school, while she still preferred print encyclopedias for her work, and she also had experience with web design and basic html coding in middle school. As the editor of her high school newspaper, Beth spent a lot of time using publishing software for print media design. While Beth wanted a computer as a high school graduation gift, she was given jewelry instead, and she saved her summer income to purchase an HP tablet laptop running Windows 7 that she used for all of her schoolwork in 2010 and 2011. Beth was active on LiveJournal in high school and maintained a Facebook profile, which she checked once a week during this study to keep up with friends in other cities and states, and she had a Twitter profile, which she was required to create for a class at the time of my study. While her personal use of social network sites was minimal, Beth also maintained the social media accounts for a local food co-op as their outreach coordinator. Beth primarily updated her information from a laptop computer, as her cell phone did not have a data or texting plan, and she used social network sites more frequently for her job than for her personal use. I was unable to follow up with Beth about her social media use in 2016.

Sandra. Sandra, a white undergraduate art and design major at the time of this initial study, was also a fashion blogger, photographer, and enjoyed making craft jewelry projects. Sandra grew up in the Chicago suburbs and first used a computer at home for games and in elementary school for games and typing papers. Sandra considered herself self-taught on the computer, and she used computers primarily to discover, share, and edit media from an early age. She was burning CDs of songs she downloaded from Napster by the time she was in fifth grade. Sandra used AOL instant messenger throughout middle school and primarily used the computer in high school for word processing, music, and editing images taken with her digital camera. Sandra joined Myspace in high school, primarily because musical groups she was interested in were using the service; she joined Facebook in high school as one of the first high school students among her peers to join the site. Along with Facebook, Sandra had accounts on the following sites at the time of this study: Twitter, Google, LinkedIn, Flickr, YouTube, and LookBook. Sandra owned a Mac laptop, from which she updated most of her information on social network sites, but she also updated Twitter from her iPhone using the app Twitterific. Along with her personal social network site use, Sandra also managed the online presence for an art museum while studying abroad in Norway, working with their communications department to promote and report on special events through their Flickr account. Sandra was also one of the initial research participants with whom I was unable to follow up with in 2016.

Jack. Jack was a white graduate student at the time of the study, who grew up in Tucson, Arizona. Along with his work as a graduate student and teaching assistant at the university, Jack was a musician, blogger, and also a father of three. In 2016, Jack had graduated with his PhD and was an assistant professor at a research university. Jack had profiles on the following services during this study: Facebook, Twitter, Myspace, Google, Tumblr, Flickr, Picasa, Vimeo, YouTube, lala—a music-sharing social networking site—and two blogs on Blogger. In 2016, Jack also had an Instagram and an inactive LinkedIn account. He also contributed to another music-themed blog that provides music reviews for regional concerts. Jack began using computers in elementary school on a Macintosh computer, primarily for what he described as "Oregon Trail kinds of computing." His family did not have a computer in their home until Jack was in high school, and he pointed to one of his best friends during that time as a technological literacy sponsor. His friend worked for AOL and assisted Jack in getting online by giving him a free screen name. Through this account, Jack participated in chats and posted to message boards. Jack has always used a computer to access music as well, and when he was in high school, he used to download 20-second clips of The Smashing Pumpkins samples from their new album, *Mellon Collie and the Infinite Sadness*. At the time of the initial study, Jack used both a MacBook and an iPod touch to connect online and to send messages through social network sites. He also sent updates to Twitter and pictures from his cell phone. By 2016, much of Jack's social media activity had moved to his mobile phone. Along with maintaining a Facebook profile, a neglected music profile on Myspace, a Tumblr account, and two separate blogs, Jack also maintained four different Twitter accounts throughout the course of this study.

Esther. Esther, a white, Jewish graduate student and a teaching assistant at the time of the initial study, was also a blogger and a knitter, sharing projects and participating in events with her fellow knitting friends online. By 2016, Esther had also graduated with a PhD and was an assistant professor at a 4-year college. Esther grew up in Philadelphia and as a child shared a computer with her siblings at home; she used the Apple 2C primarily for games like Family Feud and Wheel of Fortune. In middle school, she began to use the computer to write stories, including typing, printing, and making them into homemade books. Esther used both a MacBook and an iMac at the time of the initial study, and in 2016, she also used a mobile phone for social media. She had mostly lapsed profiles on Myspace and Orkut, and she used Facebook, Twitter, and blogged through LiveJournal and WordPress. She was still maintaining her blog on WordPress in 2016, and she added Instagram and YikYak to her social media activity. The social network site she used most frequently, however, was Ravelry, a site specifically for knitters.

Esther joined all of these sites in graduate school, prompted by friends (Orkut, Twitter), musicians she enjoyed (Myspace), and even students (Facebook). Esther considered herself an occasional user of Facebook, with Ravelry consuming the majority of her online time and attention.

Becca. Becca was a white graduate student and teaching assistant who grew up outside of Phoenix, Arizona. Becca first used computers in elementary school for playing educational games on Apple 2e machines, and her family purchased a computer for their home when she was in eighth grade. Before the computer, Becca typed school projects at home on a typewriter. In eighth grade, Becca also took a technology course, using different programs for music and graphic design, as well as word processing. Becca cited her father as a technology literacy sponsor at home; he worked in tech support for mainframe computers, and often assisted her with computer questions at home. Becca gained access to the internet at home during high school and used it to research topics for school before getting an email account as a senior in high school. In addition to her roles at the university as a graduate student and a teacher in the Undergraduate Rhetoric Program, Becca also participated in a university belly dancing troupe, placing some of their performances online, as well as maintaining a store on Etsy, where she sold jewelry that she made. During this study, Becca was active on Facebook, Etsy, and Academia.edu. Becca used a Dell laptop to update her social network sites, primarily from home and from her office. I was also unable to connect with Becca again for a follow-up.

2013 Participants

Jordan. Jordan was an African American junior and journalism major at the time of our interview. He reported that he had lived with his grandfather since he was 9, and therefore "had to navigate the virtual reality thing pretty much on my own." He had an old Macintosh computer growing up, but only used the computer for schoolwork—"typing and solitaire"—because he didn't have patience with the dial up internet connection. Jordan used a 4-to-6-year-old laptop for basic functions: social networking, web surfing, and word processing. He had two Twitter accounts, one was more of a personal account and another he used to share news-oriented information and links, connected to his major and desired future occupation. Jordan was a prolific writer and editor for the student newspaper and kept a current events news blog. While he had Twitter linked to his phone, he only used Facebook on a desktop computer. He noted that he joined social media accounts, especially Facebook, because of "peer pressure."

Friends wanted to connect with him through that platform, and so he felt a need to join. A self-described "photography snob," he also found Instagram unappealing because of its reliance on mobile phone camera images. Twitter was therefore the platform he used most frequently.

Angela. Angela, a Lebanese American junior and psychology and journalism major remembered first using a computer at 8 years old, when she began using instant messenger. She described her technology skills with an emphasis on their shortcomings. She soon learned that her hunt-and-peck keyboard methods were inadequate: "It would take forever for me to like send an IM message, and then everyone would always IM me back, 'wow, you type so slow.'" Her sister created an AOL account for her, but Angela reported that she learned everything on her own and shared the one family computer with her siblings. While she used to use Myspace, she moved to Facebook when many of her peers did, and this was the only social media site that she mentioned using frequently during our interview. Angela had what she called professional social network accounts on Twitter and LinkedIn. While she was occasionally required to use Twitter for a class, she did not use either Twitter or LinkedIn as frequently.

Stephanie. Stephanie was an Italian American senior and journalism major at the time of our interview. She noted that she first used computers in kindergarten, where she had to share one computer with a whole class of students, and began typing classes in school in fourth grade. She primarily used a large IBM computer at home growing up, where she had access to the internet through AOL and used it to play games. Stepphanie first joined social network sites in middle school, when she used Zynga, and then moved to Myspace and Friendster in high school, followed by Facebook. At the time of our interview, she had a "really old" MacBook she used mostly for schoolwork. She had accounts on Twitter, Facebook, and Instagram. She checked Facebook every few days and used Twitter to follow journalists and news organizations, as well as musicians and music journalists, as an "aspiring music journalist." Instagram, though, was "for fun." Stephanie also had a LinkedIn profile, which she did not use frequently, and a Spotify account where she shared music interests and activity wth friends and contacts.

Francesca. Francesca was an Italian American junior and journalism major and noted that she first used computers in elementary school, where she learned to type, but she used a laptop that did not have an internet connection at home growing up, primarily to play games. At the time of our interview, she had a MacBook that she used for school projects, social media, Skype, and other communications. Like Stephanie, Francesca joined Myspace but no longer used the account. She used

Facebook frequently to keep in touch with friends, and she also used two different Twitter accounts as well as an Instagram account. The Twitter accounts were separated into a more professional account for journalism and a personal account that Francesca used primarily to retweet content. As a journalism student, Francesca maintained a WordPress blog, which was connected to her Facebook account. She therefore often shared content from her blog with her Facebook contacts.

2016 Participants

Caroline. Caroline was a white sophomore and English major. Facebook was the first social media platform she signed up for, and she did so in order to connect with her high school friends and to share photos. At the time of our interview, she had accounts on Facebook, Instagram, and Snapchat. While she checked Facebook occasionally to stay updated with her friends, she posted most frequently on Instagram. Caroline noted that, for her, social media was primarily for sharing photos. She rarely posted Facebook statuses or shared text content, preferring to share photos with her contacts instead.

Sam. Sam was a white sophomore and English major. They[3] adopted social media platforms early, and Sam described joining Gaia Online and Club Penguin as a child. Gaia Online allows users to create an avatar and interact with other users in an online environment, and Club Penguin is a similar virtual world. Sam joined Facebook in middle school and had profiles on Facebook, Twitter, and Instagram at the time of our interview. Sam had a public Twitter account and mentioned their 1,500 followers in our interview; they were active in both music and activist circles and had their content retweeted by social justice activists. They also had four different Instagram accounts: one for selfies, a private Instagram account (described as a "finsta[4]" account) for close friends, one for aesthetic photos, and a fourth account to share posts on music and other media content.

Nicole. Nicole was an African American master's student in English. She started a Facebook account when she was in middle school but did not use it very often and started posting to it more than a month before our interview because she had a Facebook group that was used in one of her graduate courses. She also had accounts on Twitter, LinkedIn, and Pinterest. Nicole reported that she began using Twitter for a previous job she had, where she composed and sent tweets for a state government organization. Nicole did not share many personal updates on her social media, and she did not use it to connect with friends and family very often. She reported that she used Pinterest most often to find natural hair photos, apartment decorating ideas, and recipes.

Amy. Amy was a white doctoral student of English. She was a returning student and therefore joined social media as an adult. She reported that she signed up for a Facebook account in 2007 at the prompting of her coworkers in order to connect with them outside of work. She noted that it felt like peer pressure from her coworkers to join Facebook. While Amy had a Facebook account for almost 10 years at the time of our interview, she had joined Twitter and Instagram more recently. She used both Facebook and Twitter frequently—Facebook to keep up with friends and family and Twitter to keep up with the news. Instagram was more for family photos and to share family news and content with other relatives. Amy described herself as a Facebook "addict," noting that she spent considerable time on the site scrolling and interacting with others.

DATA-COLLECTION METHODS

As noted above, the investigation of situated literacy practices across online and offline spaces relies on a multifaceted research methods approach. In conducting these situated case studies, I collected data from four different sources, and the initial data collection occurred over the course of 2010 to 2011, beginning in March of 2010. The follow-up interviews were conducted with four of the participants in April of 2016.

1.   **Research interviews:** I conducted periodic, open-ended reflective interviews with each case study participant. The interviews began with a semi-structured organization, and the first formal interview for each participant focused on questions about their personal histories with literacy and technology. The second interview for each participant consisted of a profile tour of the social networking sites they belong to (more on this below.) After these first two interviews, I conducted periodic interviews, occurring every 2–4 weeks, focusing on recent social networking site activity and other changes to participants' social networking site use. These interviews lasted from 30 to 60 minutes, and the topics were dictated by the participants, though I frequently asked questions about specific actions taken on social network sites, focusing on literacy practices and on identity representation. Each interview was video-recorded and transcribed for future analysis. The research interviews served two important functions in the study. First, they provided a guide through the textual data I collected on online activity. In each interview, the participant and I discussed specific activity they engaged in online since we had last met. These interviews helped me to understand the interactions that each participant deemed important, and this insight guided me through analysis of participants' online texts. Second, the interviews

served an important triangulation function. Through each interview, I was able to verify my own interpretations of participants' online activity, and participants were able to discuss their motivations and provide their own perspective to the conclusions I was drawing from their work.

2. **Online texts:** The second primary means of data collection was the collection of texts that participants contributed to social networking sites. Aside from one exception, research participants allowed me to follow them on the social network sites they participated in. For these research participants, I observed their activity online, and I collected the textual record of these interactions. The means by which I collected this data depended on the social networking site and the ways in which the participants used it. Two research participants, for example, were quite active on Twitter and sent occasional tweets to Facebook, but their activity level on Facebook was lower, and they rarely updated the site independently from Twitter. For these research participants, I collected the tweets they sent in a separate document, but I did not collect the Facebook data unless it was activity we specifically discussed in our interviews. For research participants who did not use Facebook, I kept track of their activity on the site by visiting their profile pages periodically, which contained a record of their status updates, as well as the images, links, and other content they had shared through the site. I kept note of specific activity to discuss in our next interview. For the research participant whom I did not follow online, I used a video screen capture program to record our interviews, and we primarily talked from the computer during our interview sessions, as she gave me background information on some of her recent activity online. Each research participant had accounts on special interest social network sites that were not central to our interview discussions and used occasionally by the participants, such as last.fm and LinkedIn. In these cases, I kept a record of the participants' pages, but did not actively collect data on interactions on these sites. Such activity was often discussed in our interviews, at which time I referred back to the textual record on the sites. For the follow-up study, the interviews covered material that spanned the 5-year period, but I only collected social media posts from the 2 months prior to April 2016.

3. **Time-use diaries:** The third element of data collection involved time-use diaries, which I adapted from Bill Hart-Davidson's (2007) own time-use diaries, as a means to visualize the different documents that made up a workplace writing project. Hart-Davidson described time-use diaries as a means to study situated writing practices and to collect activity that would be impossible for me to observe in an unobtrusive way. I asked each participant to complete a time-use diary based on Hart-Davidson's model in order for me to visualize how their social network site use was distributed across their daily activities. Completing a diary for the length of the project would be time intensive and produce a large amount of data, and so I requested that participants pick three "average" days through which to record their social network site use, asking them the time of the event, the message and its purpose, and the

technology through which the message was sent (mobile phone versus computer, for example). Hart-Davidson (2007) noted that diaries could be a means to facilitate dialog between the participant and researcher and to add contextual information (p. 163). Through these time-use diaries, I was able to track literate activity as it was embedded within my participants' daily use of social network sites. We further discussed these diaries in follow-up interviews.

4. **Profile tours:** During one of the initial interviews I conducted with each research participant, I asked each person to take me on a "profile tour" of their social network sites. This tour was a means through which we could discuss identity representation on each site and would allow the participants to speak from specific elements of their identity representation—for example, profile pictures or specific written descriptions, but also to gain insights into participants' attitudes toward privacy settings, friend lists, and other elements of social network sites. These profile tours were recorded using the video screen capture software program called iShowU, developed by shinywhitebox. This program was chosen for its compatibility with Mac computers, its low cost, and its flexibility in recording video in several different formats. I did not conduct profile tours again in 2016. I used a number of similar methods to those used by Leon and Pigg (2011), but each method had a different focus based on the nature of writing on social network sites. Given the nature of short but frequent activity on these sites, recording a sustained writing session with video screen capture was not possible, but more reflective profile tours allowed me to gain access to participants' concepts of their online identities and reflections of their composing decisions.

Given the distributed nature of literate activity, I cannot pretend that I have captured a complete picture of these participants' literacy experiences on social network sites. Collecting data from these various sources, however, allows me to develop a multifaceted picture of literate activity in connection with social networking sites. The research interviews, for example, allowed me to gauge my own interpretations on comments that participants posted online, as well as to gain background information unavailable in the textual record.

I conducted the interviews with additional participants in 2013 and 2016 to connect the findings of my primary research participants to those of other undergraduate and graduate students, to add perspectives of a more diverse group of participants, as well as to gain additional perspectives on what might be common themes. While these interviews included profile tours, they did not include time-use diaries, digital text collection, or multiple interviews. For these reasons, the experiences of the original seven case study participants play a larger role in the following chapters. The primary themes that I derived from this data, however, include experiences of all 15 participants.

CONCLUSION

The specific methods listed above are not the only or the best way to study literacy practices on social media platforms, and I do not present them as such. Social media research involves a number of complicated challenges for writing researchers, as I've detailed in this chapter. This approach allowed me to gain an overall descriptive picture of my research participants' activities and their perspectives and rationale as they negotiated different social media platforms.

I must also acknowledge here that my approach was a bit ad hoc and low tech. Other researchers have described using technology-aided methods for data collection, including Twitter scraping, checking in with participants via text message, and using other tools to ease data collection and analysis (Pigg et al., 2014; Wolff, 2018). Many of these capabilities either did not exist at the time that I collected the initial data for this research project or I was unaware of them. Others were beyond the realm of my technological expertise. It is important for writing researchers to continue considering and exploring the potential options for studying distributed literacy practices, particularly those in digital environments. Each new method brings with it its own issues of research ethics, and it is imperative for writing researchers to consider those as well.

I also argue in chapter 1 for the importance of considering privacy and consent as networked. As I outlined in this chapter, there are real concerns regarding the use of social media data outside of context and without the knowledge of the social media users whose content is being studied. While there are situations in which these particular research approaches are called for, I argue that is crucial for writing researchers not to just consider information that is publicly visible on the internet to be public information able to be studied. Writing researchers should reflect on ways to study online activity that respects individuals' information and experiences that also places those interactions in context beyond the textual record available online.

This chapter considered many of the methodological and ethical questions that writing researchers face when studying social media, as well as the methodological decisions I ultimately made for this study. Chapters 3, 4, and 5 outline digital literacy practices that were clustered around three central challenges my research participants confronted when using social media: navigating audiences, managing data, and representing identities in the context of those audiences.

3
NEGOTIATING AUDIENCE
ACROSS PLATFORMS

As described briefly in chapter 1, social media has an audience problem. The first decade of social media use is filled with cautionary tales
of individuals posting something that moved far beyond one's original
or intended audience. Viktor Mayer-Schönberger began his 2009 book
Delete: The Virtue of Forgetting in the Digital Age with a story about Stacy
Snyder, a student who lost her ability to earn a teaching license because
of an image of herself at a Halloween party on her Myspace page that
she captioned "drunken pirate." While she was of legal drinking age and
the photo did not show her consuming anything immediately identifi-
able as alcohol, her university still denied her the credentials necessary
to achieve a teaching license, for conduct "unbecoming of a teacher"
(Mayer-Schönberger, 2011, p. 1). She later unsuccessfully sued her university about this decision. Snyder's case served as an early cautionary tale
to social media users about the ways that information persists online and
is also available to others beyond its intended audience. The internet,
Mayer-Schönberger noted, doesn't forget and therefore doesn't forgive.

The example of Justine Sacco presented a similar case, but one whose
impact was more consequential because it occurred within a single
platform, Twitter, and at a time when Twitter had 204,000,000 users
(Statista, 2018). On a flight to South Africa in 2013, Sacco, a strategic
communications professional, tweeted, "Going to Africa. Hope I don't
get AIDS. Just kidding. I'm white!" According to Jon Ronson (2015),
Sacco didn't expect any of her 170 followers to reply to her offensive
joke. By the time she had landed in South Africa, however, she was the
number one trending topic worldwide on Twitter through the hashtag
#HasJustineLandedYet. Ronson (2015) includes just a few of the Twitter
responses in his summary of the incident, from moral outrage: "In light
of @Justine-Sacco disgusting racist tweet, I'm donating to @care today"
to calls for her to be fired from her position: "We are about to watch this
@JustineSacco bitch get fired. In REAL time. Before she even KNOWS
she's getting fired." Others were caught up in the entertainment of a
scandal unfolding in real time: "Seriously. I just want to go home to go

https://doi.org/10.7330/9781646424023.c003

to bed, but everyone at the bar is SO into #HasJustineLandedYet. Can't look away. Can't leave." Someone even went to the airport in Cape Town to get a picture of her when she arrived. Sacco's "joke" was incredibly distasteful, yet Ronson's *New York Times Magazine* story presents a sympathetic portrait of her as a hapless individual caught up in the "Internet outrage machine," fueled by social media technologies that allow a specific user's message the ability to move far beyond its intended audience. In his book *So You've Been Publicly Shamed*, Ronson connected stories like these to the 18th and early 19th centuries, when public shaming was also a form of punishment, in order to question contemporary digital practices.

As writing researchers, we might attribute these kinds of examples to a lack of user foresight and knowledge or we might point to the technology itself in not allowing more nuanced controls to restrict one's audience. We might see Snyder's case as an unfortunate situation of someone whose image was taken out of context, or we might see Sacco as deserving of the digital shaming that came afterward. Both of these cases, though, indicate a wide mismatch between one's intended audience and one's actual audience on social media and the problems that this disconnect can cause.

As described earlier in this text, a key digital literacy practice needed to participate on social network sites throughout the first decade of their use involved managing and navigating multiple audiences across different social media platforms. Using information from my participants' social media use and their interviews, in this chapter I detail how these specific individuals managed multiple audiences to represent themselves, communicate with others, and manage information across multiple platforms. This activity requires not only a sophisticated awareness of audience, but also an understanding of site structure and the ability to emphasize different aspects of identity with different audiences.

As noted in chapter 1, many of the concerns of my research participants connected to audience can be understood through the concepts of *context collapse* and *rhetorical velocity*. It is often difficult for social media users to write to specific audiences when that friends-and-followers list is flattened into one contact list. Similarly, it is challenging to write on social media when that writing is also circulated beyond one's original audience. As one of my research participants discusses later in this text, it is this practice of copying and circulating that a writer cannot control. While a comment or update may be written, or an image or video shared in a specific rhetorical situation for a specific group of people, given the ease of circulating information online, that information often does not remain in its original rhetorical context. Negotiating these rhetorical situations to represent oneself, then, is a complex literate activity that involves a number of different strategies and considerations. This chapter describes some of the approaches my research participants used in order to negotiate these complex situations across social media platforms. As noted in chapter 1, we can think of these strategies as fitting into two broad categories: (a) proactive or invention strategies to generate content for social media platforms in order to reach digital audiences and (b) defensive strategies that both respond to and anticipate potential audience problems.

CONTENT AND TECHNOLOGICAL AFFORDANCES

All of the individuals discussed in this study used their own perceptions of audience based on their experiences connecting with others in both online and offline contexts. They also used site architectures available to them in order to help manage these different groups, including privacy settings, smaller and restricted groups, and other approaches. On the surface, adjusting the audience for a post by hiding it from specific individuals or adjusting one's privacy settings does not appear to be a complicated or sophisticated practice. Yet it requires an awareness of the conventions of that specific platform, an understanding of news feed algorithms and how visible one's content will be, and knowledge of a number of other social media tools in order to share information effectively. All of these factors also changed frequently over the first decade of social media. This chapter, then, describes the situated digital literacy practices these writers used to both create content and to share it with their intended audiences. Each of the writers described in this study used the available means of persuasion by composing content and utilizing the technologies available to them.

As Lunsford and Ede (1984) noted, an audience is in part invoked or signaled in language choices made by a writer, and all of the writers I have studied here do the same. They use specific language, sometimes specific hashtags, as well as images and other multimodal content, to signal or invoke a particular audience or audience stance. At the same time, these writers also use the technological affordances and structures available to them through social media platforms in order to both invoke and address specific audiences.

For the individuals I describe here, this negotiation between content and technological structure in reaching and responding to audiences was constant, continually refined by each new status update and each new comment from an online contact. Lunsford and Ede (2009) later noted how writing in digital environments allowed more of a constant reciprocity between writers and audiences (p. 48). John Gallagher (2018, 2020) also argued that the ways that writers in online contexts shift their conception of and their response to audiences real and imagined are based on online comments. While each writer I describe here developed approaches that worked for them, these solutions were dynamic and constantly in flux.

MANAGING AUDIENCE BY ACCOUNT

One proactive strategy that a few participants used was to create distinct accounts on the same platform for different audiences. At the beginning of this study, several of these individuals created multiple accounts on the same social media platform in order to reach a specific audience with more targeted content. Ronnie, an undergraduate math major at the time of the initial study, was a self-described "early adopter" of different social media platforms. He frequently established an account on a social network site when it started in order to "claim real estate" on the site in case it became popular. Ronnie noted that he started his Twitter account in this way, and he also set up accounts on other social network sites—Academia.edu, Tumblr, LinkedIn, and others—in this same way. This practice allowed Ronnie to claim the same screen name across the web and represent what he saw as the part of his identity that stayed constant across the different social network sites he belonged to, before developing a more tightly crafted persona specifically directed to a particular audience or community he wanted to reach through the site.

At one time, Ronnie had three Twitter accounts: one he called his primary, "stream of consciousness," account that he updated an average of 20 times a day; one connected to a music Tumblr account; and another connected to his blog, which simply linked to his recent blog posts. Ronnie saw these separate Twitter accounts as something that made it easy for his audience to follow more targeted information, as he described in an interview:

> I guess that's just more for benefit of people who are following me in certain capacities. If they just want, like, music updates, then that's what that Twitter's for. Then they don't have to follow my actual Twitter and see all the random stuff I talk about.

Splitting up the information he shared by platform was Ronnie's way of ensuring that his audience was interested in the information he shared.

While Ronnie used Twitter, Facebook, and other platforms constantly throughout an average day, he also developed more specialized content for what he called his "musical alter ego." he maintained a Tumblr blog, a Facebook fan page, a Myspace music page, and a PureVolume account under that name. He described the reasons for the separation of these sites related to audience. Ronnie described his musical identity this way on his PureVolume account, which is a site for musical artists to share their work, very similar to Myspace music pages:

> Sure, I certainly enjoy going by my real name every now and then but this is "Creative [Ronnie]." The [Ronnie] that people don't get to see because he never has enough time in the day to write music and usually spends his time just performing it. :)

Ronnie signaled in the profile description here that this particular social media profile has a specific purpose: to share the music he's written for those who are interested but perhaps do not see that side of him very often. For people who were not his friends but were interested in his music, this strategy enabled him to direct specific content to a specific audience, as he explained:

> And I guess I segment it cause if I want, if people are going to look at my musical self, they don't, they're probably not interested in seeing my blogging self, or you know the photos I take on Flickr or whatever, so I keep that separate more for them, not so much because I don't want them to see my other self. That's why I think, okay, they're here just to see my music, so that's what I'll just give them.

Ronnie's Tumblr account, which he linked to his specific Facebook fan page, worked the same way. He used this page to share both audio recordings of music he wrote, videos from jam sessions in his apartment, and other music-related images—all information he kept off of his primary Twitter and Facebook accounts.

Through Ronnie's musical alter ego, he created a specific audience group populated by musicians and fellow music lovers who were interested in his work as a musician but perhaps less interested in his personal life. While many social network site users maintain profiles for more professional audiences and aspects of their identity, Ronnie chose a different name to make the separation more complete. In creating a stage name, what Ronnie described as an "alter ego," Ronnie constructed an identity that he marked as different from those he presented using his other screen names. Ronnie stated that he was not concerned about connecting his music to his other online identities and he did, in fact, list his real name on the Facebook page for his alter ego. He did not link to his other social media accounts through the music accounts, however, demonstrating that he wanted to keep the two separate. A large part of the literate activity that Ronnie engaged with on social network sites involved managing content for specific audiences to construct his identity. Ronnie's use of Facebook and Twitter demonstrated how he negotiated flattened audience structures to share information and represent himself for both groups. Through his musical alter ego, Ronnie conceived of a particular audience and created a kind of profile page and persona in response.

Many of the individuals I interviewed in 2016 also split their social media accounts for this same purpose. Sam, as noted in chapter 2, had four different Instagram accounts. Their public Instagram account used this as a profile description: "my life told in selfies," and the images Sam posted to that account consisted entirely of self-portraits. The second account was a finsta account, which had less censored content that was shared exclusively with close friends. Sam described their finsta account this way: "I post the worst things. That's kind of where I just vent, because I don't have that many followers and they all know me and it's just kind of like a joke." The third account was what Sam described as an aesthetic Instagram account, where they posted "arty pics." Because their primary Instagram account was exclusively for selfies, in order to post more interesting photos and ones without people in them, Sam created a third account. The fourth account Sam created was mostly on hold at the time of our interview, and Sam noted that they were planning to post music and music-related content on that account. Like Ronnie, then, Sam split information on one specific platform by both audience and type of content. While one Instagram account was private and contained jokes and content for only close friends, the other accounts were public, defined by thematic content that would interest different audiences.

Jack, one of the graduate students in my initial data-collection period, frequently adjusted his three different Twitter accounts based both on his current needs and response from different audiences. At various times throughout the data-collection period, Jack maintained three different Twitter accounts: a long-standing personal Twitter account, a more professionally focused Twitter account about academic research interests, and one account for teaching. Jack had identified specific audience groups, and he presented himself to those different audience groups in distinct ways: as a teacher on one account, as an academic on another, and his out-of-school identity as musician and music critic on what he labeled his primary account.

When I first interviewed Jack, he had recently retired his academic Twitter account. He noted that no one followed the account, as he had already made connections with academics through his personal account before starting the second one. He described it primarily as a "container for links," most of which he also retweeted in his primary twitter account, and stopped using after 4 months, having sent only 25 tweets.

He was using a separate account for his teaching, however, which he had created to communicate with students without "subjecting students to personal tweets." He required his students to check the class Twitter account frequently. Even though only four or five of his students tweeted regularly, Jack stated that he found tweeting to be a valuable activity to engage in with his class. Keeping the class tweets on a separate account was a way for Jack to manage his different audiences on Twitter. In an interview, he mentioned a tweet he had sent out via the class account the night before, reminding students to send him their writing reflections before the end of the night. Jack stated that he didn't want announcements like this tweet going out to all of his other Twitter followers:

> I could have created like a hashtag or something like that that would have made that specific tweet go to, um, my students, but still, if I sent that through my regular account, everybody that follows me would see it, and like, what, what would the point of that be? I don't really know. It's weird, and so I don't know that I would be comfortable sending out that kind of tweet that obviously has an audience that can respond to it and the information there is important, um, but I always feel less comfortable just sending it out to the world. [. . .] Whereas if I created my own account, I could make my tweets much more specific to that class, and at the same time not disrupt or annoy other people who might follow me for those particular reasons with these kind of, you know, very directive tweets.

While Jack could have used the language of his tweets or specific hashtags to indicate that the content was meant for a student audience, he instead decided to more explicitly divide his audience by using a completely separate Twitter account. Jack noted that he often saw other academics tweeting with their students on their own primary Twitter accounts, but he didn't feel comfortable doing the same, even as he worried he wasn't giving students a good example of how most people use Twitter:

> On the other hand, I see people like [name of scholar] who uses Twitter for her teaching as well. I've noticed this semester. I guess it's not like that big of a deal, like I see things come through that's obviously for her students, and I think that's maybe one of the things about Twitter that you have to get used to is that . . . you don't have to read every single post.

Despite these conventions, Jack justified these two different accounts based on their separate aims and audiences. He saw the student account tweets as distinct from the rest of his tweeting practices, and it was easy to streamline these tweets through a separate account.

After about a month, however, Jack noted that he kept missing his students' messages because he did not log into his class account regularly enough, and he stopped using the account specifically for his students. He was still concerned that he would be subjecting the other people he connected with on Twitter to class information, but this just seemed easier, and was along the lines of what other Twitter users did. He stated in an interview: "I have no idea. I see people tweeting about stuff that has no bearing on my life, and I guess it just becomes kind of noise. So I guess I'm now noise for some people every once in a while."

In describing his choice to return to one Twitter account, Jack relied on the activity of other Twitter users, his followers, and other academics to justify that what he was doing was a common practice. He used language features instead to indicate the tweet's intended audience; by using a class hashtag from his regular Twitter account, the rest of his followers would understand and ignore those tweets.

For most of my initial data-collection period, Jack used one Twitter account to connect to the different audiences he belonged to—musicians, music bloggers, friends, academics, and students—despite concerns of context collapse. While Jack was constantly changing his mind about a narrower audience for some of his Twitter content through those other accounts, some sample tweets from Jack's main account reflects these mixed interests. The following tweets share more of his personal reflection on his life as a student:

> Still have 8 students' double-papers to grade—Got Willie Nelson promoting his new b'grass album in concert on the dvr. Let's do this. 8:31 PM Feb 27th, 2011 via TweetDeck

> Super busy 10 days ahead. Much writing, coding, reading, +writing to do. Today I'm hoping to ease it by with the Junip and S. Carey records. 12:36 PM Dec 1st, 2010 via TweetDeck

> ahhh.. just registered for 8 hours of "thesis research" for next semester. Feels good. (as I'm sure it will until I begin said research) 2:24 PM Nov 18th, 2010 via TweetDeck

After abandoning the class-specific Twitter account, Jack also sent tweets to his students for class announcements, using a class hashtag:

> #classhashtag students: All but done w grading your projects. Look for them back tomorrow sometime. Great work overall, guys. I'm super impressed. 12:09 AM March 1, 2010 via TweetDeck

> #classhashtag folks: Love this video a girl made stranded in the Pittsburgh airport. Check out her editing/music choices. http://twurl.nl 8:35 AM Feb 23rd, 2011 via TweetDeck

> #classhashtag students: don't forget I need ur (double)write-ups tonight by midnight (& hey, rest of the world: I teach. I tweet. why not both?) 8:59 PM Feb 19th, 2011 via TweetDeck

These tweets demonstrate Jack's use of both language and hashtags to indicate the intended audience for these specific tweets. Both by using a specific class hashtag and focusing the language of the tweets on class-specific content, Jack indicates a specific, smaller audience for his posts. The final tweet shows Jack addressing two audiences and acknowledging this awkward flattening of audience that often occurred—and continues to occur—on Twitter, as well as his self-conscious feeling about that audience.

Along with tweets focused on his identity as a teacher and graduate student, Jack's personal Twitter account also included tweets related to his musical interests and his online identity as a music blogger and reviewer:

> The three middle songs on the new Band of Horses are turning into my favorite jams of the summer. (Blue Beard, Way Back Home, Infinite Arms) Fri Jul 23, 2010 via TweetDeck

> Heading to Pitchfork today (or is that p4k?). I have this song in my head (substitute "llama" with "hipster"): http://youtu.be/ Fri Jul 16, 2010 via TweetDeck

> I'm thinking more about the pumpkins (writing a review tonight on tomorrow's EP release) 11:28 PM Nov 22, 2010 via TweetDeck

Jack began writing music reviews in graduate school and connecting to the music community on Twitter became more important, which also gave him new writing opportunities, as indicated in the music-specific tweets above. With his music connections, Jack was able to attend almost 50 concerts for free, he mentioned in an interview, but more important was the networking power of Twitter:

> This whole network of maybe these music writers that I've become associated with because of Twitter, like I got this job writing for this blog through Twitter, and I've kind of, I don't necessarily have any kind of notoriety and clout, but every once in a while there's a little bit of like, oh, I wrote this piece for this blog and it gets picked up, you know, and retweeted, and that's the first time I've ever had any of that, right. Like most of us don't get our stuff, we don't get our stuff published kind of across the web.

Twitter gave Jack a different audience outside of academia, as well as opportunities to publish in different genres and venues outside of academic journals. This social media platform allowed Jack to reach and cultivate a new audience for his work and to pursue his personal interests as well. Around this time, Jack also revived his academic Twitter account, which he used to share content related to his research interests and degree program. I discuss this Twitter account in more detail in chapter 5. In this way, Jack kept updates from his classes and research to the academic account, while his original and primary Twitter account was for music-related content and more general observations.

Jack found a way to combine the tweets he sent for the music community to his daily life experience as well. He also often tweeted about his personal life, recounting moments with his children:

> At ihop for free pancakes. My daughter just ate one of those butter spheres they put on the top of the short stack. 6:51 AM Feb 23rd, 2010 via txt

> Convinced my boy that Buzz Lightyear's tagline is actually "To infinity . . . and your mom!" HIS mother will be so pleased. 2:59 PM Nov 24th, 2010 via TweetDeck

> Another cute malapropism from my daughter this time. "Hey Daddy, when I put my hand on my chest I can feel my heart beep." Sun Jul 25, 2010 14:21:13 2010 via TweetDeck

The music-oriented tweets are directed to both an audience of fellow music fans and bloggers, but the combination of these tweets, along with descriptions of everyday activities, indicate that Jack was comfortable sending out updates on diverse topics to a relatively wide audience. After abandoning his class-specific Twitter account, Jack used hashtags and references to specific content as an indication of the intended audience of his posts. Jack followed the conventions of many other Twitter users he followed by sharing these updates with a flattened audience of all of his Twitter followers.

Throughout the course of this study, Jack shaped his message and also his persona on Twitter through connections with what he considered distinct audience groups. In considering how he should share information and represent himself on this site, Jack relied on others in each of the different communities of practice he was reaching—primarily musicians and academics—to model his own updates on their identity performances. Jack followed the mentions of one music writer on TweetDeck, so he would see tweets from anyone who tweeted this person's name. This was a way for Jack to not only find other musicians to connect with, but to get a sense of how other musicians and music writers interacted together in this space. In our interviews, Jack often brought up other academics and their tweeting practices as examples to consider the ways that these academics represented themselves on Twitter. Jack learned the tweeting conventions of specific audiences by joining distinct communities of practice, observing their own practices in using Twitter, and responding in a way that created a dialogic process. As Jack interacted more with both musicians and academics on Twitter, he refined the ways he reached different audiences as a result. Through this process, he found two Twitter accounts to be a better way to represent himself to both of these audience groups—academics and musicians—with whom he was interested in connecting on social media.

By 2016, Jack maintained two different Twitter accounts, but for different purposes and audiences. He had abandoned the academic account and had moved all of the academic Twitter conversation and networking to his primary Twitter account. Jack no longer wrote music reviews, and he noted that he had unfollowed most of the music bloggers, bands, and critics that he used to follow. So, while he sometimes tweeted about music and topics related to music, he used his Twitter account primarily to connect with other academics in his field, sharing information at conferences, thoughts on teaching and research, as well as recent publications. Jack often connected with academic colleagues on Facebook, and Jack noted that both personal and professional conversations with other people in his academic field occurred on that space. Twitter was the place Jack reserved for more professional conversations, as well as jokes:

> There's fewer people on Twitter that know who I am personally, so when I tweet on Twitter it might be more about just kind of like general kinds of stuff I think is interesting, or jokes, you know, like Twitter is not for anything if not for joke telling. So yeah, I'm trying to, maybe there's a little more sense of trying to be cool on Twitter more than on Facebook, and then Facebook is a little bit more comfortable to be myself.

What Jack is describing here, I would argue, is a Twitter account that is more performative than his Facebook account. In 2016, Jack shared jokes about popular culture content and events, as he noted here, as well as live tweets from academic conferences, information about publications and calls for papers, as well as content about the university at which he had an academic appointment. Jack noted that he used to be worried about saying the wrong thing on Twitter, but by 2016 he had cultivated a sense of the academic audience of colleagues that he connected with on Twitter, as well as the kinds of things he posted to connect primarily with other scholars in his academic field.

In 2016, Jack's second account was one he used anonymously. He participated in what he called a reform-minded and activist movement connected to his religious affiliation, and he used that account specifically to connect with individuals in that community. This group was one he saw as almost completely separate from the more academic and personal audiences he connected with on Twitter, and it was also one that he didn't want to connect to his offline and professional identity. The anonymous account allowed Jack to follow fellow progressive reformers and activists, listen to conversations, and join in a bit safer of an environment. He described this decision in terms of both the complex nature of these conversations and a reluctance to get into political and religious debates on other social media platforms, especially Facebook. With this second, anonymous Twitter account, Jack sought out these more nuanced conversations about faith and about ways that reform conversations can enter the church. He noted:

> I don't engage in conversations generally that are binary, right? So I'm not like flaming out some like [conservatives]. I just don't, you know, but . . . I will engage folks in conversations that are complex conversations about various issues, you know, to varying degrees of, on varying levels, but most of my talk about that particular part of my life happens offline.

Les Hutchinson (2017) discussed the ways that anonymity on Twitter allows users the freedom to connect with new content and audiences and to join new conversations outside of their offline circles and identities (p. 203). This Twitter account allowed Jack to find a group of like-minded people and begin to have these conversations in online spaces as well. He noted that he might be having these conversations more as he began an academic project connected to these issues and, in the future, this audience group might be something he would decide to fold into his primary Twitter account. At the time, though, he saw it as something separate that he was trying to explore through an anonymous account. He also explained in our interview: "Digital tools help you to articulate those kinds of complexities in ways that weren't available before." Jack could join these groups and segment things a bit by audience by creating a completely different Twitter account with a different news feed, followers list, and username, allowing him to join distinct audiences in ways he felt he controlled.

Throughout this study, Jack used Twitter to enter new spaces and conversations in order to eventually join the community and discussion. He first used this approach in academic circles back in 2010, and second, in this religious community and space in 2016. Using different social media accounts on the same platform for distinct audience groups allowed Jack to join different communities of practice in a way that allowed him to observe groups, learn about the ways they used social media, and begin participating as a part of that community. While Jack's social media use did change over the course of this study, we can trace a trajectory of the ways he became more comfortable in the different communities he joined over time by first observing their interactions on Twitter.

SPLITTING AUDIENCE BY PLATFORM

While Ronnie and Jack both created multiple accounts on the same platform to segment audience or to reach different groups, most of the writers in this study instead divided audience by platform. For most of the undergraduates in this study, managing a wider audience on Facebook meant navigating context collapse and controlling information and updates for a larger group of people, including high school classmates, parents and other family, and friends from other places. In 2010 and 2011, Twitter was for a smaller audience, for closer friends and college connections, but this changed over time. In 2013, most of my participants reported using Twitter for news, and in 2016, one undergraduate used Twitter to reach large activist audiences and one graduate student used it to reach professionals in her field.

Sandra, an undergraduate art and design major, was an early adopter of Facebook when it began to allow high school students on the platform in 2005. In 2010, Sandra had had over 600 friends on the social network site, and like other research participants, her audience on the site ranged from family members, high school friends, close college friends, acquaintances, a few TAs from her courses, and even a former employer and mentor. Communicating with these different audience groups was not something that Sandra found to be a challenge. She stated that for the most part she saw Facebook as the place to keep up with her acquaintances, because she spent more time connecting to close friends in other settings—these were the people she lived with or called on the phone for frequent chats:

> I think the only thing I really use Facebook for is really keeping in touch with acquaintances, because my close friends, I'll just pick up the phone and call, or I live with them, or like I can just, we're close, it's not like with Facebook where it's just so like kind of half, it's like a half communication sort of.

With such a large group of people, Sandra noted that her primary purpose for using Facebook, besides commenting on friends' content and occasionally posting her own status updates, was to share photos:

> I don't take pictures every weekend when I'm hanging out with my friends, but when I was, I studied abroad, and I uploaded an album of photos like

once a week. And I loved doing that, and I loved the commentary between people, and how you can comment on the photos, and back and forth.

Sandra uploaded images most frequently when she was studying abroad in Norway for a semester. Not only was she taking photos more often, but she felt they were images that had a broad appeal among the audience groups that she connected to on the social network site, and it was content that would also create interactions and commentary between the different groups that she connected with. After Norway, Sandra's photo updates of other trips, outings, and social events around campus were items that she frequently shared on Facebook. Her Facebook wall was also a place where friends left questions and updates for her, but she posted less frequently.

Sandra used Twitter with a smaller group of friends, around 20–30 people, that made up her core friend group on the site, although she connected with others as well. Sandra followed 87 Twitter accounts that included friends, other personal contacts, companies, and news publications. She also had 86 followers on the site. Sandra's father, for example, set up a Twitter account to communicate with his employees, but also followed her from his company account and has her tweets sent to his phone. Much like Facebook, then, in implicit and explicit ways, her parents and other authority figures served as an actual and imagined audience that Sandra used as a marker to determine what to post online. Sandra's audience and the external influences from friends, family members, and other authority figures considerably shaped her social media use.

Sandra kept her Twitter account public, so anyone could visit her Twitter profile and see her updates, even if that person did not have a Twitter account, but she was more open about the content she shared on this platform because of her low number of followers. At the beginning of the study, Sandra had been using Twitter for almost a year and enjoyed following the kinds of conversations she would have with other Twitter users. She updated Twitter more frequently than Facebook, and she also was less reserved about the kinds of things that she would post about:

> Sometimes it's way less, and sometimes it's a lot. Like the other day I was at the library. All I was doing was complaining via Twitter. I think of Twitter, there's like a couple things its good for. You can complain so well on it because it's kind of like untargeted, and it's also a place to kind of like record thoughts on the go. The other thing that I think is particularly what I use it for when I follow people is to find new things. A lot of people use it as a connecting, because it's like a conversation, it's a

conversation that you let other people into, which I really like. And I try to avoid complaining, but generally when I'm happy, I'm not tweeting. I also just because I'm generally a bad texter. I can't text when I'm out with my friends, or walking or anything that's not sitting in a chair. So they're all very concentrated at certain times of the day, which means class, which is why I use it to complain.

Sandra used Twitter as a place to record stream-of-consciousness kinds of thoughts. When she was alone and bored, or studying and needing to create a connection with others not in her location, she used Twitter to feel connected, to record thoughts while she was alone, and to have a kind of "conversation," as she described it. Happier thoughts and more social moments were for engaging and connecting offline, and she did not leave as much of a record of them on her Twitter account. As Sandra noted, this use of her social network site accounts was also dictated by the technologies through which she used them. She often texted her updates to Twitter; in 2010, this was a common way for Twitter users without smart phones to update Twitter while away from a computer. Therefore, the difficulty of texting on a phone without a QWERTY keyboard limited Sandra's Twitter use. The ways that technology shaped social media use for these research participants is discussed in greater detail in chapter 4.

Sandra's Twitter updates, in fact, did contain a large number of tweets that she categorized as complaining. During the first semester of data collection, Sandra was enrolled in Chinese Art, a required course for her art history major that she disliked, and this course was featured prominently in her tweets:

> done with chinese art forever!!! cookie time 10 May 10

> 3 more pages stand between me and the end of chinese art. why is this so hard? 9 May 10

> jewelry studio failure and yet to start studying for chinese art. #totally screwed 21 Apr 10

She also used her Twitter account for her multimedia writing course and would occasionally tweet updates and questions about her projects to her classmates and her instructor:

> this video project is absolutely killing me. #thelibraryisreallyhot #imovieis theworst #sticktowritingessays 5 Apr 10

Sandra also frequently tweeted when she was studying in the library:

> i thought I was distracted at the library, but there's a girl in front of me watching sitcoms. I highly doubt its a subject of a thesis 12 Dec 10

I understand the library is crowded today. I will share my table with you, but please for the love of god, stop socializing. #imlookingatyou 12 Dec 10

if you're in college you're too old to wear perfume that smells like cotton candy #musingsfromalibrary 1:43 PM Oct 3rd, 2010 via web

Sandra's tone, references to campus locations, and discussions of experiences and complaints common to her friends and classmates around finals time, for example, indicates that these tweets are meant for herself to vent as well as for this smaller group with which she had a shared experience and would understand the library setting around finals time, for example. While her Twitter account was public, the specific content of her tweets embedded in her daily experience marked them for a smaller audience. She did not share these kinds of updates on Facebook. In these ways, Sandra used both language and platform to manage audience.

For many of the social media users described here, there was some amount of overlap between their audiences on different platforms, or they used multiple accounts on the same platform. By 2016, however, more of these participants described their social media audiences as segmented by platform. Alexis, an undergraduate media studies major at the beginning of this study, used Facebook and Twitter with an overlapping set of audiences in 2010, but by 2016 had segmented audiences by platform. Alexis noted in 2016 that Facebook was for friends and personal contacts, Twitter was for professional content—Alexis worked in social media marketing—and Instagram was more of a private, anonymous account she used for posting photos. Along with Facebook and Twitter, Alexis also used Instagram as more of what she called an anonymous photo diary, of "whatever inspired me." Alexis noted:

> Instagram is the only account, is the account that I have made public, but I don't have any personal, any pictures of myself or my friends, any personally identifiable information other than maybe a picture of my room or some decoration.

She noted that she used Instagram more for herself than for others and saw her audience as more personal for herself. While she posted more frequently on Instagram than on Facebook, her posts averaged one to two per week. Her Instagram account was composed primarily of daily minutiae with few people: coffee cups, street corners, work cubicles, and scenes from both local and international trips. As Alexis noted in her follow-up interview, she saw her Instagram account as having more of an audience of one: herself, as a photo diary and record of daily life. For Alexis, Facebook was private-facing, Twitter was public-facing, and Instagram was separate from the other two. In this way, Alexis organized her audience by platform and completely separated her audience and purpose on each different site in distinct ways.

Jack approached Instagram and Facebook in much the same way. While Facebook was a place to connect with others in his academic discipline, he described it as much more of a casual place where he shared mostly family photos of his children, vacations, and more local places and cultural events for the city he lived in. While Jack's Instagram photos occasionally made it to Facebook, he noted that he used Instagram for a smaller audience of personal friends, and more of "an intimate collection, in terms of like people that follow me, are the people for whom I am posting for." He also had a series of photos and a specific hashtag he created for unique items he found at his local thrift store, for example. Jack didn't want to post too frequently on Facebook, and he only posted things he felt comfortable sharing with a wider audience. On Instagram, though, he felt fewer restrictions with his posts: "I feel more comfortable posting a lot pictures to Instagram, if that makes sense. Because that's what the content is, and therefore, so where I was on Facebook, I am more likely to only share you know, cool ones, like that one, right? Like something that is special for one reason or another." Jack saw Instagram as having a more specific audience and one where more personal photos and content were more acceptable. While there was some overlap between his Facebook and Instagram audiences, the Instagram audience was a closer circle of closer friends and family, and Jack found that dividing audience by platform was a successful way for him to separate both his audience and purpose in sharing different information.

Ronnie also split audience by platform and often moved discussions on wider audiences to more private and small group conversation tools. While Ronnie had always used his Facebook account for wider audiences, he noted in 2016 that much of his Facebook usage was more to "share ideas" and less about his daily lived experience:

> I don't know if this is just cause I'm older or because people use, like, say, Facebook differently. But back in college, it, you'd always post photos of like a party you went to or you'd use it to kind of meet up and coordinate with people. I still use Facebook events and stuff, but it's not as heavy use as it used to be for me. It's more about sharing articles and big life events. That sort of thing. I mostly focus on like sharing ideas. And links to other things. And less focus on individual events of a person's life.

Ronnie's social media activity on Facebook confirmed that orientation. His posts included sharing photos from other Facebook accounts, like the therapy dog Norbert, and YouTube videos from people like Adam Conover (who hosted the TruTV program *Adam Ruins Everything*),

Figure 3.1. Ronnie's Instagram post from The Wizarding World of Harry Potter.

Lin-Manuel Miranda's interviews with Emma Watson, as well as photos and posts from a trip to the Wizarding World of Harry Potter at Universal Studios (shown in figure 3.1), and occasional photos of food and social outings, as well as some information about voting in the 2016 Democratic primary for his local area.

He noted that much of the content he shared on Facebook was governed by his audience:

> Like that's a very controlled image [on Facebook]. Like that would kind of better reflect how I might present myself in real life situations talking to those people. And in some ways it's also like an amalgam of all that too. Cause if I'm hanging out with my family it's obviously going to act differently than if I'm hanging out with my friends. Um, and, you know, different groups and that, but like on Facebook I don't spend any time to target different groups, it's just like, it doesn't push specific content straight to them. There, I'm kind of just being more myself. [. . .] The thing on Facebook, the audience has gotten larger. And with that I haven't been as specific with what I post. A bit more conservative with it.

While Ronnie visited Facebook a few times a day, in 2016, he noted that he didn't post on the site as much, and that "conservative" Facebook behavior was at least in part governed by the diversity of his audience on the site and its resulting context collapse.

For this reason, he often moved content to more private channels and small group chat platforms. He sometimes used GroupMe for conversations with smaller groups, and a portion of his online interaction had moved to group text messages as well. Ronnie noted that he didn't often use or share information from Facebook's On This Day memory feature that pushes content from users' older posts from years past. His friends on Facebook started sharing screenshots from the Facebook memory function in their group chat, primarily about Facebook notifications that they had become friends on Facebook on that day several years ago. Ronnie noted that this was a way for him and his friends to share information with each other without sharing it with a wider group. Ronnie noted, "Cause like we wanted, this was something cool that we wanted to share but we didn't want to share it through Facebook." The Facebook memories feature is there to be shared with friends on Facebook. But rather than using Facebook's share button as the site encourages, Ronnie and his friends took screenshots of the memories and content and shared them in a different platform entirely. They deliberately chose a different audience and used tools available to them in order to share this content with a different audience.

Other participants chose different content for specific platforms to reach certain audiences. While Sam had four different Instagram accounts to separate different kinds of Instagram content, they kept political content and information specifically on Twitter and did not post about it on Instagram and Facebook. Sam described being part of a student protest movement at their university in solidarity with Colin Kaepernick's protest for racial justice. Sam shared content and tweeted information about protests using the dedicated hashtag for the protests. They noted in an interview that Sam's Twitter account was chosen by the group to share information because they already had 1,500 followers. As Sam described:

> As a group we decided to have me do it, is because I had a platform already, so it could be exposed to the most people. That one was my most, by far. That tweet that was retweeted by both of them [Colin Kaepernick and Shawn King], was by far my most, my highest, with several thousand retweets, several thousand likes. [. . .] The feedback was like combination of people supporting it and hating it, as with most things that go viral on the internet.

Using principles of rhetorical velocity, Sam and their collaborators wanted the information to spread as widely as possible. Sam deemed the tweets successful, as they received several thousand likes and retweets; the tweets containing photos and other content from the protests were also retweeted by Colin Kaepernick himself and activist Shawn King. In this instance, Sam chose to share information on Twitter rather than another social media platform in order for that content to spread widely and to reach their desired audience: a wider public beyond the university, including other racial justice activists.

The individuals in this study, then, proactively directed their social media content to specific audiences. That involved not only signaling the intended audience through the language and content, as described in this section, but also using structures available to them, such as dividing content by profile and by platform.

NICHE SOCIAL MEDIA AND AUDIENCE

While social media use had at least somewhat consolidated into a few large platforms by the end of the first decade of its use, at the beginning of the decade, frequent social media users like those described here used a number of different sites for different purposes and hobbies, including last.fm, Goodreads, Flickr, YouTube, Pinterest, lala, and the social network aspects of Spotify. Each individual described in this book split audience by platform to a certain extent, but a few of this study's participants used more niche social media platforms to reach specific audiences.

CYWORLD

Alexis, for example, used social media to connect to distinct audiences from different places and points of her life, including friends in Korea, high school classmates in the United States, friends from her university, and also contacts from her church youth group. While she used Facebook to connect to individuals in all of these groups, she used other social network sites to connect to smaller and more specific groups of friends. Alexis used Cyworld, a Korean social media platform started in 2002, to keep in touch with her friends from Korea, along with Korean American friends with transnational connections.

Alexis saw Cyworld as a place to update her Korean friends about college life in the United States. She described her audience this way:

> Cyworld I think, it's really different from Facebook and Twitter, because just because—I don't want to use the word audience, but—the friends who come to my the site would be mostly um, just native speakers of Korean in which they don't know English as well as the people on Facebook and Twitter do, so I would write up stuff mostly in Korean, but also time to time because there's so many Koreans who are also bilingual, on Cyworld, I would type write in English too sometimes, so it's different.

With her Korean friends, Alexis saw herself primarily as an American college student, and she wanted to represent and share photos of her travels and her campus life in a way that represented the American university experience for her Korean friends. Given this smaller and more specific audience, her updates on the site were also more personal. She noted in an interview:

> I think the social networking site that I use for Cyworld I think, let's say from Facebook I wouldn't . . . write stuff that's too deep inside of me, or about feelings, or about how I feel and stuff like that. Let's say I wouldn't get too moody on Facebook, let's put it that way, just because it's too exposed, and I don't need 300 more people knowing about how I feel, you know, and what I'm going through. So when I want it to be a little more confidential, I think I put that . . . on Cyworld, because just less friends on Cyworld and it's not like, you don't have a news feed. [. . .] So it's not like Facebook where when you log in you just see the whole thing, of people and what they're doing and stuff. You actually have to go to their site, to like their profile page to see what they wrote or what they uploaded and stuff.

The content that Alexis shared on this platform was distinct both through language and technology. Alexis often used Korean on Facebook and Twitter as well, as she connected with Korean friends and Korean American friends on both platforms. She chose to create and use a profile on Cyworld, though, specifically to reach a smaller audience of friends in Korea. She also adjusted the content she shared on this platform because of its interface. Without a news feed, Alexis felt that she could share more personal information. Alexis used Cyworld, then, for the specific audience she reached through the platform, and she noted that the content she shared on the site was also shaped by the platform's design itself.

While Alexis used Cyworld to connect to her friends in Korea in 2011, she noted in 2016 that she stopped using it for about 5 years but had recently picked it up again. Alexis called Cyworld "almost a dead site" and returned to it as a way to share her thoughts in a "more private" space away from "the hyper connectivity with people [that] I just felt like I can't do that on Facebook or Instagram or Twitter." She stated in an interview:

> Recently, I went through a break up, so um, I just jotted some things down that I had learned from the relationship. Um, didn't go into too much details as to, you know, why we broke up or what happened afterwards. Just things that I learned in general, like that type of stuff I wouldn't mind being public. But if it was, you know, actually about naming names and what happened, that would stay private.

Cyworld was a place she felt comfortable sharing and processing her thoughts in the aftermath of her breakup, where fewer people might see it, though she still didn't list names or too many specific details. She did not share any information about it on her other social media accounts,

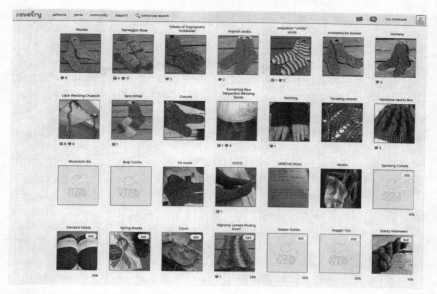

Figure 3.2. Esther's Ravelry project page.

however. When asked why she put the information online at all, she explained her use of Cyworld this way: "I like typing. I guess I just want it somewhere online just in case my computer crashes or something you know I can always have access to it." While Alexis's original Cyworld audience allowed her to share information about her life to friends back in Korea, by 2016, the disappearance of Alexis's audience on Cyworld allowed her to write essentially for an audience of one.

RAVELRY

Esther, a graduate student at the beginning of this study, also used a niche social media platform called Ravelry to connect with a more specific audience group (Esther's Ravelry project page can be found in figure 3.2). Launched in 2007 by Cassidy and Jessica Forbes, Ravelry is a niche social network site that was designed by and caters to a knitting community. Cassidy Forbes is a web developer solely responsible for designing and maintaining the site, and her wife Jessica Forbes is a knitter and blogger who wanted to create a more centralized database of knitters' projects. Writing in *Slate* magazine in 2011, technology journalist Farhad Manjoo called Ravelry "the best social network you've (probably) never heard of" because of its focus on a specialized and devoted community as well as its features and structure specifically designed for that community. In 2020, the site had 8,500,000 members (Basu, 2020). The site lets knitters organize their yarn collections, buy and save patterns, represent their finished and in-progress projects, learn new techniques, and most importantly, interact with other knitters by friending other users, joining groups, and participating in forum discussions. The forums represent particularly active parts of the site, as individual Ravelry users design and run contests, swaps, knit-alongs, and other activities that encourage individuals to learn new techniques, share resources, and meet other knitters.

danah boyd and Nicole Ellison (2007) argued that social network sites are different from more traditional online communities that organized individuals around common interests. boyd and Ellison noted that individuals primarily connect with people on social network sites that they know from their personal, offline networks, connecting with family members, friends, classmates, and coworkers. As a social network site, Ravelry is unique in that it asks users to connect with others through common interest rather than shared personal histories, and most individuals who interact on Ravelry are people who have never met before. Ravelry allows users to represent themselves through a screen name of their choosing and a profile picture, and the convention on the site is that individuals do not use their real names.

Esther used the Ravelry platform to connect with other users—those she had never met before who were similarly engaged in knitting activities. Ravelry figured prominently in Esther's daily online activity since she joined the site in 2008. During the initial data collection for the study in 2010, Esther checked the forums that she participated in on Ravelry every day: "Like normal people check their Facebook feeds, I don't know if normal people do that, but people check their Facebook feeds to see updates. I check my forums obsessively, so this is what I read most of the time." The forums allowed her to connect with other site users, see others' project updates, and interact with other knitters.

Ravelry gave Esther a forum to share and connect with others about her hobby, but more importantly, to show off her hard work with an audience who appreciated it:

> I want to show them off, and it feels really hard to show your knitting off. Like, I just feel in general, I can even wear something and people don't notice it, or necessarily say anything about it, and socks are especially hard because nobody sees them. They're on your feet, so unless I give them as a gift for somebody, or if I'm knitting in a public place and people are around. Non-knitters don't necessarily ask me questions about my knitting

all that often. So I feel like I really want to show it off, you know, I put a lot of effort into it. I want to have pictures of it, and I want to put them up.

Rather than asking individuals to represent themselves through consumer items like their favorite books or movies, Ravelry features users representing themselves through items they create. Esther's "ravatar," or profile picture, featured either her image showing off a recent finished project, or more frequently, a close up shot of that project—either modeled by her or a friend—usually socks, which Esther knit most frequently. When Esther began a new knitting project, called a cast-on post, she posted a picture of the yarn she chose from her "stash," what Ravelry calls one's collection of yarn, and then she posted progress photos as she continued to work on the project, along with an FO (finish-off) post. One of her major projects in 2010 was to knit the chuppah for her wedding, and she joined a group of others doing similar projects. Esther frequently participated in online activities called knit-alongs, which took place in specific groups, and asked individuals to post their progress updates on their projects, which fit certain parameters set by the group. Individuals posted progress updates along with other members, and the knit-along culminated in randomly drawn prizes for members. Esther was active in the Sock Knitters Anonymous forum, for example, and completed a knit-along that asked members to complete a project from a pattern in a specific book or by a specific designer. Esther also often participated in swaps, where members traded handmade items or yarn, and pools, which paired members to characters in a certain reality TV show, such as one Esther participated in tied to Project Runway. Members discussed the program as they posted project updates. Because the character Esther was randomly paired with came in second on the show, Esther received a prize when she finished her item. These activities, while focused on knitting, also encouraged site users to discuss personal likes and interests as well as popular culture events. Esther also participated in groups connected to other aspects of her identity, including a chuppah-knitters board, an academia group, a feminist knitters group, a group called Jewish Fiberholics, and other similar groups.

Esther participated in several clubs on Ravelry run by knitting stores and dyers, where she paid a fee each month and received yarn and other items at discounted prices. The connections that Esther made through these clubs also continued offline. Esther participated in a club through a yarn store in St. Louis that also sponsored a retreat each year; for 2 years in a row, Esther attended the retreat, met other members of the club in person, and participated in activities and classes while on the weekend trip in St. Louis. She posted pictures and stories both to her blog and to Ravelry after the retreat, and she stayed in contact with several of the other knitters afterward. Esther's participation in a variety of different forums and activities on Ravelry allowed her to make connections with other knitters online, and these connections also moved beyond the site to physical meetups as well. As Howard Rheingold (1993) noted in his discussion of online community on the WELL, for the San Francisco members of the group, in-person meet ups were also crucial in building community. For Esther, in both her online and offline interactions with Ravelry members, she was able to share content, including text and especially images, for a specific community that was connected to a specific interest, allowing her to show off her knitting skill and to develop those skills by connecting to other knitters. While the rest of the writers in this study had the challenge of managing different offline audience groups and networks through social media platforms, Esther instead used Ravelry to meet and connect with new contacts, who eventually became offline contacts.

Knitting and Esther's connections on Ravelry also fueled some of her other social media use as well. Esther used Twitter in part to follow specific yarn dyers, as well as other Ravelry activity. She joined Twitter in 2010 in order to follow independent dyers who dyed and sold small quantities of specialized yarns. These dyers would post updates on when that yarn would be for sale and when discounts or specials sales would happen. Using Twitter allowed Esther to stay updated in order to buy new yarn. Esther began to follow other designers who posted their patterns on Ravelry as well. Many of Esther's tweets focused on conversations about and surrounding Ravelry and her knitting activity:

> Talk like a pirate day! If you post something on a ravelry pirated thread, it translates your post into buccaneer speak. Coolest thing ever! 12:32pm, Sep 19, 2010 via Tweetdeck

> @ravelry, oh no! bad timing, just trying to claim yarn in a swap : (1:24pm, Aug 19, 2010 via Tweetdeck

> World wide knit in public day, on a cruise boat! [link to blog] 10:05am, Jul 19, 2010 via Tweetdeck

> Just finished knitting the chuppah and the crochet bind off. Just blocking and fringe to go. Yay! 12:24am, May 14 via Tweetdeck

Although she was posting on Twitter, the content of Esther's tweets demonstrates that she was directing her posts to a Ravelry audience and community as well. The same was true of Instagram. Esther also

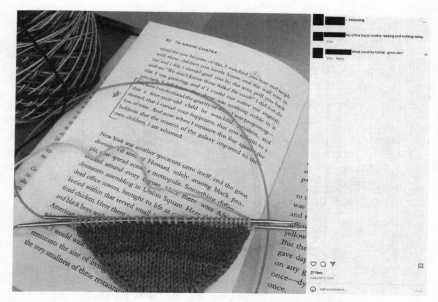

Figure 3.3. A typical reading and knitting post on Esther's Instagram page.

joined Instagram in 2013, and while she still updated Ravelry, Instagram became the primary place she shared her knitting content and connected to other knitters. She described a photo-sharing process that started with Instagram, which she then shared through Facebook, Flickr, and then Ravelry. Esther posted pictures of her finished projects on Instagram, and she also used it to connect with other knitters and yarn dyers outside of Ravelry. For most of the first half of 2016, Esther participated in a read-and-knit-along project, where she posted pictures of her knitting projects next to the current books that she was reading (see figure 3.3).

Ravelry first allowed Esther to connect with a specific audience she did not know in her personal life: other knitters, dyers, and knitting enthusiasts. She used Ravelry to connect with this specific audience, which eventually grew out to other platforms, especially Instagram. Although a great deal of her social media activity had moved to Instagram, Esther was still connecting primarily with that knitting audience she described in one of our earlier interviews. In this way, Esther and Alexis reached specific audiences through more niche social media platforms designed for that purpose.

ANTICIPATING AUDIENCE CONCERNS AND POST-COMPOSITION

As I described in the first section of this chapter, many individuals in this study observed online communities in order to determine that group's social media conventions before entering that online space more fully. Managing audience also means taking feedback from those audiences and using that feedback to shape future online posts. In her book *Status Update*, Alice Marwick (2013) argued that social media platforms encourage users to present sanitized, happy, and acceptable aspects of themselves for online consumption, partially through norms and conventions and partially through comments and critique from others. A number of the participants in this study revised or adjusted the information they shared on different social media platforms because of either indirect or explicit comments from others. Some of these adjustments were in response to online comments or lack thereof, but much of this feedback actually occurred offline, especially from parents, professors, or other authority figures. Sometimes this feedback was overt and asked individuals to take down or adjust posts, and sometimes this was more an overt pressure, where individuals' offline networks became connected to their online ones.

Alexis, for example, had an image to uphold on Facebook; she was a church youth group leader when she was an undergraduate student. She was connected to many different people from her church through her Facebook account, which she often used to represent her commitment to her faith. In her ethnography of Korean American student communities at the University of Illinois, Nancy Abelmann (2009) noted the central role the evangelical church played in students' social lives and identities. Alexis's experience was similar to many of the students Abelmann profiled. She often cited Bible verses in status updates, and she used the Notes section of Facebook to post reflections on her faith. Her Facebook content was also occasionally policed by other members of her church, such as when someone suggested that she remove some images of herself at a party when she became a youth group leader.

After planning a youth group event for her church, Alexis posted a church newsletter reporting on the event on Facebook. With the newsletter, she also posted the following reflection:

> I hope this was a day/service pleasing to God, and that it challenged, renewed, and blessed each and every one of our members of [the church] for I was overjoyed, cried in tears, and was blessed. This is my church, my home, my family God has given to me, because you nor I cannot fight alone. I sincerely thank you: God, my own family, youth group, and my church. One body, One God. Bless you all. Love you all. Jesus loves you.

Alexis represented her faith on her Facebook page, both as a large part of her life and as a way to address the audience group of her church. The newsletter in particular was addressed to this audience, and through these updates, Alexis both addressed this audience and created community with others in her church.

Alexis was also careful about the images she posted on her Facebook page. At the beginning of my study, she had recently hidden all of her photos except her profile pictures. The reason for this was based on Alexis's awareness about the multiple audiences she was reaching on Facebook. She was concerned that friends might get worried or jealous if they saw her in photos hanging out with other friends. Closing off the photos she had already posted, as well as not posting new photos, was a way to "avoid drama." Throughout the first decade of social media, Facebook developers frequently changed how individuals tagged in photos appeared in the news feed. Alexis was therefore concerned about audience as well as the rhetorical velocity of her photos: the people who might see them and the consequences of that photo circulation was somewhat beyond her control, and these were large concerns in her mind that governed how she used Facebook. Hiding all of her photos as well as untagging herself prevented some of her Facebook audience from seeing images she didn't want them to see, which anticipated and preempted criticism. The online feedback Alexis received, as well as offline conversations with members of her faith community impacted the information she shared on Facebook and how she shared it.

Sandra also often considered what image of herself to present on social media. She described herself as cautious about the information she put on Facebook. She self-selected the best photos and often untagged herself in pictures that she didn't feel presented herself in the best light. She also considered the different audiences she connected with when she posted content, both images and status updates. She noted: "I've always been cautious of what's on Facebook. It's never anything I wouldn't want my mother to see, or my employer to see, because I'm friends with both of them."

Sandra often edited what she put on Facebook based on feedback as well. If a status update didn't receive any comments from her contacts, for example, Sandra would delete it. In this way, Sandra was constantly posting information she thought her audience on Facebook would appreciate, and then revising that content based on the feedback she received from that audience. If a message didn't receive any comments or feedback from friends, she removed it and moved on. Sandra described her choice this way: "There's no reason for them [Facebook statuses] to like exist on my own wall, why am I writing to myself? I already know what I'm thinking."

In this way, social network sites provided a real-time, continuous audience for Sandra's thoughts and images. She received near constant feedback about the information her audience found interesting and important through likes and comments; Sandra took in that feedback and used it to refine her future posts. Unlike some of my other participants, then, she did not use social media to archive or save her data with just herself as an audience. For Sandra, if the information was not to be shared with others and they didn't interact with it, then there was not a point in sharing it.

Sometimes information posted on social media also required negotiation with other audiences. While Esther was rather liberal about being tagged in photos, not all of her Facebook friends felt the same way, which occasionally caused tension. Esther's mother, for example, was unhappy about a photo of herself from Esther's wedding that Esther had posted to Facebook:

> She wanted to take the picture of her walking me down the aisle down. I was like, [you] walked me down the aisle, I'm not going to take you down. [She said] well, I don't like my face in it, and this is a professional forum. Well, I have friends that are in professional circles, and I don't want them to see the picture. And I was like, I'll just untag you.

The incident Esther recounted demonstrates the challenges of social network sites like Facebook where one's audience expands beyond a user's list of contacts to include their friends' contacts as well. Esther's mother was concerned about the ability of people from her professional life to see photos of her from more social settings that did not represent her in a professional light. Tagging individuals in photos is a functionality of Facebook that allows for the greater spread and rhetorical velocity of the photos, but it provides less control of the ways in which these photos travel, especially if those photos were uploaded by someone else. This situation leads to complicated negotiations over photos and representation, as in the example with Esther and her mother. Esther's knowledge of Facebook and its various settings allowed her to reach what she considered to be a suitable compromise that allowed her to share the photo with her desired audience groups but would prevent it from circulating in the news feeds of her mother's Facebook contacts. These clashes of audiences and concerns are frequent on social network sites, and for the most part, Esther's own concerns with context collapse kept her from updating her Facebook page more frequently.

For the undergraduate students that I interviewed, especially in 2013 and 2016, Facebook was a place only for updates that would go to a large number of people because they were connected to so many family members on the platform. Jordan, Stephanie, Caroline, and Sam were all connected to relatives on Facebook. When Sam started posting more political content on the platform, they unfriended their grandmother, who often commented on and argued with their posts. For most people I spoke to, however, posting on Facebook required a considerable amount of self-censorship. Caroline primarily shared photos on both Facebook and Instagram, but she shared more photos on Facebook, partially because of the site's infrastructure and conventions, and partly for audience. She described this thinking in her interview:

> Facebook is like, I might post forty pictures of a trip. You know, I went to Oxford this summer, so I'll have like an entire album that is trip pictures, whereas Instagram you're not going to post forty pictures from your trip. People will hate you because you'll clog their feed, and they're like "oh my goodness." But Instagram will be like, it's the best picture I took on that trip. So I guess you could look into that. It's like super filtered. This is the representation that I want to give from my life. This is me, in this one picture, whereas Facebook I have it all on there. This is for the aunts. They get to see. Or even friends, if they are interested, I'll be like "I have a Facebook album." Cause then I don't have to sit and turn on the slide show. It's a little easier. Like with little slides.

Caroline compared her Facebook album to a vacation slideshow. This kind of content was "for the aunts," relatives who would be interested in the photos from her trip but including that many photos and that much information was overload for her audience on Instagram. In this way, Caroline anticipated the reaction of the audience on both platforms and made decisions about what photos to share and how based on that information.

RESISTANCE AND CRITIQUE

The defensive strategies that the individuals in this study used to manage audience primarily involved anticipating critiques from specific individuals in their audience and self-censoring in anticipation of those critiques. While there were a number of technical and privacy tools that social media users had available to them for audience management, many of the writers discussed here instead chose not to post specific content to social media. As noted in the previous section, both Sandra and Alexis managed their photos, personal information, and other content by choosing to keep certain information offline entirely. Sandra first expressed concern in representing herself online, but as she continued to interact with others on social network sites, she stated that she was directed by her parents' rules about sharing information in online environments:

> I've always been kind of cautious about putting all my feelings and emotions, and personal stuff like on the internet. Especially when I was younger, because you know, if it's on the internet, it's free to my parents too, so like, they said that anything that's on the Internet is fair game, so if you don't want us to know, don't put it on the internet, and that's really easy to live by.

From the beginning of her social network site use, then, Sandra was concerned about the audiences she connected with through the site. While this concern was first impressed upon her by her parents, she used them as a measure of what she should and should not share on social network sites. If she didn't want her parents to know about something she was doing, she didn't put it online. In this way, Sandra internalized a type of parental litmus test to the information that she posted on social media platforms. This outside audience and the way Sandra internalized it was similar to the way Alexis described her church's audience in shaping the information she shared on Facebook.

Beth, another undergraduate student, was less comfortable representing herself in online spaces and sharing her information online. Beth joined Facebook when she graduated from high school, and she described the same reluctance and peer pressure to join that site:

> My friends were like, "we need to stay in touch," and I was like, this is actually a good point, because when I've moved, people don't stay in touch. That's why I got on Facebook, and I got in touch with my friends from elementary school.

Beth used Facebook's groups feature to organize her friends list according to these audience groups, but she did not send out different content to each one. Beth described her use of Facebook as minimal; she checked the site once every few weeks, and she updated her status on the site once every few months. She did share photos on Facebook, but often by tagging herself in photos taken by her mother or other friends, so that they would show up on her wall. In this instance, she didn't want to upload the content herself, but she instead used her knowledge of Facebook's tagging mechanisms to make that content available to her friends.

Like several of my other participants, Beth was also concerned about the information she was sending to audiences, for reasons of context collapse. She noted that she deleted content and removed herself from images because she was concerned about the information others could see, particularly her boss:

> When my boss wanted to become my friend on Facebook I went through and made sure there was nothing incriminating looking. I didn't think there would be, but, someone was making jokes about drugs on my wall post, like way back, and I was like, yeah, my boss probably doesn't want to see that and then like . . . I was somewhere where people were playing beer pong, I wasn't, and so like I just untagged myself so it doesn't show up in my thing anymore because I just couldn't figure out how to change the privacy settings so only like a specific group wouldn't be able to see certain things. And I thought this isn't worth it. I don't care about this picture so much anyway. Take it off.

Beth's concerns about her online identity and the information she placed on Facebook will be discussed at more length in the next chapter, but she often described an apprehension about putting personal information online in any context, and a lack of control about where that information would spread.

Beth was also cautious about the kinds of information that she shared online. While Beth was conscious of her audience groups on Facebook, she represented herself on the site primarily by not representing herself. She did not interact much with others, and she did not engage much with specific friend groups or other audiences, primarily because she did not see her identity representation as staying within that group. More than any other participant, Beth was concerned about the rhetorical velocity of her information into other contexts that she did not sanction. While Ridolfo and DeVoss (2009) advocated for proactively considering delivery and circulation in digital environments, Beth saw this affordance of digital media ultimately as something she could not control, and she therefore chose to manage this situation primarily through self-censorship.

In her interviews, Beth expressed being uncomfortable in online rhetorical situations, unsure how to connect with others, to share information, and to evaluate the information that others shared with her. She was also ultimately concerned about the control of her own information and how it might spread beyond the context in which she shared it. She did not interact with different audiences, and she did not express a desire to do so, primarily because she did not trust the technologies themselves, which I discuss in chapter 4.

Nicole, one of the additional graduate students I interviewed in 2016, was similarly concerned about sharing too much information on social media platforms or connecting with people who would also share too much of her information. Nicole had a Facebook account since she was in middle school, but she did not use it much or connect with many people on the site because she was concerned about connecting to friends of friends on the site, as she explained in our interview:

> I had this thing about not being on social media for a long time and kind of just keeping my profile under cover, like it's just if you knew me, you knew me from meeting face to face with me, not online. So I didn't connect with family and friends because I don't know who's in their network, and then their network would be connected with my network. And some people that I associate with, I don't want people to think that my friends associate with that kind of people. So I just kind of keep my image clean. So I don't connect with anyone.

In connecting with people on social media platforms, Nicole was worried about two things: first, the lack of control over audience and how connecting with friends of friends would expand her audience, and second, how the people she was connected to on social media platforms would define her as a person. While Nicole did not elaborate what she meant about "that kind of people," it is clear that she was concerned about her friend connections on social media defining her in some way. Nicole noted that she was connected to more family and friends on Pinterest, but it wasn't as much of a problem to connect to people through that site because she only shared links there, not her own content. Like Beth, Nicole kept a great deal of content off of social media platforms entirely, and she also did not connect with many people on the platforms.

BUILDING A SOCIAL MEDIA PROFILE
THROUGH AUDIENCE AWARENESS

As noted throughout this chapter, the individuals profiled here addressed specific audiences through both linguistic choices and through the technological affordances available to them on social media platforms. One final example from Ronnie demonstrates how he used both of these strategies to build a network of social media profiles to provoke a specific response from his friends.

On April 1, 2011, Ronnie changed his Facebook relationship status to "in a relationship" with Alison Moreau. Eleven friends "liked" his status, and four friends commented on it. Over the next several days, Ronnie and Alison exchanged a series of messages on Facebook and Twitter, tapering off around April 8. But Ronnie and his girlfriend didn't break up; she never existed. She was an April Fool's Day prank Ronnie concocted:

I decided that day, I was like, I need to prank someone really well, and um, on my news feed a bunch of people had gotten into relationships and people were doing pranks like being engaged, but they weren't very elaborate, you knew they were fake, and like, I want to really prank someone.

Ronnie described how he created this persona, using an alternate university email address and pictures from the website of College Humor's Hottest Girl of 2008. He gave her a story, telling friends that they met over spring break. He set the privacy settings on Facebook so that no one could see how many friends she had, but her profile pictures and all her information were visible. He listed her as graduating from a high school not far from his hometown, but not one that any of his friends had attended. Ronnie found a number of pictures of this girl with a camera, so he played up photography as a hobby for his character as well. Ronnie wrote her detailed profile on Facebook by copying and editing sections of favorite movies and music from his female friends' profiles. He also made sure that her writing style was much different from his own, using the convention of some social network site users of repeating the last letter of words multiple times for emphasis. For example, these are some of the Facebook and Twitter updates Ronnie wrote as Alison:

> Register for fall classes tomorrowww . . . Graduation seems right around the corner. Not sure how I feel about that . . . :/
> Blah, I miss my family alreadyyy. . . . :(Summer, I'm pining for you!
> Just arrived home for the weekend. Looking forward to seeing Amy tomorroww!
> It's so nice out todayyy <3

Along with the repeated letters, Alison also used hearts and exclamation points, stylistic features that did not appear in Ronnie's own updates. Ronnie also used an equal sign for his own emoticons online at the time, so he consciously made sure that Alison used colons instead.

Ronnie and Alison had many public conversations on both Facebook and Twitter. Ronnie had his laptop logged into his Twitter account and his iPhone logged into Alison's Twitter account. Like many Facebook users, they shared links, primarily music videos in their case.

Ronnie often emphasized Alison's physical location, either somewhere on campus, or at home over Easter weekend. Ronnie's sister, who was in on the joke, suggested that Alison should be present at their Easter dinner, and so Ronnie posted the following on Twitter: [happy easter! having a lovely meal with @skippy96 and @alison_m]#fb[1] Alison also had a number of conversations with Ronnie's friends who friended her, both people who were in on the prank and those who weren't, including discussions about hometowns, majors, and plans for after college.

While Ronnie told a few people about the prank from the start, within a few days most of his friends on Twitter knew it was a joke, and by April 9, Ronnie had changed his relationship status. Several people expressed their concern over the end of Ronnie's relationship, while others were angry he had pulled off this prank. This situation led to a final tweet from Alison's account: "Some people just have no sense of humor . . . :/ So, who's up for some fun and games?" And this tweet from Ronnie's Twitter account: "[just killed one of my characters, @alison_m. today is a sad day for creativity]."

Ronnie's creation of Alison's Facebook and Twitter accounts was certainly not a new practice online, and this kind of activity, which Sherry Turkle (1995) described as identity play, is well-chronicled in her book focusing on Lambda Moo, *Life on the Screen.* I wouldn't suggest that Ronnie's creation of this character allowed him to experiment with his identity, as Turkle did in her text, though his reliance on some gender stereotypes to create Alison is reminiscent of what Lisa Nakamura (2002) labeled "identity tourism." While text-based MUDs and MOOs have faded in popularity, internet users do create fake profiles all of the time. Friendster, an early social network site, met its downfall by trying to police fake accounts, and fake celebrity accounts are common on Twitter. Yet identity is also created through sustained interaction with individuals across multiple platforms. As filmmakers Ariel Schulman and Henry Joost chronicled in the 2010 film *Catfish,* creating a persona on a social network site involves not just one person but an entire network of corroborating individuals and activities. Because many of the people individuals connect with through these sites are also those with whom they have connections offline, these interactions frequently traverse online and offline boundaries, such as Ronnie's interactions with his roommates. Ronnie tried to keep up this aspect of his fake character with the frequent references to location. Part of Ronnie's inability to keep up the fake profile, then, lie in an inability of this character to participate in all of the forums, online and offline, that she plausibly should have.

In Ronnie's creation of Alison, he relied both on a close attention to language and his knowledge of Facebook and Twitter tools and platform architecture. By pulling content from friends' profiles and consciously reproducing certain discourse conventions, Ronnie created believable Facebook and Twitter profile pages. He knew that he had to hide Alison's friend list to prevent suspicion, and also used other site tools and conventions to make the content believable at first glance to his audience: his friends and contacts on Facebook and Twitter. This example demonstrates how Ronnie was able to use his knowledge of social network site structures and settings, genres and discourse conventions, and a sophisticated sense of audience to construct social media profiles that, for a time at least, passed for authentic within these structures. He knew what language to use (repeating letters, references to popular culture, specific hashtags), which genres (short wall posts, authentic-looking photos, and other Facebook comments and Twitter replies), and which settings to change (privacy and wall settings) to reach an audience of his peers.

In some ways, Ronnie's profile construction served two purposes. First, it allowed him to experiment with ideas of identity, genre, and authenticity. As he noted in an interview, he thought people were often too willing to accept the information they saw on social media at face value, and this incident allowed him to make that point with his own friends. Second, it allowed him to perhaps not perform a new identity, but to try out a different role for himself, one in a relationship with another person. There is much about Alison here that is idealized; from the photos from College Humor, already held up as an idealized standard of beauty that is also white and blond. Her interactions with Ronnie, as well as with his friends, allowed Ronnie to create an idealized representation of a girlfriend, as if to experiment with the idea itself.

In our 2016 interview, Ronnie reflected on what he always described as "the April Fools prank." He called it "a kind of Turing test," and he explained that he did it mostly as an experiment to see if he could pull it off. While his approach might seem obvious and even cliché now, Ronnie created the Alison profile before "catfishing" became a common, or at least well-known, internet practice. He also noted that people's expectations about who was human and who was a bot, which he called the 2016 version of the Turing test, was based more in evaluating the authenticity of the language used. Ronnie instead saw that authenticity as based more in photos in 2011:

> I think the emphasis now is like can you spot a robot or a chat bot based on their speech patterns. Photos aren't like a test of if they're like human or not like they used to be.

Ronnie noted that this prank would have been more difficult to pull off in 2016, and it wasn't something he would do again. Ronnie reflected:

> That was a lot easier to do back then and I think I was more willing to exploit that. Um, as a college student. Versus now it would be harder to do and I would like realize that it's possible but I wouldn't act on it as something I would do.

While Ronnie identified a way to exploit the means through which his friends and other social media users verified and judged online content in 2011, he had also identified an issue with the way that social media users created online identities in a way that allowed deception, at least on the surface. While Ronnie believed such a deception to be more difficult to pull off in 2016, around the time of our interview, the Internet Research Agency in Saint Petersburg was engaging in a very similar practice. As the investigation conducted by the Intelligence Committee in the U.S. Senate found, Russian operatives created fake profiles on social media platforms, including Facebook and Twitter, using photos of Americans with assumed names and identities, in order to expose and create divisions among the U.S. electorate and to help Donald Trump to win the 2016 presidential election. While Ronnie discussed this prank as an innocuous experiment, he also identified an affordance within the social media platforms he used that would be exploited by a different group of social media users with less innocuous aims.

PEDAGOGICAL APPLICATIONS

This project is intended to engage with and describe the self-sponsored literacy practices of individuals on social media platforms, yet there is much that this research suggests for pedagogy as well. Chris Anson (2017) argued that social media "can provide forms of tacit learning—especially about discourse—that mirrors learning encouraged and expected in school" (p. 310). Anson, among other scholars, has advocated for a connection between social media literacy practices and academic ones in the college writing classroom in order to encourage rhetorical awareness and "facilitate the transfer of discursive ability across diverse communities of practice" (p. 310). Social media platforms, however, present as many teaching challenges as they do opportunities. Instructors should consider the many implications for asking students to create profiles and/or to connect through social media with their classmates.

I close this chapter and the two that follow with a few suggested pedagogical applications of this research. These are general approaches rather than specific units or lesson plans. Some of these approaches are ones that I have used in my own teaching, while others are not. While I emphasize the first decade of social media throughout this project, many of the literacy practices that individuals engaged in during that decade apply to the following one as well, and many of these suggestions can continue to be adapted to newer social media platforms and practices.

Joining Online Discourse Communities

Each of the writers in this study used site structures, such as different profiles or different platforms entirely, to address specific audiences. While a platform is not an audience, different communities can form on different platforms, where many of the members are connected through the same network or use site structures to organize (hashtags on Twitter and Instagram or subreddit pages on Reddit). As I described in this chapter, several of the writers in this study used social media platforms to observe and later join specific online communities. Jack, for example, followed both academics in his field and music bloggers on Twitter and observed their conversations on the platform before joining in conversations with others in the community. Esther did the same with knitting communities on Ravelry and also followed them to Twitter. Studying an online community and observing both their discourse and social media conventions is a process that has a clear analogy for academic communities and other discourse communities. Assignments that ask students to identify specific writing conventions on social media platforms for both familiar and unfamiliar communities, for example, would allow students to observe how these writers use language and technical affordances (everything from hashtags to digital stickers to other features) in order to effectively communicate within that community. In his dissertation study of writing instructors and their students using social media for pedagogy, David Coad (2019) described one instructor who designed an assignment asking students to observe and then join a specific Reddit community. Approaches like these allow students to study online discourse communities and apply that experience to academic ones.

Using Genre Conventions

Each of the writers in this study also learned to identify and internalize the conventions of key social media genres in order to reach specific audiences. Ronnie, for example, studied the Facebook profiles of his other friends in order to create a profile his friends would believe was authentic. Esther used a specific knitting community genre of posting both cast-on images at the start of her projects as well pictures of the final product. Particular types of tweets, for example, exist as genres, as well as particular types of Instagram posts: selfies, food photos, and even, more specifically, latte art.

Studying specific social media genres allows students to both further explore their tacit knowledge of these genres as well as observe how genre conventions structure both the form of a particular text and the audience's expectations for it. For example, I start my multimedia composition course each semester with an image essay project, and I provide students with a number of options based on common social media genres, including the gif reaction essay, the Twitter thread, and image macro memes. When introducing this project, we spend a great deal of time as a class bringing in different social media genres, discussing their conventions and variations, and then applying students' takeaways from this project to other genres, both academic and beyond. Similar approaches to social media genres in the classroom would allow students to explore how content, technical constraints, and community conventions combine to create a specific genre.

Visibility Through Technical Structures

Each writer described in this chapter also used the technological affordances and constraints of specific social media platforms in order to shape their audience. A focused classroom activity based on this literacy practice might be a conversation around effective hashtag practices. André Brock (2012) described hashtags as "a user-created metadiscourse convention" that began as a way to categorize tweets, but they soon became "an expressive modifier" (p. 534). Louis Maraj (2020) argued that hashtags are "a 'remediated' form of commonplaces and/or commonplace headings" (p. 48) that allow students to critique and resist dominant ideologies and to "shape public knowledge and the deep ecologies they denote" (p. 49). Each of the individuals I have profiled here used hashtags as a way to both find online communities to join as well as direct their own messages back toward those communities. In her study of the YouTube practices of young adults, Patricia Lange's (2007) research found that the adolescents she studied used obscure tags on YouTube in order to prevent their content from being discovered by a wider audience. Alternatively, Abby Dubisar and Jason Palmeri (2010) described a student whose video remix went viral on YouTube because he was able to gain visibility through the tags he used when he uploaded the video.

Maraj (2020) described a hashtag assignment he used with students that asked them to use Tumblr as a commonplace book. Each student chose quotes, images, and examples from their class readings and shared them on Tumblr, using a series of hashtags to describe and interpret the reading, as well as to reblog and engage with classmates' posts. This assignment, Maraj argued, "aims to conceptualize hashtags as a tool for analysis, research, and curation" (p. 59). It serves as an example of a strong reflective assignment that builds from the platform affordances of Tumblr as well as the rhetorical function of hashtags in order to promote reflection, analysis, and synthesis in a writing course.

In addition, the Lange (2007) and Dubisar and Palmeri (2010) examples show social media users who effectively crafted their texts for rhetorical velocity, either to prevent circulation or to increase it. One particular classroom application, then, might be to challenge students to design social media content that most effectively uses the platform's technological affordances to circulate their content (including strategic hashtags and other settings), and then to design social media content to be shared only within a particular group to which they belong or to otherwise limit its audience. Such an approach asks students to explore the technical tools at their disposal to reach their audience more effectively and to shape their content toward that audience.

CONCLUSION

This chapter explored specific literacy practices that the individuals in this study engaged in to manage their audience challenges. Each writer used proactive strategies in shaping audience by creating new social media profiles, splitting audience by platform, and using specific language and genres in order to reach their intended audiences. Many of the undergraduates in this initial study uploaded fewer updates on Facebook, where parents and sometimes even grandparents could see them, and shared more on Twitter, where their audience was primarily their friends. Others, like Jack, created multiple accounts on a social media platform to better manage audience.

These writers also used defensive strategies to keep information off of social media platforms, including self-censoring information and restricting audience through platform settings. Sandra noted in an interview that she had taken up advice of her parents that anything she didn't want to be public, she shouldn't put online. While some used different groups and permissions features to restrict content for different groups, for most it was easier to keep that information offline entirely. In many situations, the people I have discussed in this chapter carefully considered the information they were sharing online and whether or not to post it. When different people in their lives connected with them on social media platforms, they often reevaluated the information they were sharing and adjusted accordingly. Beth noted, for example, how she "cleaned up" her Facebook page after her boss friended her, and at many different points during this study, each person evaluated the information they shared with others in much the same way.

Each participant integrated these social media platforms within their everyday lives and other technology and literacy practices. While each platform did not dictate specific actions, they did provide certain constraints, and each person described here had to analyze and evaluate these constraints and decide on their rhetorical strategies accordingly. Social media platforms, then, were intertwined with the ways these writers reached audiences and connected with others, and, as Berry et al. (2012) described, they used their understandings of these affordances to craft messages and approaches that were compatible with their own social and material circumstances. In the following chapter, I will turn my attention more specifically to the social media technologies themselves in shaping user experiences.

4

MANAGING DATA AND TECHNOLOGIES

In her 2013 *College English* article, Jessica Reyman argued that not only do writing scholars and teachers need to consider the use of what she described as the "social web" for teaching, learning, and writing, but that we also need to understand the implications of generating data on these platforms. She argued, "We have not fully examined the related, inextricable act of generating data as part of composing processes" (p. 515). While writers in social media spaces upload content and information, they also create data, a broader category that for Facebook includes "a plethora of information types: name, email address, birthday, gender, status updates, photographs, comments, friends, groups, likes, recommended links, tags identifying people or locations, searches, browsing activities, messages, metadata from uploaded content, information about the devices used to access the site, including IP address, information from advertising partners about shopping activities, and information from partner services" (p. 519). Rather than considering data created by social media users to be without authorship, Reyman instead argues that we see it as cocreated by the user and the platform:

> It is the interaction between humans and technology that results in the productive act of composing data: as users view, contribute, and share with social and participatory Web technologies, with other texts, and with each other, they become collaborative agents in generating data. (p. 526)

Beck and Hutchinson (2020) note that most scholars in computers and writing who have taken up concerns of privacy have "tak[en] a stand against widespread surveillance and the decrease of privacy protections online" (p. 3). They point to the detailed and complex literacy practices required to evaluate technologies that share personal data, to read and understand privacy policies, and to make personal decisions on what to share and not share (p. 7). In this chapter, I examine the ways that social media users cocreate data as part of mutually constituted human-technology assemblages allows us to expand our frame of analysis

https://doi.org/10.7330/9781646424023.c004

beyond individual social media users and to consider their role in larger networks and systems of information.

Throughout the first decade of social media, writers using these platforms struggled to make sense of and adjust to the ways that social media companies used their data. As described in chapter 4, managing audience through social media platforms involves developing literacy practices to negotiate both specific audiences and site designs themselves. Managing one's information, access to it, and its circulation are activities that social network site users engage in within the structures of these platforms. When sites redesign their interfaces, organize information differently, shift policy and strategy, and change privacy setting configurations, writers change their practices as well. As these design changes affect so many individuals, such issues often lead to public concern and even backlash.

One of the first controversies about data management and design changes on social platforms involved an outcry about the Facebook news feed feature, introduced in September 2006, which fundamentally changed not only how users engaged with the service, but how visible their information was on the site.[1] Another Facebook controversy occurred in 2009, which grew to a breaking point by the spring of 2010, when Facebook rolled out its new Connect feature. Facebook Connect, an advertising program that also aimed to put Facebook logins and passwords across the web, drew not only media criticism and public panic, but also separate complaints filed by Senator Charles Schumer and the Electronic Privacy Information Center to the Federal Trade Commission. The critical mass of 500,000,000 users in 2010 concerned about the use of their information on the site caused panic and also a reflection on the ways social networking sites like Facebook had changed and were changing their use and treatment of users' data.

A number of events precipitated this public outcry, beginning with a December 2009 notification users received on the service prompting them to review their privacy settings. While this move seems to have been prompted by complaints that users didn't review or understand their privacy settings, the default option on the site for most categories switched to users' information being visible to everyone, resulting in those who hadn't paid attention to the notifications to have their information exposed to anyone on the internet. In April 2010, Facebook announced the Facebook Connect program, which changed the way information is displayed on users' profiles, linking them to former Fan, now called "Like" pages, and a larger program called Social Plugins that allows Facebook "Like" buttons to be placed on outside websites, linking people through their Facebook pages to numerous other places online.

It was unclear how much information Facebook was sharing with other companies through what they called social plugins, and the web, television, and print media exploded with stories attempting to explain the changes and to comment on their larger implications. The media coverage came from those who typically write about Facebook, such as technology site *ReadWriteWeb, Wired,* and *Slate,* but also stories across a range of media outlets, from the *Wall Street Journal,* to stories on Yahoo's finance section with titles like "Seven Things to Stop Doing on Facebook," a cover story in *Time* magazine, and a detailed chart in the *New York Times* mapping out all 50 of Facebook's privacy settings and more than 170 options. Facebook users circulated status updates alerting people to the new changes while educating them on how to alter these settings. The Electronic Frontier Foundation called for a Bill of Privacy Rights, and critics declared May 31 to be Quit Facebook Day. Around this time, a group of students in New York announced that they were building Diaspora, a decentralized social network that allowed users to own their own data, and this platform immediately raised over $200,000.

After almost a month of defending the site's changes, including a rather disastrous question and answer forum in the *New York Times* with Elliot Schrage, who was Facebook's vice president for public policy at the time, Facebook announced that it would be revamping and simplifying its privacy controls on May 26. These complaints ultimately resulted in a consent decree between the FTC and Facebook in 2011, which stated that Facebook had continually violated consumers' privacy rights by making their information public without warning or consent as well as misrepresenting the amount of information that third-party apps could have access to through their connection with Facebook (Federal Trade Commission, 2011). The panic slowly died down, and coverage of Facebook retreated back to the tech pages. While Facebook agreed to third-party audits of its privacy policies in the consent decree, it continued to violate the agreement in the intervening years (Tufekci, 2018).

This cycle of changes that first raises alarm, then backlash, and finally ultimate acceptance has become a familiar cycle on Facebook. Zeynep Tufekci (2018) has called these frequent public outcries and the company's subsequent need for damage control "Zuckerberg's Apology Tour," a cycle that continued every few years until 2018 when Zuckerberg himself testified before a joint session of the Senate Judiciary and Commerce Committees and the House Energy and Commerce Committee about the Cambridge Analytica scandal and the Russian disinformation campaign on its platform during the 2016 U.S. presidential election. These hearings resulted in the FTC leveraging a $5,000,000,000 fine on the company in July of 2019 for violating that 2011 consent decree by deceiving users about the privacy settings for some of their information, misrepresenting its facial recognition technology, and deceiving users about the ways Facebook used their phone numbers, ostensibly for security but later used for advertising purposes. While the fine and agreement required Facebook to establish an independent privacy committee outside of Zuckerberg's control and to implement additional security safeguards, it did not require the company to admit guilt or to implement any structural changes. The agreement also indemnified Facebook and its leaders against any claims prior to June 12, 2019 (Glaser, 2019). While the Cambridge Analytica scandal and subsequent congressional hearings led to another public outrage as well as pledges from many to delete or deactivate their Facebook accounts, the service continued to grow its international user base and had 2,850,000,000 active members worldwide in April of 2021 (Statista, n.d.).

Facebook's large user base, the visibility of its CEO Mark Zuckerberg, and the seriousness of the FTC consent decree and settlement make it a case study for issues of user data, privacy, and other concerns, but many of the problems the FTC and Facebook's critics have identified apply to other social media platforms as well. These issues demonstrate the concerns of users, society, and governments of the ways that social media companies collect and use user data. Some of the changes to Facebook that led to user outrage were based on policy alterations that Facebook did not make clear to its users, and some were about hacks or misuses of Facebook user data that was allowed on the platform, like the Cambridge Analytica scandal. Other changes were just about the visibility of information; while users' information was displayed in ways that made it more visible, the audience who could see that information had not changed. These concerns reveal the tension between what users can both understand and control about their information and what the software and interface allow users to understand and control. Tufekci (2018) noted that Mark Zuckerberg's responses to public outcry about Facebook's policies and actions usually involve revising the ways that users can control and learn about the site's privacy policies. Yet more education and transparency about privacy options does not allow users to change the underlying function of the platform itself. Individuals are ultimately given a predetermined set of choices. Default privacy settings on Facebook used to have a number of different categories of visibility: Everyone (which meant publicly available to the internet), Network (meaning the university or business network of which a user was a part), Friends of Friends, Friends, and Only Me. Users could also put their friends into groups and restrict information to discrete groups. At the time of this writing in 2021, users can select from Public, Friends, Custom, and Only Me. While the Custom option allows users to keep certain information and posts hidden from particular audiences, the options do not allow users to choose one of the older, now defunct, privacy setting options. The data that is available to Facebook itself, in Reyman's (2013) definition, is also somewhat determined by the means through which users access the site. Technology journalists more recently revealed that Facebook was collecting the text messages from Android phone users because Android had lax data and privacy safeguards, while Facebook could not access the messages on iPhones, which had greater security and encryption features (Tufekci, 2018).

In the introduction, I discussed social media platforms as an assemblage of technological infrastructure, policy parameters, governance structures, and users. Through the case studies I conducted, managing one's data within that assemblage emerged as a particular area of concern and of anxiety for my research participants. Much of this challenge, as noted in chapter 3, was about audience. Individuals were concerned about their intended and unintended audiences when sharing content on social media platforms. They were also concerned about managing their data on social media platforms themselves. Some of this concern was about visibility: Who am I writing to? What are the consequences of this writing? And who owns it? Other concerns were about the data generated as a consequence of that writing that social media platforms and their partners—including advertisers and other third-party partners—had access to. Some of this information users could control, but the Cambridge Analytica situation demonstrates that social media companies and other organizations will make use of individuals' data in undisclosed and unforeseen ways. It is easy for social media users to feel powerless, and indeed, their choices are usually restricted to a set of predetermined options. There is a tension between what users can understand and control about their data on social platforms and what the software and company policies allow them to understand and control.

This chapter describes the generation and management of data within this social media assemblage as a set of literacy practices, ones that the individuals profiled here developed in response to these challenges. When an individual signs up for an account on a social network site, this person has to consider not only how to represent themself and share content, but also what the social network site company will do with that information, how to navigate the control of their data through the site interface, and how use of the site will become integrated (or not) into their writing and communication practices. Beyond the audiences that individuals communicate with on social media, their literacy and identity practices are also influenced by the sites themselves through their design, policies, and ways that individuals integrate use of these sites into their daily practice. This chapter details how social network site users, as Reyman described, interact with an assemblage of technologies, policies, and users on different social media platforms to generate and manage data. Edwards (2020a) called this integration of bodies, devices, and digital infrastructure "deep circulation," and he noted that data flows through affective, textual, and infrastructural dimensions (p. 79). Once writers place texts into circulation, such as through social media platforms, they are subject to both surveillance and critique, Edwards argued. As demonstrated in this chapter, when users' perspectives and options are limited, they also often push back on these constraints, questioning policies, insisting on more control, and subverting the sites' intended uses. This chapter first considers the proactive strategies that these individuals used in managing technologies and integrating them within their daily literacy practices before considering their defensive strategies in navigating and using distinct privacy settings.

NAVIGATING SOCIAL MEDIA ASSEMBLAGES

Lisa Nakamura (2002) has written about the ways early discourse surrounding the internet saw it as a place, an exotic third-world location that reified Western internet users as tourists in cyberspace (p. 89). Through images like the ones she analyzed, the internet has in the past been seen as a location a user visits that is separate from one's embodied, offline life. The MUD users interviewed in Sherry Turkle's (1995) book, *Life on the Screen*, for example, drew distinctions between the worlds in which they interacted and experimented with identity, and IRL, or "in real life." Rather than viewing the internet as a place, however, ubiquitous networked computing means that the internet goes everywhere, accessed through a wireless laptop computer, a handheld tablet, e-reader, or mobile device. Users of social media platforms update their status from multiple locations, share content on the go, and have updates sent to their mobile devices. Instead of providing strict boundaries between online and offline selves, users of social media have instead integrated the platforms within their own daily lives and literacy practices.

Each of the writers in this study managed social media platforms as assemblages, made up of multiple technologies and user interfaces, governed by distinct and changing policies, and populated with growing numbers of users. As described in the introduction and in chapter 1, considering social media platforms as assemblages allows us to examine how their users navigate them at multiple levels. Kendall Leon and Stacey Pigg (2011) described the ways that graduate students engaged in "digital multitasking" and in one temporal moment blended "multiple virtual spaces that represent different goals and purposes" (p. 8). While the graduate students they studied used social media as a cognitive break from more mentally taxing work of writing academic text and reading journal articles, social media is also "where the 'official business' of academia gets done" (p. 8). Leon and Pigg described the ways that requesting and finding resources, learning about new texts, discovering calls for papers, and networking with other scholars all happened in social media spaces for graduate students. They saw this literate activity as distributed across a number of different virtual spaces, using Paul Prior and Jody Shipka's (2003) concept of "chronotopic laminations," which they defined as "the dispersed and fluid chains of places, times, people, and artifacts that come to be tied together in trajectories of literate action, the ways multiple activity footings are simultaneously held and managed" (p. 181). Writers' literate activity is dispersed through chains of daily events, and writing happens in moments between domestic activities like doing the laundry, sitting in coffee shops, and commuting.

While Leon and Pigg as well as Prior and Shipka examined academic writing, a more diverse range of writers integrate their activity on social media platforms within their daily lives. Someone might interrupt a task at work or while studying to waste a few moments scrolling through Twitter's news feed. An individual might make a few comments on a Facebook thread while standing in line at the grocery store, and someone might snap a picture of a billboard or another object on the way to work and share it on Instagram. All of the writers I studied integrated social media platforms within their daily lives and navigated these assemblages of hardware, software, policies, and people in order to do so. In the first section of this chapter, I describe the ways these case study participants integrated social media platforms and their related technologies into their daily lives. Each person took a different but proactive approach to controlling the information they shared on digital platforms.

Photos and Assemblages

The increasing importance of mobile technologies that occurred over the first decade of social media use led to an increase in image-based content on social media platforms, as it became easy for users to quickly take a photo at any time and to share that photo on social media. As Lauren Cagle (2019) identified, these kinds of digital texts are part of a complex assemblage of human and nonhuman actors: cameras, wireless networks, apps, interfaces, policies, and individual social media users. Not every participant had a smart phone at the start of this study, but those who did shared more photos, videos, and other scenes of everyday life on their social media accounts. Ronnie's social media use provides the best example of the ways that many social network site users integrated their activity within their daily lives. He had an iPhone that he carried with him everywhere, and he sent updates to Twitter frequently through his phone. He also used it to document his day through images and video, and he sent the images to TwitPic from his phone. Ronnie cited his iPhone as much of the reason that he shared images so frequently and pointed to one example where he saw an image in a bar that reminded him of his friend: "My friend's in the, he's a railroad engineer, so if any time I see a train I kinda tell him about it, so I saw that in the bathroom at Murphy's so I just tweeted him. Just like that."

The ways that Ronnie shared photos on Twitter was dependent upon all aspects of this assemblage. At the time, Twitter did not allow image uploading, so Ronnie used a popular supplementary service, TwitPic, that was designed to integrate with Twitter's API and allowed him to share photos he had taken with his phone in the moment. This technological infrastructure (both his mobile internet-connected iPhone and the TwitPic service) allowed Ronnie to integrate his social media use within his daily activity, and he connected to his personal contacts by documenting his lived experience on social network sites. Ronnie sometimes used a service called 12seconds that also integrated with Twitter to upload a short video from his phone, such as of him and his friends hanging out on the roof of his apartment building.

This specific assemblage allowed Ronnie to engage in at least one social network site most of the time, whether he was in front of a computer or just on his phone. In 2010 and 2011, the social media platforms themselves sometimes did not allow image and media integration, so Ronnie integrated different tools in new ways in order to share content. In this way, Ronnie consciously suggested different technologies to suit his individual composing needs and integrated those services together. In 2016, Ronnie engaged in much of the same practices, but most of the services he used for his composing and sharing practices were directly integrated within the apps he was using. Not only did Twitter provide seamless photo sharing, but Ronnie also used Instagram to engage in many of the photo and video sharing practices that he had previously cobbled together from different services, including TwitPic, 12seconds, Vine, and others.

Jack used Twitter in much the same way, using his personal Twitter account to link to moments from his everyday experience in TwitPic. Jack tweeted about conversations with friends and family, social events, and posted pictures of these events on Twitter, for example, taking photos that commented on grocery store runs and images from good meals. As described in chapter 3, both Jack and Alexis had also moved this activity to Instagram, with Jack sharing thrift store finds and Alexis posting frequent photos from walks, commutes, and work settings. Jordan noted in 2013 that he found Twitter's interface easier to use and more accessible on a mobile device, and therefore integrated Twitter into his daily phone usage, while only interacting with Facebook on a computer. As mobile phones and the photos they captured became a part of more social media users' assemblages, new services developed for those devices and practices specifically.

Managing Devices

In 2010 and 2011, Ronnie integrated his use of social media within his daily activity as a college student. He was often in front of a desktop or laptop computer, and he accessed social media platforms primarily through the website. He checked Twitter constantly from the website, and saw it as a habit, part of his daily routine, and something he did when he was bored. He also visited Facebook a few times each day from his laptop computer to keep up with his friends. His roommates were on Twitter as well, and the three of them had conversations in the apartment that took place partially in person and partially on Twitter. He stated in an interview:

> It's weird, we'll mention each other and sometimes when we're in the apartment, we'll talk about what's going on on Twitter and say, "hey, did you check out this tweet?" or "did you check out what I wrote on your wall?" which kind of feels weird because it kind of defeats the purpose, you know, I could just tell you in person.

Ronnie's roommates, for example, knew when he was awake in the morning not because he left his bedroom but because he sent a tweet from his phone or computer. Apartment announcements were also circulated through a Facebook group rather than through physical notes left in common areas, as I mentioned in the introduction of a previous chapter. In these ways, social media platforms served as both communication and organization spaces, some open to other audiences on the internet and some closed.

When Ronnie studied at the library, he usually listened to music through last.fm, which documented the songs he listened to and shared them with his friends. He often tweeted his last.fm activity as well, sharing the songs he was currently listening to with his contacts as well:

[#nowplaying tool. specifically, lateralus and 10,000 days. i have some arguments to settle] Sun May 30, 2010 via web

[i need to WAKE UP. #nowplaying lady gaga] 10:08 AM Dec 7th, 2010 via web

[room is arranged but needs tidying. got the pc hooked up to the music, though, so it's time to scrobble! #lastfm #nowplaying @paramore] 5:24 PM Dec 31st, 2010 via web

Ronnie's situated digital literacy practices involved chains of activity across different social network sites and mobile devices. We can see each of these individual actions as situated, embodied activities that were part of a specific assemblage and influenced by histories of the tools, including the sites themselves, used to create them. Rather than considering Ronnie's activity on social network sites as discrete and isolated actions, we instead should see that work as part of a larger system of literate activity that traverses a number of different interfaces, ones that Ronnie selected and integrated for specific purposes.

Ronnie also made stylistic choices in his social media posts—specifically his tweets—to account for the ways that he integrated different platforms in his daily social media use. When Ronnie posted updates to Twitter, he always enclosed his tweets within square brackets. Along with being a matter of style, Ronnie's brackets at one time served an important purpose. Ronnie usually updated his Facebook status by forwarding select tweets to Facebook. From 2009 to 2018, a third-party app called Selective Tweets[2] could be integrated within a user's Facebook and Twitter accounts and allowed people to repost individual tweets to Facebook by adding the #fb hashtag at the end of the tweet. Ronnie used this feature to integrate these two platforms, and he had some Twitter updates sent to Facebook. The difference in the structure of updates within these two spaces, however, sometimes gave the Facebook updates convoluted grammar. As Ronnie explained:

Back when Facebook had, when you update your status to like, "[Ronnie] is . . ." it had that "is." I put the brackets there to kind of segment it off. Even when they got rid of it, I say okay, well, my name is just kind of here. I need this to be separate. So that's where that originally came from.

Ronnie originally used the brackets in order to preserve the grammatical structure of his tweets in Facebook. As in this example, all of

Ronnie's tweets appear in this format: "[quick nap before rehearsal. i have a headache from staring at the computer screen too long]." Formerly, Facebook structured status updates with an automatic "Ronnie is" construction, so the update would appear on Facebook as "Ronnie is [quick nap before rehearsal. i have a headache from staring at the computer screen too long]," which allowed him to preserve his sentence structure and the first-person voice that was common of his updates on Twitter. After Facebook changed the format for status updates, first to just the person's name, and later dropping the name to adopt an open format, Ronnie kept the brackets, which became a signifying feature of his tweets. Ronnie noted, "I guess it's artsy. It's like my trademark in a way." They also signified Ronnie in a particular way to his friends, as he described: "On occasion I'll use my friends' Twitter accounts when they leave their computers unattended, and I'll put it into brackets so people will actually know it's me, who follow me. They'll know [Ronnie] messed with this person's Twitter account." A stylistic convention Ronnie adopted as a way to negotiate the limitations of an interface structure on Facebook became an identifying feature of his own writing online, to the point that this feature indicated his authorship in other spaces as well. His friends recognized writing in square brackets as his.

Ronnie's experience also demonstrates the complex ways in which activities on social network sites bridge online and offline spaces. Interactions were often initiated online and end in some kind of offline activity; Ronnie contacted friends through either Facebook or Twitter to plan social events for later that evening. Ronnie also used Twitter as he would text messaging to plan meetups with his friends. In one instance, he tweeted his plans to have dinner at a campus restaurant and invited others to meet him there. Sitting at a table in the restaurant, replies on Twitter were sent to his phone, and he used Twitter as he would texting, through which he learned that several of his friends planned to join him. Ronnie's activity complicated easy boundaries between sites as online and offline activity, and he made use of social media assemblages to manage his daily literacy practices.

TRAVERSING BOUNDARIES THROUGH SOCIAL MEDIA PLATFORMS

Alexis often used social network sites to manage her connections with others who were farther away. Like Ronnie, Alexis also used Facebook to network with friends, make plans, and send updates to her friends and contacts. These connections were especially important for Alexis when she was a college student, as she lived off-campus rather than with friends on campus. Alexis updated her Facebook status with her location when she stayed with a friend on campus during finals week, so Facebook was a way to keep in touch with her local college friends about her physical whereabouts any given week. Unlike Ronnie, Alexis shared few photo updates from her phone, though she did occasionally upload photos to Cyworld. While Alexis was traveling, however, she sent updates to Twitter via her cell phone in order to keep her friends updated about her travels:

> When I'm traveling and stuff and people aren't physically there with me, for example, I traveled to Michigan by myself, and I just loved constantly texting to Twitter, updating my status to other people, for those people who know I'm gone, but don't know exactly what I'm doing, you know, so my close friends gets [*sic*] updated.

Alexis used social network sites in her daily literacy practices in order to send frequent updates on her lived experience to her friends and connections.

For users without smart phones that included data plans, Twitter offered and still offers an SMS texting option for its users that involves sending tweets to a specific number via text message. This feature allowed Alexis to update Twitter easily on her travels and allowed her to still feel connected to her friends when she was away.

One of the most important people Alexis connected with was a friend in Korea, with whom she shared a group diary on Cyworld and frequently connected on that site. Because their wireless plans didn't include international rates, she and her friend would send each other "texts" by using the direct message function on Twitter. They both activated a feature in Twitter that would send private direct messages to their mobile devices via text, and they were able to stay in frequent contact using the direct messages feature as a texting service. Alexis, like many of my participants, used social media creatively to get around limitations and restrictions within the technology she was using in order to make these services work within her daily life.

For transnational students like Alexis, this constant contact with her multiple friend groups also represented important relationship maintenance with those far away. As Youngjoo Lee and Alan Hirvela (2010) noted in their study of the self-sponsored writing practices of a 1.5-generation Korean American student, participating in these different sites, particularly Cyworld, helped their research participant "establish and maintain her memberships in 'affinity groups,' that is, groups of other Korean 1.5 Generation adolescents as well as some of her non-Korean friends." Wan Shun Eva Lam and Enid Rosario-Ramos (2009) also argued for the importance of online connections, particularly blogs, for immigrant students in the United States to maintain ties with friends and with their home cultures across long distances.

Berry et al. (2012) described the various ways students with transnational experiences used digital networks to communicate across geographically dispersed communities, arguing that their co-researchers "create digital communicative landscapes, connected spaces of globalized human flows that resist a simple mapping onto conventional, physically contiguous geopolitical spaces." Alexis's experience with social network sites allowed her to connect to her various friend groups at one time from anywhere, and she used and repurposed multiple technologies in order to do so.

The social media assemblages in which Alexis participated included updating her Facebook status from class with her netbook, sharing photos of a recent trip on Cyworld, and sending updates about her location to Twitter with her cell phone. These assemblages included multiple platforms as well as multiple countries. In her online interactions, Alexis crossed boundaries of language and place quite easily, sending updates in both English and Korean to friends in the United States and in Korea as well.

While Alexis used Twitter to "text" with a friend in Korea in 2011, she used KakaoTalk for the same purpose in 2016. KakaoTalk is a free, mobile instant messaging application popular in Korea. Similar to WhatsApp, KakaoTalk allows for text-based private and small-group conversations, including photo and video sharing. Alexis reported that she used the app almost every day to keep in touch with her family and friends in Korea. Like her previous use of Twitter, she used social media applications to overcome barriers of time, space, and international cellular phone rates to keep in touch across transnational spaces. Like Ronnie, by 2016 Alexis was able to use more specialized applications and social media platforms to meet her individualized communication needs, rather than repurposing a more generalized service.

MANAGING SPACES

Writers also integrated social media platforms into specific places. Prior and Shipka (2003) described the ways that writers used "environment selecting and structuring practices (ESSPs)" (p.181) during their academic writing sessions in order to focus. These practices also translate to digital environments and social media platforms. Sandra also used a combination of desktop and mobile applications in her social media use, but technological limitations kept her social media use more to a desktop. Although Sandra bought a new iPhone during our study, she didn't use it frequently for social media updates, and most of Sandra's tweets were sent from her computer while she was at the library:

> I thought I would be doing it all the time, but generally I'm on my computer, or like, on one of the computers in the computer lab. For some reason my AT&T network doesn't work on the quad. It's like the only place I'd want remote access. Um, I think I will more over the summer, and like being at home, just because I'm just around computers less, and I'm going on vacation, and I don't want to take my computer with me.

The specific setting of the library and its desktop computer played a role in Sandra's social media use. While she wanted to use her new iPhone around campus to share updates, the technical limitations of her service provider made that difficult. New smart phone capabilities at the time allowed users to update social media more regularly from mobile phones, but Sandra was not able to incorporate those practices into her own social media use.

Using a web browser and a desktop computer, though, allowed Sandra to share details from her daily experiences while she was studying or otherwise online. The following tweets demonstrate how Sandra commented on her daily activities, primarily in her hours at the library, but also commenting on her daily activities in other contexts, through social network sites:

> Typing on windows computers at the library is proving to be stupidly difficult 26 Apr 10

> On a scale of 1 to 10 of how excited I am to be at a history final review session, im definitely at -3 9 Dec 10

> watching a romantic comedy based around ramen. #netflixmondays 2 Aug 10

Sandra used the Twitterific application to check and update Twitter on her iPhone, but the application also made her use of the service difficult. It took the Twitter client too long to load, it was "buggy," and she stated that she didn't have the patience for it. Unlike Ronnie, Alexis, and Jack, who enjoyed updating social network sites while they were away traveling, around campus, and conducting other activities, Sandra only felt the need to update the service when she was at a computer:

> I also think I think more about tweeting when I'm sitting at my computer, you know, I'm generally kind of bored. It's usually probably because I'm studying and doing work. Kind of just doing nothing.

Ronnie and Alexis utilized social media assemblages to integrate social media platforms within their daily lives and experiences, representing physical places and activities in online environments. While Sandra spent a great deal of time in the library, she did not feel the need to update her activities outside of this space online. Although Sandra reported that she expected to use her phone more to update social network sites over the summer, she didn't use them much, and continued her library updating habits during the fall semester as well, as seen in the following tweets sent during one study session:

> remember august when everyone in the library was wearing shorts. Makes all the boots and winter coats really sad. #whyisntthiscalifornia 12 Dec 10

> i thought I was distracted at the library, but there's a girl in front of me watching sitcoms. I highly doubt its a subject of a thesis 12 Dec 10

> nothing is happening on the internet. how am i supposed to stay distracted from statistics? 12 Dec 10

> haven't even started statistics . . . 12 Dec 10

> just realized I've been at the library for almost 8 hours. holy shit.12 Dec 10

For Sandra, the rhetorical situations that occasioned an update to her social network sites were specific to these contexts. In her article on the influence of place on networked writing practices, Stacey Pigg (2014) discussed the ways that writers navigated and structured "local ecologies of place, people, and materials" for their working and studying environments (p. 261). Social media, particularly Twitter, was a part of the ecology that Sandra created while in the library. While her social media use was at least somewhat restricted by technological assemblages in which they were situated, she also used them proactively and integrated them within her own writing and studying activities.

COMMEMORATING IMPORTANT EVENTS

While Ronnie, Alexis, and Sandra integrated social media within their daily lives, social media users throughout the first decade also integrated social media platforms into some of their most important life moments. Social media platforms were also used to make announcements and to signal changes, from relationships becoming "Facebook official" to announcements about graduations, new jobs, and other events. Facebook eventually added Life Events for users' timelines in order for them to mark and track important moments.

Esther was one person who integrated her own social media use into an important life event. As Esther and her husband both used social media frequently, they invited people to tweet during their wedding.

Before the event, Esther posted the following tweets:

> We're having a live twitter feed up during the wedding. Even if you can't make it, send us a message. #weddinghashtag 10:24am, May 21, 2010 via Tweetdeck

> If you tweet between 3PM to midnight Sat May 22, your tweets will appear on a screen at our wedding #weddinghashtag 10:26am, May 21, 2010 via Tweetdeck

> Getting married today! #weddinghashtag 9:22am, May 22, 2010 via Tweetdeck

During the event, wedding guests and other friends tweeted messages to the couple, and Esther then posted the following tweet afterward:

> Thanks all for tweeting my wedding! #weddinghashtag 8:54am, May 23, 2010 via Tweetdeck

Esther and her husband also included social media into their ceremony, as they updated their Facebook relationship statuses during the event for all of the guests to see. Social media platforms, then, were a part of how they organized and structured their lives, and they turned to them to mark momentous occasions as well.

ASSEMBLAGES AS BLACK BOXES

Navigating the assemblages of social media platforms means more than just choosing the specific combinations of tools that fit a writer's aims, location, and situation. Throughout the course of this study, these research participants expressed difficulty in understanding the functions of some parts of these platforms. For the writers I describe here, social media platforms were often seen as taking actions that were inscrutable; sometimes this action might be the result of a proprietary algorithm, and sometimes it was a policy change or difference. In most of these cases, though, these social media users would ascribe actions to the platform itself without distinction, and it was, in fact, difficult to determine which aspect of the assemblage was responsible.

As noted at the start of this chapter, social media assemblages are often difficult to separate into their requisite parts, and it is difficult to determine what aspect of the platform was responsible, because the result was based on the different actors in the assemblage working together rather than any separate piece. But these relationships were also "blackboxed" for their users, and it was difficult to identify the different elements involved. Latour (1999) defined blackboxing as "the process that makes the joint production of actors and artifacts entirely opaque" (p. 183). An individual does not notice the system that produced an overhead projector, in Latour's example, nor the number of individuals needed to support its use until one element of that production fails to work. Similarly, it was difficult for many of my research participants to pull apart the various influences on their social media platform experiences because many aspects of Facebook's employees, policies, procedures, and proprietary algorithms together influenced the experiences they had on the social media platform.

Safiya Noble (2018) has studied the ways that these algorithms are racially biased, reflecting societal prejudices and inequality as well as an overly white and male technology industry. Although Noble's book *Algorithms of Oppression* focused on Google and search engines specifically, her critiques apply to social media platforms as well, and their algorithms also reflect inherent biases, from suggestion algorithms to news feed–sorting algorithms that foster engagement and controversy, to other similar structures. For example, Becca frequently posted about and commented on both the ads she saw on Facebook and the ways that the site suggested that she become a fan of certain pages.[3] While the suggestions are based on algorithms that identified similarities between users' preferences and likes, it was easy to put a larger cultural meaning onto these suggestions or to consider what assumptions these algorithms might be working within. Becca stated in an interview:

> It suggests all of these Black celebrities and then says, "You are a fan of Barack Obama" underneath. And I'm just sitting here, like, this is so problematic. I just like to speculate about what they're basing these on. I mean, I guess statistically, it's like if people like this thing, they also tend to like this thing. . . . Occasionally it's stuff that makes sense, like "become a fan of the White House because you're a fan of Barack Obama," or "become a fan of Michelle Obama, because you're a fan of Barack Obama," but Will Smith, and Lil Wayne, and Tyler Perry?

While the Facebook recommendations were generated through an algorithm, Becca read them as having cultural meaning, in this case, grouping Black actors, producers, and entertainers with the president into one group. Becca described this occurrence as problematic in that it made broad generalizations based on one category of similarity: race. These kinds of situations in which Facebook did not consider the cultural meaning and consequences of its algorithms were frequent and extensive. Many of these examples were about race, but the site also faced controversy when a new feature encouraged Facebook users to reach out to their Facebook friends with whom they had not connected recently, and some of these contacts were Facebook users who had passed away.

Ronnie also had questions about how the algorithms functioned and sorted information. Ronnie and his friends spent a good amount of time on last.fm, a music-sharing social network site, considering how their activity on this site affected both their music compatibility with each other and how that activity shaped their statistics on the site overall.

Comments like these on Twitter are frequent:

@Matt And this will up our Last.fm compatibility! ^_^

[@wanderbass56(Ronnie)'oh god, ke$ha is being scrobbled to my last.fm' @Ryan_B: 'you're going to lose compatibility with everyone you know']

One evening, Ronnie's friends competed for highest compatibility with Ronnie on his musical tastes on last.fm. Ronnie started with this tweet, which linked to a screenshot of his friend's profile on last.fm, which listed their compatibility:

http://twitpic.com/xxxx—[you just can't buy that kind of compatibility. ;P @n3sam and i are clearly meant to be!]

Within 10 minutes, Ronnie's friends altered their own music choices to be listed as "super" compatible as well:

http://twitpic.com/xxxx—[actually, @jsanto seems to have the upper hand. @n3sam, you guys need to fight for my musical love!]

http://twitpic.com/xxxx—[it appears @Ryan_B wants in too . . . okay, if one more person grabs 'super' i swear . . .]

http://twitpic.com/xxxx—[@Matt is now 'super' with me . . . and i won't ss @reptilesara since she's been for a while. what's going on

http://twitpic.com/xxxxx—[add @hijohn to the list . . . that makes six 'super' friends! tonight is clearly an epic night =) glad you all[4]

Ronnie spent a good deal of time considering the criteria for these preferences and how his own activity might change and shape these preferences. For Ronnie and his friends, changing their actions in order to change settings on sites like last.fm becomes a kind of game. They interacted with each other, but they interacted with the social media assemblage as well in order to determine how it functioned. Trying to figure out these specific technologies and algorithms was also a way for the individuals I profile here to better understand how these technologies worked in order to shape their use and better integrate it within their daily literacy and social media practices. Understanding the logic would help these social media users better use these tools proactively.

Sometimes these systems were beyond users' control and these assemblages broke down in ways that made it difficult to determine where the problem occurred or how to fix it. While an actor, either an algorithm or an actual person behind the scenes, was making decisions that influenced my participants' experiences with the social media platform, it was at times difficult if not impossible to contact anyone about the issue. In November 2010, Beth tried to log in to her Facebook profile and learned that her account had been suspended. Beth recounted the frustrating process she had navigating Facebook's organizational structure in order to regain access to her account:

> It was just a pain in the butt because of course there aren't any real people at Facebook that I know of, and so I had to go through all of their different systems, and I was like, ok, I want my account back, and I finally got there, and I was typing in stuff and they're like, well your account doesn't exist anymore because it was a fake identity. I'm like, no it wasn't, and I had to go through this whole process . . . I think my account was hijacked, and they gave it back to me with no explanation as to what happened. [. . .] It was just super stressful because no one told me what was happening, and I ended up going through like 40 hoops to get it back, and I wasn't even sure that it still existed. [. . .] I was very uncomfortable about the lack of clarity about what was happening. So it's deactivated. I may reactivate it in the future, but it was just such a hassle.

Beth described her anger and confusion over this process and especially Facebook's silence on a reason for her account deactivation. Beth also noted in that interview that her mother had told her about a story she heard in the news around that time about young women around Beth's age having their Facebook accounts deactivated because of a bug. Facebook, in fact, confirmed a problem around that time regarding a glitch in the system they used to verify accounts, which caused a "small number" of female users' accounts to be deactivated (Melanson, 2010). Beth was never provided this information by Facebook, however. Beth's largest complaint, as she described in her interview, was the process. She could never discuss the issue with Facebook directly, and as she stated, "there aren't any real people at Facebook that I know of." She also described a frustrating process of being led through Facebook's flow charts, moving from one screen to the next in the hopes of finding an answer to her problem, which individuals at Facebook took too long to respond to. For Beth, this incident opened up the black box of Facebook's operations and their ineffectiveness was enough to make her leave the site.

Beth made this decision based on control. This incident made it clear to her that she did not have control of her own information on the site, and this lack of control and transparency about their processes caused her to leave the site entirely. According to news reports of other Facebook users' issues around the same time, this problem was caused by a program that helped Facebook identify fake accounts. Interestingly, while Facebook deactivated the account of a legitimate user representing an authentic offline identity, Facebook never identified or suspected the fictional Facebook profile Ronnie created that I described in chapter 3. Les Hutchinson (2017) also described how Facebook deactivated the accounts of drag queens in 2014 for not using their legal names in their profiles, requiring these users to present state-issued photo identification in order to reactivate their accounts. While Facebook attributed a situation similar to Beth's as a technical error, the 2014 situation was an intentional policy change at Facebook to attach account identities to offline identities. The assemblage of technology, employees, and policies combined here in a way that not only deactivated a legitimate account but it made it difficult enough to regain access that Beth walked away entirely. Although in most cases the actions and activities of individuals who work for these social network sites are invisible, incidents like this one break apart these black boxes and cause frustration for users when they cannot contact someone within Facebook's confusing labyrinth of help menus.

The first half of this chapter has demonstrated how the social media users I've described here manage the assemblages that make up social media platforms and adjust them to fit their own needs. Nelly Oudshoorn and Trevor Pinch (2003) noted the importance of studying users' connection to and take up of technologies and to study those technologies within "their context of use" (p. 2). Technologies are accompanied with scripts about their use, which enable and constrain certain actions (Akrich & Latour, 1992). Users can take up these scripts or resist them, adjusting these technologies for their own use through an "antiprogram," defined as "the users' program of action that is in conflict with the designers' program" (Akrich & Latour, 1992, p. 261). The writers I studied took up social network sites in their own ways to resist the expectations of the designers and their scripts. Ronnie, as described in chapter 3, created a fictional Facebook profile when Facebook encouraged its users to represent so-called authentic, and even legal, offline identities. Becca and Sandra resisted Facebook's encouragement to connect with other users, and Jack did not use the sharing software on his last.fm account.

Data management across the kinds of technological assemblages that exist in social media platforms, I argue, involves small interventions like this, ways for individuals to adapt the interfaces of social media platforms to work more effectively for their needs and to even resist the policies put forth by the platform. Johnson-Eilola (2005) used the term "conceptual objects" to discuss the ways that objects only have meaning within "specific, contingent, dynamic contexts" (p. 26), and these meanings are often not ones considered by the designers of these objects. While social media platforms often placed a number of restrictions on users' activities to occur within specific parameters, individual users adapted these guidelines for their own uses and their own meanings. It is interesting to note, for example, that many of the functions commonly used on Twitter, including retweets and replies, were functions developed by users and not the Twitter designers themselves. In these ways, many practices developed by users that adapted the technologies to their own needs became codified within the sites themselves.

PRIVACY AND MANAGING DATA

One of the most visible ways in which individuals managed social media assemblages, and one of the aspects of social media platforms they discussed most often, was privacy policies and settings. As I described in chapter 3, one of the primary issues social media users have to manage is determining not only their intended and immediate audience but also who has access to their information and how that information might travel. All of my research participants, then, spent a good amount of time and energy determining the answers to these questions and managing their data within different parameters defined and allowed by social media platforms' privacy policies and their design affordances. Each of these individuals cared a great deal about who had access to their information and what consequences that might have. Considering privacy and navigating complex privacy settings, then, was sometimes a needlessly complex task, and one of the most common defensive tools these users engaged in to manage data on digital platforms.

As noted in the introduction to this chapter, Jessica Reyman (2013) described how Facebook distinguishes between what they describe as "content and information," the information Facebook users upload and post to the platform, and data, which is the information it collects about users based on their activity on the site, their location, demographics, and other information. The individuals I studied, therefore, were concerned about privacy at these two different levels: (a) *outward facing*: information shared with their friends (content and information); (b) *inward facing*: information shared with the social platforms (data). While one of these types of privacy is much easier to manage than the other, all of the people I talked to for this study were concerned with both types and actively worked to manage them. They employed two primary strategies in managing their identities in terms of privacy: (a) self-censoring information they shared on social network sites and (b) frequently reviewing and managing privacy options on these sites.

Outward-Facing Privacy Management
Self-Censorship

As noted in the previous chapter, self-censorship was an audience strategy used by many of the writers I describe here and was often influenced by the particular communities these individuals connected with on social media platforms. Self-censorship, though, was also used as a data-management and privacy strategy. Put simply, one way to keep information private was to not put it online in the first place. Beth often employed this strategy, and she was nervous about putting herself out there online because "that is the ultimate putting yourself out there. It's accessible forever." Even though she kept her privacy settings restricted, she felt that keeping her information off the internet entirely was the best policy for her:

> I don't want people to be able to find out that much about me just, like, online. And I can see in other people and in myself the tendency just to put way too much information online, so I definitely try to keep that restricted, even though, like, it's very private. Anyone could just copy/paste off of that and take it somewhere else. So even though I know that's not likely to happen . . . I just go into it with an assumption that everything will be seen by someone I don't want it to be . . . I don't want people to be able to stalk me, so I keep it to people I know.

Like most of the individuals I interviewed for this project, Beth also had to make decisions about adjusting her profile with friend requests that cut across her typical audience groups. She cleaned or adjusted her profile slightly when her boss friended her, as discussed in chapter 3, which was her solution instead of customizing her privacy settings. Raynes-Goldie (2010) noted that the most common strategy for Facebook users in managing their privacy did not involve adjusting settings at all but consisted of, as Beth just described, "cleaning" one's profile selectively to remove offending information. As Marwick and boyd (2014) argued, however, privacy on social media is a networked concept, and Beth was not the only one making decisions about whether information about herself would end up on social media. Her friends also uploaded content about her, and Beth often untagged herself from photos, which kept the information from appearing on her Facebook wall. While the picture remained online, it was no longer connected with her identity and profile and much more difficult to find.

Nicole was the individual I studied who was most aware of and concerned about networked concepts of privacy. As noted in chapter 3, she did not friend many of her offline contacts on Facebook because she did not want to connect different friend groups together or to be defined by them. Nicole self-censored a good deal of information on social media platforms as well, keeping content to items she shared on Pinterest or to links, resources, and information connected to her academic field of study on Twitter and LinkedIn. The boundaries Nicole maintained began to cross when she had to use a Facebook group in one of her graduate classes as a discussion space. She connected with some of her classmates through Facebook then, but they began tagging her when she won an award in her field. Because of Facebook's friend recommendation and news feed algorithms, other people noticed the content and sent her friend requests. Nicole stated in an interview: "When I got the [award], all my dance friends want to be Facebook friends with me. Block block block block." Nicole not only deleted the requests but used the site's infrastructure to block the users entirely.

As discussed in chapter 3, the writers I studied had different ways of managing audience across different social media platforms. Facebook allows individuals to restrict content to or from certain individuals, previously through the groups feature and currently more selectively. While Beth set up particular groups through which to restrict content, she found changing her settings confusing and never used them. As she noted above, it was easier for her to just remove the image than to restrict access to it. Most of my research participants felt the same way, and only one of them used these groups; while they had the ability to adjust their privacy settings on Facebook to better manage these different audience groups, these writers developed their own rhetorical strategies instead.

Like Beth, Sandra frequently cleaned her profile, more in terms of cultivating a particular image of herself than in removing or censoring content. Sandra stated, "I don't like it to look like I've been on Facebook all day, even though I normally have." For Sandra, interaction with her friends on the social network site was important, and she always deleted her Facebook statuses that did not receive any comments from her friends. If her status update didn't receive a response, "there's no reason for them to, like, exist on my own wall," she stated. "Why am I writing to myself? I already know what I'm thinking." Sandra's Facebook friends, then, acted as post-publication feedback for her, and the response she received helped Sandra edit her responses after the fact. In this way, Sandra curated her profile with only the witty reflections and updates that received responses from her friends.

Sandra describes cultivating her identity on Facebook as a form of "branding," and she frequently revised information on her profile to cultivate that image:

> I do a lot of policing because I kind of like to think of myself online as like a brand. Whatever you put out there is you, and one bad image, picture, text, it can destroy it. I'm really interested in blogging in the future, and I'm in the process of designing a website, and I think that the Internet can be your business. There's no reason to destroy it. Because everyone has their own embarrassing stuff, but the Internet is solidified and permanent.

Sandra spent a good deal of time on social network sites managing this information; putting up images and updates that cultivate a particular image. This attention, Sandra noted, applied especially to photos, noting that she was "very conscientious" of the photos both she and others posted of her. Rather than using the groups feature that Facebook provides for managing content with different groups, Sandra instead managed her content through this editing and policing process.

Stephanie also reported cleaning her profiles, but over a longer timescale. She stated that she deleted much of her older content from her Facebook and Twitter accounts and deleted her Tumblr account entirely, anything that was from high school:

> I deleted a lot of old posts. Cause I mean, I never thought about that before until I realized I was graduating and I need to get a job. I deleted anything that was beyond like from high school I got rid of. I made sure I cleaned all of that up. And I'm just more wary of what I post. Like I'm not going to post all my personal business on the internet. It's not, you know, it's not necessary.

Like other participants, Stephanie cleaned up her social media content, but she also went back years and deleted old content that she felt was oversharing or placing her in a bad light.

As Alice Marwick and danah boyd (2014) described, privacy on social media platforms is networked and social; users make decisions about privacy by reading context and social situations, and privacy controls are managed in collaboration with one's friends. Alexis strictly controlled information available on Facebook, for example, but most of the information she placed on Cyworld was completely public. She attributed that difference to the site design itself. Users' information on Cyworld is organized differently from Facebook and has nothing like a news feed. A user has to click on each individual's profile in order to see all of one's updates, which changes the kind of information she places on the site. Alexis's comments here demonstrated how her identity representation was influenced not only by the different audience groups she connected with but also by the design of the sites themselves. Cyworld's lack of an algorithmic news feed—frankly, the absence of any news feed at all—influenced the amount and type of information she shared on the platform. On Cyworld, she felt that she could be more personal, because her updates, while public, weren't broadcast to all of her contacts on the site.

By 2016, Alexis had changed the way she thought about privacy on social media and adjusted the information she shared as a result. She noted in an interview that many of these changes were about both the platform designs and the audiences she connected with:

> I used to post a lot of you know, essays and just diaries. I haven't done that for the past five years. I would do it very occasionally because of the hyper-connectivity with people; I just felt like I can't do that on Facebook or Instagram or Twitter. Like I can't really post about the things that I really deeply think about or anything philosophical. It's just like, I don't feel comfortable with it. I think most people wouldn't. [. . .] I went back to Cyworld recently and have started posting again about just, you know, because I know it's almost a dead site so I know people aren't on that, and so I would make it public or sometimes just private for, public you know for anybody to see if they're interested.

Alexis noted that she used Cyworld in 2016 for something closer to blog writing, and while she made some posts private in order to use the site like a private journal, she also published more general daily life updates for anyone who might come across her page. In this way, Cyworld functioned as more of a journal or blog space for Alexis, and one that she generally felt comfortable hiding in plain sight because of elements specific to that platform.

These four individuals here point to other aspects of privacy on social media platforms—because of the networked nature of privacy considerations, data management also has social concerns and pressures with which to attend. While privacy tools allow individuals to restrict content from specific people, there is also a concern that those restricted might find out they have only limited access to this person's content, either through conversations with others about specific content or by discovering that some information appears to be hidden, as Sandra described above. For these reasons, sometimes self-censoring information before it could even appear on Facebook was the best strategy for my research participants. Friending practices were also often fraught. Beth noted that she cleaned up her Facebook profile when her boss connected with her on the platform. She felt some social and professional pressure to accept the friend request, but that connection also required her to change some of her social media practices and revise past content. Managing one's information, then, did not stop when the status update, picture, or link was shared, but continued long afterward. This kind of information management also led many participants to share different information on different platforms. When Facebook became a place where users were connected with their bosses, their parents, and other authority figures, some conversations and topics moved into different spaces: Twitter, Instagram, Cyworld, and private chat threads, in order to better manage who could see their information, as I discussed in chapter 3.

Managing Settings

Privacy settings on Facebook, as discussed earlier, changed frequently throughout the course of my study. In early 2010, these privacy settings involved a myriad of different options for sharing different information (status updates, photo albums, applications, and other information), which resulted in the *New York Times* article mapping these different settings and options (Bilton, 2010). Facebook continued to make frequent changes to their privacy policy settings, providing and adjusting different groups of users (like "Friends of Friends" or people from users' university networks), as well as adding and then removing group features that allowed users to manage different levels of information sharing for different groups. When Facebook implemented major profile design changes in 2010, the social network site also switched many of the visibility categories for items like profile pictures and friends lists to "Everyone" by default. Many of the individuals I studied read about these privacy changes from news stories or from information posted by friends, and each of my research participants changed and updated their settings.

Sandra in particular mentioned a news story she read that caused her to make some adjustments:

> I remember there being like a huge thing, Facebook is changing its privacy settings. I remember trying to read through it, and not understanding a word of it. I think I saw like a Yahoo, like one of those stupid articles

that pops up on your home screen that said like 10 things to never do on your Facebook, and one of those things was like never put your full birth date including the year, so I took off the year, and I did change it so only I could see my photos. I might have changed who can see my profile, like friends of friends or, . . . I went back to just friends.

Sandra pointed to a popular press story as informing her about the information she placed on her Facebook page, which brought up issues of reputation (through photos) and larger identity theft concerns (through listing a full birth date). Early in this research study, Sandra had most of her information open to friends of friends because, she stated,

> I'm not too concerned about privacy. I keep it friends of friends, because if I were to meet a friend in person, I would probably be pretty open and friendly. I think it's good for networking too, because if you meet someone for the first time and tell them your name . . . if people don't have a picture, or it says nothing about them and it's just a name, there goes any chance of that connection, which is like the whole point.

In discussing the reasons for her privacy settings, Sandra mentioned both her practice of only putting information she was comfortable sharing more publicly on Facebook, and in her goal of using the site for networking as well as keeping in touch with current friends. Sandra therefore used the affordances of the technology in order to better facilitate her goal of connecting with new people on Facebook. Later in the study, however, after Sandra read more about Facebook privacy issues in the press, and she began her professional job search, she restricted her privacy settings to friends only. She stated:

> I had friends of friends, and then I realized how many people that actually is because I mean, people that I was interning with over the summer from Arizona had mutual friends in common. I haven't been to Arizona since I was 7, like I don't know anyone there. So I was just like, that was just too many, too many people. I think I have like 600, not that many, but then you know, I have friends who have like, 3,000 friends. How have you even met all those people?

A Pew Internet report published in 2012 noted a lack of density in Facebook connections; on average, only 12% of a user's friends were friends with each other, so one's updates were not reaching a close-knit community of friends, but rather, a number of unconnected friend groups. Friends of friends on Facebook can, in fact, be 100,000 people (Madden, 2012). Sandra's use of Facebook's privacy settings evolved as her identity concerns evolved, and in adjusting these settings, she relied on the affordances of the technologies, popular press accounts giving individuals advice about their settings, and interactions with other Facebook users.[5]

Becca was one research participant who took advantage of Facebook's group feature, but only for students currently in one of her classes. She noted that she had a "secret folder" that she would "stash current students in" that restricted access to her photos and other profile information. For the most part, however, she kept all of her content open to anyone connected as her friend on the site. She was also kept updated on Facebook's privacy and policy changes by her friends on the site, who frequently posted on these changes:

> People [were] posting, here's how you get rid of this so Facebook doesn't stalk you everywhere you go. Some people kind of overdo that, but some of the alarmist posts that are like, oh no, quick, stop Facebook from seeing anything ever.

For Becca, revising her privacy settings on the site was a process influenced by the design of technologies themselves, as well as communications and interactions with her friends on the site. Like many Facebook users, Becca relied on communication from her fellow Facebook friends, technology reporters, and general popular press to learn about changes to the platform's privacy settings rather than communication from the site directly. While this situation suggests that Facebook's own communication about the site's policy changes might be inadequate, it also demonstrates that privacy policy changes on the site are often complicated and multifaceted. Frequent changes and multiple policy gradations can be confusing for many users.

While Sandra pointed to online news articles that informed her of changes to Facebook privacy settings and the need to make adjustments, in 2013 and 2016 younger interviewees began to discuss the ways that their parents gave them advice on what information to put online and how to manage privacy settings as well. Stephanie noted that her parents frequently gave her warnings and advice on what information to keep offline, including personal information, so she was always thinking about the importance of privacy information online from before she used social media.

Caroline and Sam, who were undergraduate students in 2016, both described a practice common for students of creating different Instagram accounts with different settings. As described in chapter 3, finsta, or fake Instagram accounts, were secondary, private accounts that these social media users only shared with a few friends. While they were called fake Instagram accounts, Caroline noted that they often presented someone's real life more, while public and more open Instagram accounts instead represented a more curated image:

> What if a Fake Instagram is your real life and the actual choices you're making and then the real Instagram is the one where everything is filtered and pretty and you know purposefully we're taking a picture now at this place. And you know, I know people who find walls. They're like "We didn't even go there, but we saw the wall, we took the picture there" like it's not even real.

Instagram's interface allowed users to register for more than one account easily and to switch between them on the app.[6] The site's more binary public/private privacy settings also contributed to the practice of creating finsta accounts, one that was public and one that was hidden.

INWARD-FACING PRIVACY MANAGEMENT

Managing privacy on social media platforms throughout the first decade of social media was not only about trying to control who could see one's information on the service. As noted in the introduction to this section, it was also about the data social media platforms collected from their users, used in advertising and sometimes shared with external partners. All of the participants in this study were concerned about sharing their information with social media companies, but most were unsure of how to safeguard their information in the face of complex privacy settings and frequent changes.

In 2016, Alexis was working as a social media marketer and analyst, and she had probably the most insider knowledge about how her data could be used. This information influenced the way she shared information online as well:

> I was a super kind of a pro-privacy person. But you know, being in the industry has made me realize there's honestly no such thing. Um, I mean companies try, yes, try very hard. And yeah, you're going to stay anonymous for the most part, but still if we wanted to, if the companies wanted to, they can find out about you really quickly. Um, but of course we can't disclose any of that information, but it does inform extracting insights and better targeting um, so, it's just, I feel like it's not there. [. . .] Anything that you have publicly available in social, you have, it's public so obviously we can find you, we know what you're going to talk about based on your behavior in social. We know the topics that you're interested in, that you're passionate about, how you feel about a certain topic.

Alexis said that while she was concerned about the information that her social media friends and followers had access to, she has little to no control about the information that companies, like the one for which she worked, had access to. She noted that if it's online somewhere, it's generally available, and while companies anonymize that data, it's not hard for them to reidentify individuals. While she was careful about the information she shared with her own contacts, she knew that this information was generally accessible to someone.

In the face of this knowledge, Alexis noted that privacy was still important to her:

> I've been a lot more cognizant and aware of the information that I submit or put out. Like some people, even though they're in the data industry, like they don't care. Like whatever's more convenient, whatever is more effective, they don't care, right? But for me, I think privacy still matters for me, um, so I try to stay away from that. I don't link all my accounts to all the crazy apps or gated apps. [. . .] I have colleagues who, and I think this is kind of true, like because the web and social are so hyper commercialized, some people want better targeted ads for them. They don't want anything that doesn't cater to their interests or needs. And so some people just don't care.

Alexis noted that she still kept content off social media platforms, did not link her social media profiles to third-party applications who might get broad access to her data, and she paid careful attention to the information she was sharing on both the front end and the back end. To a certain extent, Alexis knew the project was futile, but she still tried to retain a bit of control around her information.

Alexis was not the only research participant concerned about what I have described here as inward-facing data privacy, and several individuals in this study found ways to try to thwart company data-collection systems. Beth, for one, reported that she often kept information off of Facebook because she didn't want the company to own her data. That was Ronnie's primary concern in using social network sites as well; he was comfortable about his data being public to his contacts and the internet at large, but he wanted to own that information and remain in control of its circulation. Over the course of the study, Ronnie began to have serious concerns about privacy and ownership of his information on Facebook. Ronnie came back to this fake profile of Alison, discussed in chapter 3, shortly after Facebook changed its privacy setting configurations in April 2010. Ronnie grew concerned about the amount of personal information he was placing on Facebook and also critical of the ways many of his peers took information on Facebook unquestioningly as the truth. He went back to listing Alison as his girlfriend and also listed fake siblings. He removed his high school to list Hogwarts

School of Witchcraft and Wizardry in its place, and he changed his current employer to the Ministry of Magic. He described this decision in this way: "I guess it's some sort of a statement. So many people just kind of go with what's on Facebook and trust it. There's really no basis other than assuming people are honest."

Ronnie described himself as sympathetic to Diaspora's cause, and that in the 6 months after the Facebook privacy settings change, he migrated most of his information off of the site. In 2011, he used his blog, hosted on his own domain, to hold most of his information, including his CV. All of his profiles on social network sites linked back to this blog. He uses this organization for two reasons: he only had to update information in one place and he left as little information with Facebook as possible:

> I don't mind the information being out there. I guess having it in Facebook's hands kinda bugs me. . . . I've seen Facebook as less of a location where I operate out of and more of just a satellite social network, so I'm just taking everything I can and just moving it out and making it as minimal as possible. That's also why I don't fill out any information on any of my other social networks like Digg or Flickr. I don't fill out anything but a little blurb that says where I am and then the link that goes straight to my website. Because I don't want to maintain all of that. . . . Any information I put on there is not really telling a full picture, so I'll send people to my blog, which says things much more accurately. Even if it's just my interests and my favorite movies and stuff like that. You know, just kind of seeing how information represents me, and I guess my take on it.

In this way, Ronnie used his own blog and site to keep more of his information in a single place. Not only was it easier to update just one service, rather than the more than 15 platforms on which he had accounts, but it also allowed him to keep greater control over his data, placed on a site he owned and managed rather than one controlled by a different company.

Interestingly, as a frequent user of many different social media platforms, Ronnie had no concerns about his *information* being online and publicly visible. His blog, for example, contained a good deal of information about his everyday reflections as well as a detailed CV of both his academic and musical pursuits. What Ronnie was concerned about, however, was the back-end rather than the front-end information and privacy management. By putting primarily false information on Facebook, Ronnie prevented Facebook from profiting from that information, while also sending his peers a message about their own use of information on the site. Ronnie's anxiety over ownership of his information and his continual attempts to control its presentation demonstrated the constant work individuals like Ronnie engaged in managing one's life and identity through social network sites. Frequent technology changes mean that these practices can be both time consuming and never ending.

In 2016, Ronnie thought of privacy on social media platforms much the same way, but his concerns translated into different practices. As Ronnie was just online less often, his updates were less frequent, and he shared information less often. He did list his work and school information on his Facebook and Twitter profiles, but he used his blog less frequently and did not use it as a central hub for his information as he did in 2011. Ronnie reported in 2016 that in terms of privacy issues, his views and practices on social media had changed the most in terms of what services he was willing to adopt. In 2010 and 2011, Ronnie often joined new social media platforms in order to "claim real estate" on the site; as discussed in chapter 3, many new services proliferated over that time period, and Ronnie wanted to ensure he could use his standard screen name and identity information in case the service took off. He also noted that other people "were a bit more trusting about kind of what they saw at face value." Not only did his friends share more information, they also took more of the information they shared at face value. Ronnie's obfuscation in providing fake information back in 2010 and 2011 allowed him to make a statement about information authenticity on social media at that time. In 2016, that message was less necessary for Ronnie to make.

Other social network site users were not as concerned about these issues as Ronnie was. Jack, for example, discussed this ownership of data at length and his ambivalence about Facebook and other social network sites collecting his data. On the one hand, Jack stated, there are advantages to this information sharing:

> I guess one of the nice things about the Internet is that it does allow us to do this kind of very thing that Facebook is like capitalizing on and making a lot of money on, obviously, and some stuff. But this model they've created really just uses the Internet in the ways that the Internet can be used, um, so is it *that* bad?

Later in the interview, however, Jack compared Facebook to the large agribusinesses that own seed patents he had recently seen profiled on the film *Food, Inc.*:

> And so in that sense, there's this weirdness about how this company owns my information. And that seems kind of wrong that they can make money by, you know, selling advertisers my name as a potential person that might benefit from their advertising or whatever. So that's funky, that they own me in that way, that they're capitalizing on information that I'm giving

them about myself, and in that way they kind of seem to have, they're like that one gigantic soybean company. But that's not necessarily true, because that doesn't mean that I can't share my information in other places, and other places can't use it in similar ways and be really good at it, so I don't know. As long as like my family and finances aren't in danger, I'm not super sure how I feel about it.

As a whole, Jack had some vague concerns about inward-facing data management issues, but the dangers felt far removed from his daily lived experience. He stated in a later interview, "I don't really care if Facebook knows what kind of music I listen to." While participants like Ronnie, Sandra, and Becca were concerned about what message the music they listed on Facebook said about their identities as music fans, Jack was both unconcerned about this and about what Facebook might do with that information. Rather than defining privacy through the concerns he addressed above, Jack took a pragmatic approach that had more to do with rhetorical issues.

PEDAGOGICAL CONCERNS: MANAGING TECHNOLOGIES AND DATA

All of the participants in this study, as described throughout this chapter, were concerned about the ways the information they post on social media platforms could be used, both by their friends and followers and by the platforms themselves. This finding suggests a need to consider how students' information is collected by online platforms used in the classroom and to assist students in better managing their own data. Since blogging became a practice used by writing instructors (Gurak et al., 2004), students have been sharing their writing in public and semipublic digital spaces. In requiring students to use public spaces for connecting with others and sharing classwork, writing teachers should also be reflective and conscientious about the writing in digital environments they require from students. Alexis noted that when she conducted an online search of her name, the public blog she was required to keep for one of her classes kept coming up. While Alexis was concerned about being represented by her classwork and the many reading responses she wrote that semester, she also didn't want to completely hide the blog or delete it. Similarly, Beth joined Twitter as a requirement for that same class. While she kept her tweets protected, she was resistant to using the service and never sent more than a handful of tweets. Nicole also was required to use a Facebook group for a class, and her increased Facebook use allowed people from other aspects of her life to find her more easily on the platform. When writing teachers ask students to post information for class online, we should discuss this work and its online presence within students' broader digital identities and information-sharing practices. We can think of these implications through both inward-facing data and privacy management of the platforms themselves and outward-facing data management to publicly available internet content.

Inward-Facing Data Management

Scholars such as Chris Gilliard and Hugh Culik (2016) and Amidon et al. (2019) have raised concerns about the ways that a variety of information technologies use student data and information, from Turnitin.com and course-management systems, to blogs, social media platforms, video conferencing tools, and other educational technologies meant to track students and their information. Writing instructors should always consider the ways the particular tools they are using in the classroom will collect and use student data, especially if that use is required in the classroom. As well as carefully selecting the tools used in class, instructors can also make these topics a subject of class conversation. Analyzing privacy and data-use policies and discussing their implications for users' privacy will help students to understand the ways that social media platforms and other internet services use their information. Drawing their digital identity profiles and connecting those profiles to what Estee Beck (2015) called the "invisible digital identity" will also allow students to trace their own information around the web and better understand the implications of privacy policies and data collection. Beck (2015) also provided some guidelines for teaching students about tracking technologies in order to assist them in making informed choices about their data use. In considering data management a digital literacy practice, writing teachers can provide space within their own courses, especially digital and multimodal composition courses, for these conversations. Colleen Reilly (2020) and Jenae Cohn et al. (2020) both present ways of discussing surveillance in writing classes by asking students to analyze their digital data trails and by analyzing Google Docs privacy and surveillance issues. Involving students in these conversations can help them consider how their own data is used.

Outward-Facing Data Management

Blogs, website builders, and social media platforms themselves allow writing instructors to better integrate multimodal composition into their classrooms; they also provide students with tools through which to collaborate and help them to reach authentic and wider audiences for their work. Writing instructors should also consider the ethics of requiring students to use these services in the classroom as well as how visible students' information will be. Asking students to use Twitter in the classroom, for example, might help class communication, build community, or teach students to craft succinct and pithy messages, but it also might open students up to harassment. Their tweets might also become visible for the wrong reasons. Students might be wary of a class requirement of joining social media platforms that they had consciously decided not to join (Vie, 2015). For students who have deleted their Facebook accounts, for example, creating a class-specific Facebook group might bring up a number of concerns and challenges.

Allowing students to keep their information under a pseudonym or a password-protected account on blogs or website-builder platforms will allow students to retain control over their information. Class conversations about how students can turn a class blog into a portfolio after the class by highlighting only one's best work could assist students in building this professional online identity as well. I utilize both blogs and website builders for digital portfolios in my multimodal composition courses because of the digital affordances that they allow students. I give students the option to use pseudonyms on these sites and to create password-protected posts and pages, if they wish, with a common class password in order to keep the students' writing accessible only to the class. I also have a conversation toward the end of the class about how students would like their class projects and information to persist online. I tell students that after the class is over, they can continue using their blogs and portfolios for their future courses or professional use, or they might decide to remove some information or delete the accounts entirely. Presenting the class with different options allows them to consider how they would like to continue to share their work online, and our class conversations remind them that they can make decisions about how their work is presented. While these are not the only options to bring discussions about data management into the classroom, they represent two ways of considering students' data-management and privacy in social media and other online contexts.

CONCLUSION

Social media users not only need to understand how to craft information to reach the right audience but also need to know the mechanisms through which they are generating other kinds of data. Managing one's information during the first decade of social media use required that social media users learn how to navigate social media assemblages, understand privacy policies, adjust privacy settings frequently when platforms changed strategies, and make decisions about what to make public, what to keep private, and what to keep offline entirely. Identity management, information management, and audience management all flowed through social media platforms and the assemblages in which these individuals found themselves.

Each of the people I studied learned to navigate these assemblages and to manage their data on social media platforms in ways that worked for them. Julie Cohen (2012) argued for the importance of "the play of everyday practice" in individuals' representations of self within networked technologies, emphasizing the places where the design and structure leave gaps and allow users' agency in their own representation and control of information. While many accounts and criticisms of social media platforms emphasize data surveillance and lack of privacy, individuals like Ronnie and Beth managed to find ways to push back against the designs and constraints of the programs themselves to assert their own agency. While users' perspectives and options were often limited, they also often pushed back on these constraints, questioning policies, insisting on more control, and subverting the sites' intended uses. These writers, while influenced by the design of these web platforms, had agency in these interactions and responded to changes in site structure and policy in thoughtful and reflective ways that demonstrate the importance of viewing these concerns as part of individuals' literacy practices.

5

MANAGING IDENTITY IN
PROFESSIONAL SPACES

Alice Marwick's (2013) ethnography of Silicon Valley companies in the early days of social media spent a good deal of time describing bloggers and other online entrepreneurs that Marwick called "microcelebrities." These individuals shared a large amount of information, sometimes staged and performative, on social media platforms for self-promotional purposes, attention that some were able to leverage into personal brands and careers. By the end of the first decade of social media, Instagram "influencers" and celebrities promoted products and shared their lives with their digital audiences for a living. While none of the individuals I studied through this project turned social media into a career in that fashion, their use of digital platforms also became integrated into their professional lives. While the writers I discuss in these pages met challenges in reaching audiences, social media platforms also gave them opportunities to reach more professional communities and to make connections.

Though not true of all social media platforms used by my research participants and discussed in this study, the majority of social network sites popular during the first decade of social media emphasized individual identity representation. From the first social network sites, like Friendster and Myspace, to the mid-decade arrival of Instagram, much of the activity surrounding these platforms emphasized identity representation through profile construction, image sharing, and activities that presented oneself through likes and dislikes as well as friend connections. As boyd and Ellison (2007) argued, these spaces through which to interact online "are primarily organized around people, not interests" (para. 37). Social media platforms "are structured as personal (or 'egocentric') networks, with the individual at the center of their own community" (boyd and Ellison, 2007, para. 37). Ellison and boyd's (2013) update of their social networking site definition emphasized that while those identities were still central to these sites, they were co-constructed with other users through interactions, testimonials, and

https://doi.org/10.7330/9781646424023.c005

engagement with others. As individuals made composing decisions through these sites, they also decided how to express themselves for specific online audiences.

The individuals whose social media literacy practices I describe in this book had the most challenges and questions when it came to navigating questions of identity representation in professional spaces. All of my research participants faced moments of professional transition throughout the course of this study. The undergraduate students were approaching graduation during my initial data collection phase in 2010 and 2011, and the graduate students all navigated dual identities as students and teachers while also becoming full members of the academy. The additional participants I interviewed from 2013 were all journalism students, quickly approaching their own graduations and potential careers in media. The individuals I interviewed in 2016 were also learning to navigate professional spaces. This chapter explores the third challenge individuals faced in using social media platforms and the literacy practices they developed to manage it: representing their identities for professional audiences. Representing oneself and one's work for professional audiences on social media platforms requires a management of both audiences and data. The literacy practices I describe in this chapter, then, are extensions of those discussed in chapters 3 and 4.

PROFESSIONAL IDENTITIES AND ONLINE SPACES

An inevitable result of studying undergraduate and graduate students in this project meant that I was studying individuals at moments of transition and enculturation. In a transitional space between school and the workplace, upper-level courses in students' majors not only allow them to practice more advanced disciplinary work but also provide them with the opportunity to develop professional identities in these fields. The graduate students I spoke with for this project were also entering professional spaces through their coursework, teaching, and professional development, and some of that work took place on social media platforms as well.

This chapter considers identity construction in those moments of adjustment and change in entering new communities. Lemke (2008) demonstrated a need to understand identity in how it functions as a mediating term between social-structural phenomena and lived, interactional experiences (p. 17). There is a tension between scholarship that discusses identity that is tied to gender, race, and class categories and a professional identity that is situated within a specific workplace or professional community of practice. Lemke highlighted this distinction between "identity-in-practice on the short timescales of situated small-group activity" (p. 18) and concepts of identity that exist over a lifetime and are framed according to "larger institutional scales" (p. 18). Lave and Wenger (1991), Casanave (2002), and Prior (1998) discussed how students and writers become enculturated into professional fields through education and academic writing. Through the construction of self via discourse, writers create new identities as they enter new communities of practice. Moving into and through academic spaces, though, often does not translate to the fields and communities that students will enter after college. In their study of engineering programs, Eliot and Turns (2011), for example, have found that these programs often focus more on professional activities and networking and less on what it means to enter that community of practice, to work, and to think as an engineer. As Lave and Wenger (1991) argued, gaining entry to these communities is often about identities, which is the element that Eliot and Turns (2011) found missing in their study of engineers. Lave and Wenger note the importance of education in assisting students with shaping their identities in ways that allow them to become members of these academic, and later professional, communities of practice. Entering professional spaces and cultivating these professional identities can be a challenge, particularly for students without models to follow and points of entry to professional spaces more tied to communities of practice based in work than tied to academic spaces.

It is important to keep in mind the race, class, and gender dynamics of professional identity construction as well. As André Brock (2020) argued, identity representation is always political, and Christina Cedillo (2020) called attention to the ways that social media platforms present concerns for multiply marginalized people in professional settings. Using the examples of three academics on Twitter, Cedillo argued that social media platforms are mechanisms of social control through which "members of vulnerable groups are rendered hypervisible by social media logics that depend on systemic biases epistemologically" (p. 145). Building professional identities, then, presents additional concerns for multiply marginalized people who can be both more visible in social media spaces and more easily reduced to one aspect of their identity, such as their race, as Brock (2020) has also argued. In addition, definitions of the word "professional" are also based in concerns of race and class that privilege white and middle-class logics.

The primary ways that universities have assisted students in entering these communities are the traditional ones Eliot and Turns (2011) mention: alumni connections and networking programs. Yet students at many universities do not have access to these kinds of alumni and industry connections for professionalization, leaving students at less connected institutions at a disadvantage. These networking activities at all institutions are also more concerned with the immediate goal of employment opportunities, ignoring the importance of assisting students in developing professional identities to join and contribute to professional communities of practice.

Patricia Boyd (2013) discussed professional identities by drawing on Herminia Ibarra and Jennifer L. Petriglieri's (2010) definition as centered in "the various meanings attached to oneself by self and others" in professional spaces, combining a social identity (centered in social roles and groups) with a personal one. She also pointed to the importance of business writing courses not only in practicing professional discourses but also in creating professional identities, which she did through online discussion boards and assignments that asked students to compare discourse in academic and professional communities. Social media presents both opportunities and challenges to students in representing their work in new ways and gaining entry to professional communities of practice. Through Twitter, LinkedIn, and other online networking spaces, students can learn about, gain entry to, and begin to join professional conversations in their fields. These sites open these professional communities of practice in new ways with lower barriers to entry. Many of the participants in this study first considered approaching professional communities through defensive identity-management strategies like removing content and untagging photos, yet there are more proactive approaches to professional identity representation as well. I discuss both in this chapter.

OBSERVING AND ENTERING PROFESSIONAL DIGITAL COMMUNITIES

Social media platforms provided some of the writers I profile here with the opportunity to find, observe, and gradually join professional communities in digital spaces. Ronnie joined Academia.edu, for example, while he was working as a math research assistant during the summer. Although he was considering graduate school, he was only beginning to think of a more developed academic identity for himself. Setting up an account on Academia.edu was a way for him to begin to participate in that space in the hopes that this professional identity continued to grow. Setting up this profile allowed Ronnie to connect with and observe other academics and to consider the information they found most important. It was one of the ways that Ronnie gained access to particular communities and more specialized community spaces.

Sandra took a broader view of joining professional spaces through the more general social media platform LinkedIn. She joined LinkedIn and began using it to network with professionals in her field as she was job searching. Constructing an identity as a professional in order to secure employment that will lead to a career is something students approaching graduation have always done, but during the first decade of social media they began doing it in online spaces as well. Sandra was uncomfortable with this process of creating a profile for this more professional audience. She called LinkedIn "the death of every college student" and expressed his discomfort and unfamiliarity with this particular community:

> I hate that stupid site because it's so serious. There's no component of fun, at all, and you know that you're not going to stay in college forever when you actually have to update your resume and say actively looking for a job. It's just, like, terribly depressing.

Sandra described the site as a "business portfolio" where she listed key information from her resume and connected to former coworkers and other professional connections. She limited her personal contacts on the site to people she knew in real life, but because users' information is public, she used the site to network during her job-search process. She noted that before she had an interview with a particular company, she looked up those interviewing her on LinkedIn, which helped her present herself, her skills, and her past professional experiences in a particular way. While this was an aspect of identity representation that Sandra was uncomfortable with, using this site specifically for a professional audience helped her land a permanent position after graduation. For the undergraduate students, then, social media platforms could be a place to think through positioning oneself for professional audiences, even including networking with potential professional audiences.

Many of the undergraduate students I interviewed in 2013 had accounts on LinkedIn as well but did not find it particularly useful. Many of them were potential journalists going into the media industry, and they found Twitter to be much more helpful and relevant. Stephanie, for example, noted that she created an account on LinkedIn when she was looking for internships but had since lost her password. She had only connected with one former high school classmate and her high school principal through the site. Jordan did not have a LinkedIn account. Angela, a psychology major, had an account but did not use it frequently. She had originally signed up for the site using a shortened version of her last name, as she had on other social network sites, but she was unable to change her name later. She also noted frustration with the site's interface because it asked her for her industry every time she logged in. She said in an interview: "Every time I try and change it it's like 'What industry do you work for?' I'm just, I don't work for an industry." Many undergraduate students, then, felt like they should be on LinkedIn for job and networking purposes, but both the site's design and their lack of connections on it made it difficult for them to use.

Nicole, on the other hand, used LinkedIn more than she used Facebook or even Twitter. She noted sharing items connected to her academic discipline and education. While she connected to professionals in her field on Twitter and shared related content there occasionally, Nicole posted more of it on LinkedIn. She also shared content related to HBCUs and related news on LinkedIn. She described the difference in the ways she used the two platforms this way:

> But LinkedIn, I do share articles and things, so I would say my audience for LinkedIn would be people like me, so teachers in the field, English, teachers of like disadvantaged populations, cause I came from like an impoverished neighborhood, so teachers who work with those type of students, just anybody that's, I think it would be a more older audience, so it's more a professional audience, so when I tag things it's articles like "How Can We Help African American Males Succeed?" Or like, articles like that, so, I'm not really like, Twitter is like I'm giving advice and help to students, but my LinkedIn is like how can professionals help students.

While Nicole saw both of these as professional spaces, she saw Twitter as reaching students and LinkedIn as a space to connect with fellow professionals.

Jordan also used Twitter frequently, both in his personal life and to share his journalism, blogging, and other writing. He described his professional identity on Twitter this way:

> It's a less offensive version of my Facebook personality. I've never actually thought about my professional identity because I try to be relaxed and informal. [. . .] I'll say like quasi-philosophical thoughts that I have, or I'll say something funny. It's pretty random. I've never actually thought of consolidating it to be professional and refined, suit and tie kind of thing, you know. More like Levi's and a T-shirt kind of thing. That's my personality on Twitter.

He had one Twitter account he described as his "more professional" account with fewer followers. In our interview, he also reflected on advice he'd been given from one of his professors on creating engaging content on Twitter:

> Yesterday I got advice from Professor [name removed]. I was going through my grandfather's old things cause my mama told me, "You get the first pick of the litter. Go down there and see if anything you like, rummage through his things, see if you like anything, and then you can have it." So I live tweeted that. But I was talking about his shoes or whatever and how his swag is really high and mine is really low, and I was kind of impressed with my grandfather. And [professor's name] said that I should have posted pictures. I should have live tweeted pictures along with it.

Jordan tweeted in both personal and professional capacities, but because Twitter was becoming an important platform for journalists, his professor even gave him advice on ways to create engaging content.

As discussed in the previous chapters, Jack also used Twitter in professional spaces and found it particularly effective for assisting him in building his identity as an academic and in entering a professional community of scholars. In 2010, Jack was required to tweet for a graduate course, and he used that opportunity to revive his academic Twitter account, which he is still using along with his personal account. At times, he tweeted material from both accounts simultaneously, but at other times, these two accounts had distinct topics and distinct audiences. Jack described this decision as one he made as his research interests developed; both the academic tweets and the music tweets were becoming more specialized. Given the success he had in networking with musicians and writers through his primary Twitter account, he saw the potential for a Twitter account focused specifically on academic issues to work the same way.

Jack often commented on the culture of academia in this account, as well as his ideas of himself as an academic:

> Oh, so I guess I sense the power of Twitter in that way, and so I want to represent myself to this other group of people when I'm becoming more comfortable talking about academic things there, and I suppose as I get more and more comfortable in that community, that I'll want to interact with those people more often as I get to know them, and meet them maybe at conferences, or read their work or whatever. I see the Twitter network as a way of staying connected and interested and having people know who I am and that kind of thing. All this stuff is kind of important when I get a job.

As these interests developed, he saw the increased tweets about music and musicians as separate from and distracting to a more academic tweeting audience. In an interview, Jack described his continued anxieties about identity representation on Twitter in this way:

It's kind of like this split identity thing. Like, I, if it was me, and I was like an academic, I would be annoyed by my music tweets because I do it pretty much all day long. I guess I'm concerned about self-presentation as an academic, like I want to be considered as a scholar in this community, not as like a music blogger, and so, that Twitter account is more about trying to like, have a digital presence, so at least people will know who I am when I go to these conferences.

When Jack revived his academic Twitter account, then, he saw it as a way to mark his identity as an upcoming researcher in the field and to let others know who he was, in terms of his academic research interests rather than his music tweets.

Jack noted that when he had used an academic Twitter account before, he hadn't followed anyone on that account, and therefore had difficulty gaining followers. When he restarted this academic Twitter account, Jack unfollowed many of the scholars he had connected with through his primary Twitter account and followed them on his academic account instead; he ended up following about 100 people. When we discussed this change in an interview shortly after he made the switch, he considered the change to be successful, as several scholars he had connected with on his primary Twitter account had already switched to sending links and communicating with him primarily through his academic account. The tweets he sent from this academic account was a range of reflections on academia and academic culture:

> Learning how to be a scholar is like seeing a sticker and thinking, "Andre the Giant? I didn't realize he had a posse!" [link to blog] 1:33 PM Sep 15th via TweetDeck

> Been thinking about the observation of new grad student that everybody talks about how busy they are. Academics have a culture of busyness. 9:07 PM Oct 6th via TweetDeck

> It's true, but why? Is our projected busyness evidence of our "seriousness" or devotion to our work? Or a trick to guard against more work? 9:18 PM Oct 6th via TweetDeck

> If you have an answer, I'll have to read it tomorrow. I'm busy grading right now. 9:19 PM Oct 6th via TweetDeck

Along with these tweets, Jack also often discussed scholarship through his academic Twitter account, sometimes tweeting questions for his own research, and sometimes tweeting quotations from his reading:

> To what extent is sound textual? For example, can we submit musical discourse to the same kinds of critical analysis we give other text? 1:34 PM Sep 16th via TweetDeck

"Composition is not writing anymore; it's composition" K.B. Yancey (qtd. in Halbritter's "Musical Rhetoric in integrated-media composition") 2:45 PM Nov 11th via TweetDeck

Jack also frequently retweeted from his academic account, passing along links he came across or from groups he was affiliated with, including tweets from groups like the Humanities, Arts, Science and Technology Alliance and Collaboratory (HASTAC) and news sites like NPR. Jack saw this academic Twitter account as a way to discuss his developing research interests, to connect them to material he found online, and most importantly, to network with like-minded scholars. Given that he had connected with different academics through his primary account before revitalizing this second account, Jack sometimes had difficulty parsing out what activity should appear on which account, and who he should connect with on each account:

> Let's say I went to a conference and met one of these people that I follow on my [academic] account. And we find, oh yeah, we're actually like, friends, and at that point, when the connection becomes something more than just something that's useful academically or for that kind of networking, then that person might graduate into the other feed, into the other place. Because then I know that if they're following me in that other site then they care about the stuff that I'm listening to, with the stuff with my kids that I might tweet about, and whatever. It's like, it's a more personal space. . . . But maybe it's just a weird, like schizophrenic thing. It's really, as you can tell, I'm really weird because it feels like, it feels a little crazy, right, to separate yourself in that way. And I'm not somebody who like uses the web to do this kind of identity play like that really.

Parsing out this inevitable overlap was something that Jack constantly struggled with in representing his identity with the different audiences he engaged with on Twitter. One means by which to manage issues of context collapse is to use different accounts for different audience groups. Jack saw a number of advantages to approaching his social media use, especially on Twitter, in that way. This practice presented problems, however, because boundaries between audience groups are always porous. Jack considered some of his Twitter contacts friends who also happened to be academics; these individuals could follow both of his Twitter accounts, and some of them did. But Jack described challenges in trying to determine how to reach these individuals and through which account to do so.

A later discussion of Jack's use of the academic Twitter account was a bit more tempered. He noted that he tweeted from the academic account "every once in a while." If he was tweeting something that was related to the academic process, as he described it, "something that is both kind of academic-y, or is related to academic process," then he often tweeted the information from both his personal and his academic Twitter account, unless it was overly technical: "If it's like technical kinds of things, like stuff that people in my quote 'real world' wouldn't care to know about then I'll just keep it out," he stated in an interview. He further explained:

> Like yesterday, I was tweeting about something, like, deep thought I was having about academia, and it like applied across the board so I just did it from both. So I wonder if that's obnoxious for people who follow both of my accounts, for them to show up right next to each other at the same exact time. I don't know.

Jack, therefore, made frequent decisions about audience, and where the information he wanted to post on Twitter crossed audience groups; he occasionally sent those tweets from both accounts. While his decision to do so was ultimately based on the audience he felt he was reaching through each account, he often questioned whether or not the dual accounts and audiences was the right decision when there was some overlap.

Jack had about 70 followers on his academic account in the fall of 2010, but only connected with or talked to those contacts he had already made on his personal account. Even if he didn't often talk directly to other academics via this account, he still found the connection valuable, and it was also a networking opportunity he planned to continue:

> Anyway. I think that over the next year, as I make an effort to be more active in things like conference communities, and I start thinking about publishing, I start making connections between the names on my Twitter list and stuff that they're writing and that kind of thing, maybe I'll have a better sense and be less paranoid about this kind of thing, and maybe if I have, by the time I have something out maybe, like, I eventually will publish something, then I'll feel more justified in interacting with people. I just kind of feel like the new kid, you know? That's not a very good metaphor. I don't know all the dance moves yet. Nobody is circling around me while I do all kinds of hiphop moves. "Go [Jack], go [Jack]!"

Jack created his academic Twitter account to share information and connect with other academics in his area, but he didn't feel entirely part of that community yet. While Twitter was a space for him to connect, he measured his own role in the community through more traditional academic genres: conference presentations and journal articles. He still saw traditional gatekeepers in the field as marking his inclusion (or not) within the discipline, and he was still learning "the dance moves," as he described it.

The connections Jack made with scholars on Twitter were different than those he made with people he knew in the music community, and those were connections that Jack saw as having an important, but perhaps less tangible, payoff. Jack was, however, very excited to receive a reply from someone he referred to as a star academic and a frequent tweeter:

> He replied to me once. And I was kind of like, this guy isn't responding to me, this is crazy. And it was also something really stupid too, like I was joking that my hair was getting long enough that I could comb it and look like Justin Bieber, and he said something, congratulations, or something like that. But it felt cool to be noticed, you know, by this person.

Even though the conversation was about something unrelated to academia, Jack was excited that this academic noticed him and commented, as he felt it gave him some sort of notoriety. For a graduate student like Jack beginning to enter the field, this kind of connection was important for him in order to build connections, even casual ones.

Jack later described the ways that his social media use has also opened up opportunities for him. He stated, "There are several moments in my social media history where having a Twitter account and being involved in a certain community has really done a lot to help me do stuff." Building connections with colleagues on Twitter gave Jack built-in acquaintances when he started to attend conferences; he described how Twitter helped him network for a job, and he also found out about an acceptance for a journal article publication through Twitter before receiving the official notification via email. He became involved with Twitter early in his graduate program, around the same time that other academics were joining Twitter. Joining Twitter then put Jack on an equal playing field with other academics, including junior and senior faculty, who were joining the platform at the same time. While Jack still placed value in traditional institutions and gatekeepers (like conferences and journals), Twitter allowed Jack to reach these gatekeepers and stakeholders more easily. Jack's Twitter use developed with Twitter itself, and it allowed him to create productive connections that have continued to help him through his career.

Jack also compared his approach to a few other graduate students, up-and-coming scholars, and others whose use of Twitter involved making bolder claims or pronouncements that sometimes started heated arguments and what Jack referred to as "flame wars." Jack compared that approach to his gradual joining of an academic community on Twitter by first listening to conversations, working through issues of different audiences, and balancing audiences on different Twitter accounts before finally joining the conversation himself. Jack found this approach to be particularly effective for helping him build his professional networks.

Esther only connected to a few academics on Twitter and saw it primarily as a tool to enhance her conference experience rather than a place where she could join academic conversations on a regular basis. While she sometimes used conference hashtags to join online conversations at an academic conference, she did not use social media much to connect with others in her field. Becca, however, joined Academia.edu before her academic job search, primarily to enhance her professional online presence and to connect with other scholars doing similar work in her field. While Becca found little interaction happening on that social network site, through the duration of her time on the job market she received notifications from Academia.edu when someone searched for her name on Google and clicked on her Academia profile. Becca did not develop a website for her job search; she noted that web authoring was not one of her professional strengths, but she found Academia.edu to be a forum for which she could easily share some information about herself and her work as a scholar.

CENSORING INFORMATION

The defensive strategies that participants used in reaching professional communities paradoxically meant actively hiding their content from those communities. After his initial introduction to Academia.edu, Ronnie primarily kept personal information off of the site. While Ronnie represented himself as a musician and listed his performance portfolio on his website (see chapters 3 and 4), he was less concerned about making connections professionally online or about the potential of professional contacts or potential employers discovering his online information. In 2016, Ronnie noted that he had a LinkedIn profile at one time, but he deleted it. He didn't want to be contacted by recruiters, and he was also concerned about having his entire work history publicly on the internet. He stated in an interview, "I didn't feel comfortable with that at all." Ronnie noted that while he sometimes did social media promotion material in his previous job, he was the research participant who used social media the least in a professional capacity and preferred to keep his professional life separate. This was perhaps surprising given how much time he spent on social media as a college student, but the connections that he cultivated through social media connected less to his professional goals.

Alexis was often concerned about audience and ways that personal and professional audiences blended on social media, and she often received advice from friends about managing her information for professional audiences. In 2011, Alexis was frequently concerned about who could see her information and what effect that would have. Much of this concern was prompted by a friend who worked in media and gave her advice about closing access to her accounts while she was looking for a job. Alexis always kept her Twitter account private and always restricted content on Facebook to friends only. Alexis stated:

> I value my privacy, like, I don't want people knowing what I'm doing because Facebook and Twitter is just a constant like status update. I don't want a third party, someone that I do not know, to know what I'm doing or where I am constantly.

She wanted to share this information with her friends, but she didn't want individuals outside this group to have access to it.

During her job search in 2011 as she was planning to graduate from college, Alexis used her Facebook settings to restrict access even further, hiding her pictures, closing her Facebook wall to friends' posts, and finally, hiding her wall altogether. Much of this was about control; she could not control what her friends were posting on her wall, and therefore sought to minimize any potential problems that could come about. By closing her wall entirely, which hid all of her own updates as well, Alexis took it a step further and ensured that even her own language couldn't be misinterpreted. Alexis's strong restrictions on her Facebook account was probably an overreaction. Given her privacy settings, no potential employer would be able to see more than her profile picture unless she approved a friend request. Alexis's management of her privacy settings gave her peace of mind and control about her information, although it had no effect on potential employers' ability to see her content and did shut her off from her friends. She used the tools available on Facebook to manage her privacy, but she used them with an abundance of caution that went beyond what the public or potential employers may have been able to see of her information. She noted:

> Nowadays I feel like while Facebook still is kind of like that [. . .] it's so convoluted with professional networks too cause as you're in the, as you're in the industry your colleagues, your former colleagues, or even your boss are gonna add you sometimes. I don't think that, it's not always ideal, and so I do feel like there is limitations as to what I can say and share on Facebook compared to what I did before, and so I think I have really kind of phased out of Facebook because it has been too, it's almost like a LinkedIn, although I still have my friends and families on there.

In 2010 and 2011, Alexis was concerned about managing different friends, family, and church connections on social media, but in 2016, some of those audience concerns with context collapse expanded in a different way to be focused primarily on her coworkers and even supervisors. These audience groups put further restrictions on what Alexis felt she could say or share in a way that made Facebook, as she described, "almost like a LinkedIn."

Alexis used a metaphor of two different social events to explain the ways she considered Facebook and Twitter to be different platforms for different audiences:

> I just feel like even Facebook [. . .] if we used to compare Facebook as the family dinner, and then Twitter as kind of a cocktail party because you're chatting with people you don't know, you're creating a professional network, you're following you know these art . . . music bloggers, um, reporters and they follow you back and you're having these conversations with people on the topics that you're caching [i.e., following and saving content] about whereas Facebook you're sharing everything in your life: "Oh this is what I had for dinner, Oh I'm in Chicago," and just you know your friends, those kinds of contexts.

Alexis noted that while she had coworkers who used Twitter professionally and worked to cultivate a large following primarily of professionals, like the cocktail party she described, she was "not very active" on Twitter. She noted that she primarily consumed content on the service instead, saving and retweeting links for her to read or reference later, rather than actively engaging with other professionals. She stated, "Twitter sometimes for my own sake. For example, if I see something, a graphic I find really interesting, I use Twitter more as a note taking device." If Twitter represented more of a professional audience to Alexis, it was one that she did not engage in as much, preferring LinkedIn for a professional representation of herself and her work, and Facebook as a space for more personal content for friends and family.

Becca also restricted access to her Facebook profile during her search for an academic faculty job, noting that she tried to influence and direct the first impression search committees might have of her when looking for her online:

> I did make my Facebook profile unfindable to people [who] weren't friends of friends because I didn't want people just randomly looking me up and making judgments about me based on the first thing they saw there, when they hadn't even talked to me, because like I said, for me it's more of a friend space, so I didn't want people who I didn't know at all but were in a space to judge me to be here [on Facebook].

While Becca maintained her philosophy of representing her whole person rather than separating her personal and professional identities, she acknowledged that controlling this first impression was an important part of her online representation and crucial for representing herself as a professional: a teacher, scholar, and writing researcher:

> I don't feel like they're separate. I feel like I don't have that strong of a web presence for my professional identity yet, and I feel like the presence I have that does in a way blend some of those things isn't something that I want to be just open to just anybody who stumbles on it, and it really took being on the job market and realizing that people were Googling me and stuff that made me be like, you know, I probably don't want just any random person to stumble into my profile [. .] I don't hide personal stuff from people that I actually interact with professionally, but [. . .] I didn't want someone searching the web for me and being their first, their first introduction to me to be a picture of me bellydancing when they're looking for a writing teacher. You know, it just seems incongruous in ways that are not incongruous to me but maybe to other people.

The academic job market was a point of friction for both Becca and Esther, in that they had to consider another set of external audiences online and even in social media spaces. The rules for using social media while on the academic job market were not—and as of this writing are still not—fixed. Both Becca and Esther received competing advice from different professors and mentors about what and how much to share online. Esther was more concerned about sharing information about the location of campus visits and other potentially sensitive information with her graduate student colleagues and her family, but Becca spent more time considering how to represent herself professionally to the different audiences that might happen upon her social media profiles. Most of these concerns, as well as our conversation about these concerns, centered on her Facebook page and her profile picture. Since she was connected to many of her professors and even other academics in the field on Facebook, considering how she represented herself in this space was important. The "Friends of Friends" privacy setting on Facebook, for example, could include quite a large number of people. As Becca described above, she approached her online representations while she was on the job market not as a process of cleaning up her social media accounts but more in terms of the type of first impression she wanted to cultivate.

TEACHING OTHERS

Esther frequently discussed using her own social media experiences to teach her students. She shared some scholarship about the academic area of fat studies via Facebook and Twitter with a student who was working on a project in that area. She also noted that she and the student got some attention from an unwanted audience when she live tweeted the presentation at her college's undergraduate research presentation day:

> [Esther's student] wrote a thesis project on fat studies, and some of the feminist sites started bringing up a lot of kind of fat studies—for public consumption, articles—and I started posting them to my Facebook for a little bit and linking her, so they could see them because we were working on the thesis together, or she was writing the thesis, but I was mentoring her. And so I wanted her to see those articles and actually, when she presented at the Liberal Arts Symposium last year, some people posted like troll-y posts to her Twitter when I . . . live tweeted her presentation.

Esther noted that her student was rather adept at pushing back against this online harassment and holding her own in the Twitter conversation about her project. But this example demonstrates how easy it is for a conversation on social media to move beyond one's intended audience into other areas, and women and topics concerning women's embodiment are frequently topics for this kind of harassment.

Esther also found her use of social media with her students important for their understanding of digital media. She noted:

> I really loved the tweeting that happens at conferences and the students don't really realize that world at all. I mean they really don't, and the faculty don't understand it either. So there are a lot of faculty that are, like, technology is ruining everything and our students are, they don't read anymore, and then you know, there's just a lot of lamenting about technology and how bad it is. So I just, I try to help my students understand that technology is a tool and it's not bad or good. It's just what you make it.

In this way, Esther used her own social media use and her live-tweeting practices to teach students not only how to live tweet a more academic event, but also how to use the platforms effectively and deal with problems when they arise.

Finally, Esther's students were also an impetus for her to join LinkedIn, which she used not so much to connect with other professionals in her area but as a means through which to keep in touch with students, as well as her university. She noted a recent experience when a former student announced a promotion at her job, and Esther sent her a message to congratulate her. Esther, then, continued to use a variety of digital tools to connect with students during their time at her college and after they graduated. She also worked to move them into professional communities, partially through social media.

TEACHING INTERVENTIONS

Both Jordan's and Esther's example demonstrates that there are roles for writing instructors to play in assisting students with building professional identities. During the initial data-collection phase for this research, several of the individuals I worked with were searching for full-time jobs. Both Becca and Esther were participating in the academic job market for tenure-track positions, and Alexis and Sandra were both looking for entry-level positions in their fields of media and fashion retail, respectively. Concerns of online identity representation took on a greater sense of importance during this process, and each individual changed her privacy settings in order to better control how her information spread online and how much prospective employers could learn about her through an initial Google search. While Becca was initially unconcerned about blending personal and professional identities on Facebook, during her job-search process she determined that she did not want her belly dancing pictures to be the first material a potential employer saw about her in an online search. She then tightened her privacy settings and revised some of the information on her Facebook page in order to better control her online persona. Sandra also revised her privacy settings on Facebook during her job search, when she realized just how many people she shared with under her previous "Friends of Friends" privacy setting.

Becca and Sandra also joined other social network sites in order to represent professional personas online. Becca created a profile on Academia.edu; while she constructed the profile first just to "give somebody something gratifying if they Googled" her, Becca found the account to be important when the head of a search committee for a position she had applied for began following her on the site. LinkedIn was helpful for Sandra not only because she could easily create a professional presence and network with others, but also because she could look up information about the individuals at a specific company who were interviewing her. Neither of these women spent much time on these sites, but they both found the ability to create a basic profile that could serve as a professional online presence for prospective employers who were searching for them online.

Esther and Alexis approached their online presence during the job search differently, without building much of an online professional identity. Alexis relied on the advice from others in her social network on how she was displaying her information to others. But most of the advice Alexis received was negative: *Don't show your photos, don't let people write on your wall.* Alexis managed her online identity during her job search primarily by shutting it down. Esther said that she kept meaning to create a website for her teaching portfolio and other materials, but she never found time to do it. While Esther used social network sites less frequently during her job search because of time constraints, she did not change much else about her digital persona except for removing her family member's post about her travel for campus visits. Sandra and Becca's experiences suggest that cultivating a digital professional persona through the use of a professional social network or through a personal website would have served them both well.

Perhaps as a way to avoid situations in which students are judged for social media content they upload, many are given advice to tighten privacy settings and remove photos when they begin to look for jobs as they leave school. Social media use while actively applying for jobs is often seen through a negative lens: do not post publicly, do not share photos, and be careful about what information is available online. danah boyd (2014) has argued that this type of paternalism does not give young people the opportunity to engage in thoughtful online interactions. Similarly, this advice may help students consider the wider audiences of their content, but it does not allow students to use digital technologies proactively, to connect with professionals in their fields, or to share their professional work with a wider audience.

Yet using online communities creates other types of inequity. Goode (2010) emphasized the importance of a "technology identity" in how individuals have access to computers and the ways that they incorporate information technologies within their daily lives, noting how these inequalities perpetuate throughout students' educational careers. For everything from registering for classes to using library resources and specialized software in their major's classes, Goode noted how these technological skills are often assumed within universities, and students without skills in these areas quickly fall behind. These inequalities, I argue, continue to follow students after they leave the university. Presenting a professional digital identity through social network sites and personal websites has become an increasingly important aspect of the professional job search. But for students without access to professional discourses and fewer experiences with technology, the emphasis of a digital professional identity creates new disadvantages.

TEACHING PROFESSIONAL IDENTITY

While in many cases my research participants were skilled at reading rhetorical situations online and responding accordingly, they also had a good deal of fear and anxiety about those representations, particularly when it came to a professional identity. Alexis, for example, removed information about herself, but she did not create a profile that may have helped her create more of a digital professional presence. Her experience suggests a place for educators to encourage students to consider a digital, professional persona: an online portfolio that could highlight a student's best work at the university and help them to construct an identity as a professional, or a profile on a social network site that would help a particular student join a professional community. This emphasis is not only relevant in terms of the goal of securing employment but also encourages students to be public writers and intellectuals who are able to use their rhetorical skills in digital environments to highlight their best professional talents.

Students should be encouraged to consider their online professional identities in a more productive way rather than through a deficit model. Rather than asking students to hide information or take it down, there is an opportunity especially for writing teachers to assist students in considering their online presence in a productive way in order for students to showcase their work and their skills and even to network with potential professional connections.

Digital Portfolios

In several of my classes, after conducting the initial phase of this research project, I have asked students to build digital portfolios to showcase not only the work they completed in my course that semester but also the work they have done throughout their classes at the university in order to highlight their professional skills, build digital professional identities, and to construct a place online that would assist them in developing a digital online presence. I have assigned this project for multimedia composition courses, digital journalism courses, and classes for preservice teachers. While the focus was different, based on the aims and goals of the distinct student groups, the portfolio allows us as a class to have conversations about professionalism, digital data management, and digital and professional identity representation in various online spaces.

Within each course, I positioned the discipline students were entering as a community of practice within which students would interact and develop professional identities. This course happened after students had taken several previous journalism courses and were familiar with the genres. Teaching online genres and digital journalism allowed students to consider not only the affordances of the digital media for their own stories but also the possibilities for networking, promotion, and participation with other journalists online. For other courses, I encouraged students to examine the professional websites of people in their chosen fields: teachers, communication specialists, speech pathologists, and others, in order to analyze and examine conventions for professional websites and to understand how professionals represented and positioned their digital presence.

Digital portfolios are, of course, not new, and in many ways, the portfolio I asked them to create is incredibly conventional. But I wanted students to feature work they had done in this class, and I also wanted them to go beyond the course and to represent themselves in professional ways in order to build an overall professional persona that they might carry with them as they leave college. I encouraged my students to reflect on the work they had done throughout their college careers and consider how to represent the best of what they've done at the university in a way that highlights their skills. Paired with the other digital composing we accomplished that semester, this project culminated with their own entry into a professional community of practice. Through this project, students not only developed comprehensive portfolios featuring the work from the class but also took the opportunity to feature their past work, for journalism students, and for preservice teachers, their teaching philosophy statements and detailed teaching experiences.

Jordan, Angela, Stephanie, and Francesca all created these digital portfolios, and the interviews I conducted with them after our class also included a discussion of the digital portfolios they created. Each student created a WordPress or Weebly site—one they planned to continue using. Stephanie noted that she hoped to keep working on the professional portfolio she developed for the class and continue to use it to showcase her work. Francesca also planned to keep using her WordPress site as well. Angela noted that she was happy with the site, and it allowed her to showcase the digital projects she was most proud of. But as a psychology major, the portfolio had less usefulness for her moving forward. Jordan created a site more for his personal writing than his journalism. While he noted that he planned to use the site moving forward, it was less connected to a professional community of practice than some of the other students' projects. So, while these portfolios gave some students a means through which to highlight their professional work beyond the classroom, they were more useful to some than others.

I began these teaching activities without any large or ambitious goals in mind. I hoped to have conversations with my students about building a professional digital presence for themselves in a way that was productive rather than reactive. There is a good deal of potential with social media and with other digital composing tools in assisting both graduate and undergraduate students to move conversations about digital identity representation from a defensive rhetorical practice into more of a productive and preemptive conversation. While I have closed each chapter with some general approaches and suggestions for bringing social media and social media scholarship into the classroom, many social media scholars in rhetoric and composition have developed detailed and sound pedagogies for integrating social media into teaching (Buck, 2015; Coad, 2013; Faris, 2017; Mina, 2017; Shepherd, 2015). I only suggest here that writing and rhetoric scholars and teachers can assist students in thinking through productive ways to represent themselves online in digital spaces and in discussing professional identity with students. While the rules for using social media in professional settings are forever changing, writing scholars can also assist students in navigating these changes.

CONCLUSION

Social media self-branding strategies, Alice Marwick (2013) has argued, result in online identities that become "safe for work," without any personal or potentially embarrassing information, becoming bland, corporate versions of individuals. While her argument remains specific to the tech industry, concerns about professional identity and audience have the possibility of creating a similar situation for both graduate and undergraduate students. As individuals use social media for professional networking and for showcasing professional work and interests, there is a danger for students at all levels to simply be creating neoliberal, safe-for-work identities that force them into easily consumable, uncontroversial selves, ones seen as unthreatening to white and middle-class hiring managers and hiring committees. The expectation to participate in these online spaces also contributes to a blurring of boundaries between work and personal selves in a way that contributes to the always available working culture of late capitalism, as Marwick also critiques.

Rather than considering a digital professional identity as a monolithic concept, though, the experiences of these students instead suggest a multiplicity of different ideas of what it means to be a writing researcher and academic. Esther's introduction to Facebook was through her identity as a writing teacher, and she took the most conservative approach in connecting with scholars in her field on social media. Becca ultimately changed her privacy settings and her profile picture as she prepared for the academic job market, but she also expressed a conscious effort not to censor other aspects of her identity in academic circles. Jack continually revised how he represented his identity for the different audiences he connected with on Twitter. Nicole found ways of addressing both professionals and students on LinkedIn and Twitter. The experiences described here suggest viewing the ways that graduate students develop professional identities not as a process narrative of enculturation but instead through dialogic interactions with multiple communities in digital spaces. The approach that seemed most successful for Jack, and to a lesser extent for Becca, was a "personally professional" identity that combined more professionally oriented content with everyday minutiae, for example. Notably, this approach was not the one Nicole took, suggesting that "personally professional" means something different based on race and gender.

Developing a professional identity through social media does not happen just through building a profile but also in the accumulation of specific moments of interaction with different audiences and communities. Esther and Becca chose to manage their professional identities as they approached the academic job market by revising privacy settings and removing information. While these activities may change one's initial identity presentation at the surface level of the profile, the approach does not consider the ways that this data can persist online, through tagged photos, information shared by other social media users, and archives or databases. This digital record, so to speak, becomes even more important for younger students. As students develop a longer history of online activity, stretching back to high school and even before, the persistence of personal information affects one's ability to manage or alter it, thus becoming an even more important consideration in developing professional digital identities.

While this study has taken a practice approach to identity, this identity construction also interacts with individuals' other identity categories, including race, class, gender, ethnicity, and sexual identity. While Jack's more personal updates were well received, and Jack more actively sought out professional communities on social media, both Esther and Becca were ultimately concerned about presenting some aspects of their personal identities to professional audiences. In terms of the undergraduate students, Ronnie moved away from any kind of conversation about his professional identity in digital spaces, while Alexis was always concerned about the border between personal and professional communities and spaces. While I cannot draw larger conclusions here beyond these case studies, upholding a professional image and representing a professional persona in online spaces was both more important and more fraught for the women included in this study. While these case studies cannot offer conclusions about the role of race and gender in professional identity representations, the data presented here also cannot be separated from these identity categories.

This balance between the personal and professional has important implications for student mentoring as they begin to network with professionals—and for graduate students and other scholars—through social media. Developing a professional identity in coordination with social media platforms requires graduate students to navigate multiple audiences as they work to develop their own sense of identity as teachers and scholars. Yet digital spaces are always in flux and the rules for acting within them are contested and constantly changing. Studying digital professional identities require similarly flexible frameworks. Viewing digital professional identity as multiple and enacted through interactions that strike a balance between content that is more professional and content that is more casual can help writing researchers better understand the role of social media as part of students' professional identity representation. This research suggests a personally professional identity as a potentially effective one, though not the only one, available to students at all levels who are developing professional digital identities through social media.

6

BEYOND SOCIAL MEDIA'S FIRST DECADE

In her book *How to Do Nothing: Resisting the Attention Economy* (2019), visual artist Jenny Odell argued for a reorientation away from what she describes as the "always on" nature of social media and its inevitable draw for our attention, arguing for the replacement of #FOMO, the fear of missing out, with #NOMO, the necessity of missing out—or, as she compromises, "#NOSMO, the necessity of sometimes missing out" (p. 22). Odell is hardly the first to call for moves away from social media. While calls to delete and deactivate Facebook began with its first privacy backlash, moves to step away from social media of all kinds, sometimes described as "digital detox" days were common throughout this first decade of social media.

By 2010, the middle of social media's first decade, scholars and cultural critics were also beginning to reflect on the implications of social media on individuals and society. In her book *Alone Together*, Sherry Turkle (2011) expressed concern about the futures of individuals whose relationships are mediated through technologies such as social network sites: "We recreate ourselves as online personae and give ourselves new bodies, homes, jobs, and romances. Yet, suddenly, in the half-light of virtual community, we may feel utterly alone. As we distribute ourselves, we may abandon ourselves" (p. 12). For Turkle, the identities that individuals created online were inauthentic and separate from their offline identities. Similarly, Jaron Lanier (2010) bemoaned the difficulty of fitting identities and friendships into the boxes available in a Facebook profile. Representing oneself by filling out boxes on a profile was reductive, and "that reduction of life" was broadcast to friends to eventually become the truth (p. 80). Representing an identity online is reducing that identity.

In her ethnography of Silicon Valley and the microcelebrities and bloggers that shaped social media over this period, as noted in chapter 5, Alice Marwick (2013) argued that social media disciplined selves into palatable, corporatized identities. Social media platforms restricted

https://doi.org/10.7330/9781646424023.c006

self-expression and connection within a narrow range of behaviors, not only by the site designs themselves, as Lanier argued, but also through their panoptic qualities of social surveillance and limited range of behaviors expected through social media etiquette. The consequences for moving outside of that narrow range of behaviors was potentially quite high, as Jon Ronson argued in his 2015 book *So You've Been Publicly Shamed.*

Christina Cedillo (2020) has argued that these consequences are different and more pronounced for those with marginalized identities. As described in chapter 5, Cedillo noted that dataveillance, the monitoring of populations or specific groups of people through the collection of different data points, has its roots in colonialism. Combined with what she described as "identity-avoidant frameworks," (p. 133), such as colorblind ideologies of racial difference, the effect is one of surveillance of multiply marginalized people while making invisible the surveillance systems through which that surveillance happens. Since the end of the first decade of social media, scholars such as Cedillo, Safiya Noble (2018), and Ruha Benjamin (2019) have demonstrated the ways that digital technologies, including social media platforms, reinforce and exacerbate systems of racial inequality in ways that are sometimes less visible but just as powerful. While Turkle, Lanier, and Odell all expressed a desire to step away from social media platforms, it is never simple to step away, and in many cases, it is impossible to opt out.

Turkle, Lanier, and other critics of social media platforms have often overlooked two things: (a) the ways that other institutions, societal structures, and technologies have always restricted the identities of historically marginalized people in particular, as Brock (2020) and Benjamin (2019) have called attention to, and (b) the role of the users of these social network sites and their agency in using them. Social media platforms do encourage certain behaviors, prescribe certain conceptions of identity through the fields available on profile pages, and reduce a myriad of human connections and relationships under the common word of "friend." The writing that individuals engage in on these sites is also limited to the means of expression available on the site, as discussed in chapter 2; these sites restrict HTML design options allowed on web pages, for example. These platforms are also embedded within established systems of racial inequality, which continue to privilege whiteness in digital spaces that often still assume the default internet user is white and male.

In studying users of social media platforms, the actual situated digital literacy practices they engage in, and the ways that individuals creatively work within these constraints to produce sophisticated rhetorical responses to others, we can better understand the role that these sites play in individuals' lives. As noted in the introduction, social media platforms can be understood as assemblages of technologies, corporate interests, policies, and user practices. This project has examined user practices closely in order to consider the ways that individuals manage these assemblages, navigate technological affordances and social conventions, and assert their own agency over these technologies. As noted in the introduction and discussed in more detail later in this chapter, limitations of on my own research design and focus have left this project with fewer generalizable contributions to make on the role of race—and to a lesser extent, gender—in social media's first decade, yet I felt it was important to open this final chapter with an acknowledgment of the way social media platforms have also reproduced much older systems of inequality.

This book has examined situated digital literacy practices in the first decade of social media's popular use in the United States. Throughout this first decade, individuals who used the internet frequently had to learn to manage audiences, identities, interfaces, technologies, privacy policies, new genres, new terms, and new etiquette about what to share in which spaces. A close study of the interactions of individuals on social media can help us to better understand the important meaning-making activities that take place on social platforms and how individuals navigate the multiple social and technological influences on their writing practices in online environments. This research project, which examined these issues for 15 undergraduate and graduate student writers, makes some observations on the use of social network sites to represent one's identity for different audiences that have important implications for the study of writing in digital environments and for the teaching of writing. This chapter summarizes this case study research and discusses its implications for our understanding of literate practices during the first decade of social media and points to directions for future research in writing studies.

DIGITAL LITERACY PRACTICES IN SOCIAL MEDIA'S FIRST DECADE

In order to successfully communicate and connect with others on social media platforms, individuals developed specific literacy practices for managing what many saw as their challenges: navigating multiple audiences, managing data and adjusting to policy changes, and balancing both personal and professional information on social platforms. Social media platforms make visible the various influences on literacy in digital environments, including social and cultural influences on literate practice through interactions with various communities and their discourse conventions on social network sites. They also include technological influences on literacy through writers' interactions with the social network sites themselves—negotiating site interfaces, managing data through different privacy settings, and navigating various computer software and hardware in connecting to social network sites, from laptops to smart phones and other mobile devices. Studying writing in the 21st century requires a focus on the ways in which social influences on literacy work with technology to shape writers' experiences.

Not only did these writers construct identities by building profiles on a multitude of different social media platforms, from popular sites like Facebook and Twitter to Cyworld, Last.fm, Ravelry, and LinkedIn, they also engaged in a variety of complex literacy practices. Alexis, for example, posted poetry and reflections on her faith to the Notes section of Facebook and longer updates on her life as an American college student on Cyworld. Ronnie shared a near constant stream of his thoughts to his contacts on Twitter, uploading video and audio of musical compositions to Tumblr and Facebook, and navigating a number of different technologies and audience groups in creating profiles for and interacting with others as Alison, the fictional persona he created. Jack cultivated connections with multiple audience groups through different Twitter accounts, and Esther showed off her knitting as well as her writing skills in showcasing projects on Ravelry and in using social network sites to share posts from her blog about these projects.

The acts that individuals engage on social network sites represent important literate activity, and the writers I studied integrate their use of these sites within their daily lives. As noted in the introduction of this text, this generation of students writes more than ever, and most of this writing happens in digital environments like social network sites (Duthely, 2018; Grabill, 2010; Lunsford et al., 2013). While writers create distinct texts in these environments, the writing work they do is best seen through the study of digital writing that Collin Brooke (2009) advocates, focusing not on discrete texts but on "medial interfaces," the ways in which writers constantly interact in digital environments to create texts that "are but special, stabilized instances of an ongoing process conducted at the level of the interface" (p. 25). Through a focus on these situated digital literacy practices, we can see the complex ways the writers I studied navigated these influences to represent themselves on social network sites.

Managing Audience

One of the most challenging aspects of managing social media involves navigating audiences both through the ways that multiple audiences collapse into one friends or followers list but also how that information can travel beyond one's original audience and intention through what Jim Ridolfo and Danielle DeVoss (2009) called rhetorical velocity. Jack's use of Twitter demonstrates this concept in the ways that he continually developed new Twitter accounts for new audience groups. Jack first moved back to one Twitter account based on his observations of how other scholars and writing teachers were using the site; because it was easier to tag his class-related tweets with a specific hashtag, Jack felt no reason to have a separate account that represented more of a teaching persona for his students. Throughout the course of this study, however, Jack observed conversations within two distinct communities: music bloggers and reviewers and academics in rhetoric and composition. As Jack began to represent himself in ways that more clearly fit within these distinct communities, he created two accounts again in order to represent himself more clearly both as a music critic and as a young scholar refining his research for his dissertation. Participating effectively in both communities involved sending updates of interest to each group and interacting with other group members. In order to participate, Jack needed to successfully conceive of a specific audience on this social network site and to know how to best use the means at his disposal (an image, quick bio, and ability to send text, links, and other content) in order to represent himself as a member of that community.

While Jack created two different accounts on the same social network site, other participants used different sites to conceive of and interact with distinct audiences. Alexis, for example, saw Facebook as the place through which she communicated with her church youth group members and therefore represented her identity as a youth group leader on that site. She used different elements of Facebook, including updating her status, sharing images, and posting longer reflections in the notes section in order to represent herself as a reflective Christian and to encourage others she connected with to do the same. On Twitter, however, her purpose was quite different and involved communicating more intimately with a smaller group of friends, posting complaints and travel updates to those interested in her daily activities. Like Jack and the other participants in this project, Alexis was able to analyze the online rhetorical situations in which she participated and to use the affordances of those sites (uploading images and text, using the Notes section of Facebook, and the ability to text to Twitter while on the road) in order to represent herself effectively for each audience. In 2016, Sam chose to place more public and political content on Twitter not only because of their larger audience of followers on the service, but also the way that content would travel.

The individuals I profiled through this study continued to adjust their social media use and their audiences as the social media platforms changed. In 2010 and 2011, the undergraduate students shared less information through Facebook, and these individuals understood that their audience on these platforms was larger and might include their parents and even grandparents. Twitter was for a closer group of friends. Ronnie, Alexis, Sam, and Nicole, however, reported that Facebook was more a place for friends in 2016, while Twitter was for larger public audiences. While both Ronnie and Jack used to share images on TwitPic of fleeting moments with friends or walking around, by 2016 Instagram filled that role for them and some of my 2016 interviewees, while Alexis also moved her travel photos from her Korean friends on Cyworld to a wider audience on Instagram. Managing audiences required analyzing audience on each platform, understanding who one was reaching where, and adjusting the information one shared accordingly. It was also a process that was continually shaped through interaction with that audience. As John Gallagher (2018) has argued, online audiences are not only about production but also distribution, and the experiences of the case study participants I profile here demonstrate the need for continued research on conceptualizing and managing online audiences.

Managing Data

Along with audience, social media users had to understand how their information was being used. This required a knowledge not only of adjusting the visibility of one's data but also of how online activity generated data used by the social media platforms themselves. Each participant had unique ways of managing these social media assemblages and integrating them within these individuals' daily activities, and most writers customized that experience. Ronnie and Jack used a variety of different third-party services that worked with Twitter in order to customize their experiences. Ronnie, Jack, and also Alexis took frequent photos with their mobile phones and uploaded them to social media platforms, integrating multiple technologies and services within their daily literacy practices. While Sandra primarily used Twitter only when located in a specific space and Jordan did the same with his Facebook use, Alexis used a variety of different platforms to connect with others while she traveled and with friends and family in Korea.

The participants also customized their privacy settings in order to better manage others' access to information. While Sandra was originally comfortable sharing all of her information with friends of friends (an option for one's privacy settings on Facebook), she changed these settings as she learned how many people she might be reaching in that way. Beth kept her privacy settings as closed as possible and even disengaged from Facebook altogether over control of her information. Sandra, Becca, and Alexis revised their privacy settings when they were on the job market as well. Although each writer I studied had a good deal of knowledge about the way privacy settings were configured on each site, many of them expressed difficulty in keeping up with the frequent changes to these settings, particularly on Facebook. Rather than spending time poring over their different options on the site and checking them frequently, the participants in my study developed other strategies for managing their information, primarily involving self-censoring information and keeping certain topics off the site. Important digital literacy practices on social media platforms, then, also involved navigating and customizing site interfaces and managing privacy settings.

Building Professional Digital Identities

At different points in this data collection process, each of the individuals who were part of this research study used social media platforms to reach audiences of professionals and managed their data with different professional audiences. Without much guidance from professors, mentors, parents, and career counselors, each individual I interviewed for this study found a way to manage their information and present a professional digital persona to a group of people in order to network and make connections. Throughout this first decade of social media use, the rules for these kinds of interactions were not, and are still not, settled or stable. For the graduate students, it was not clear if an active social media presence would help or hurt them on the job market. For undergraduate students, activities usually centered around cleaning up their social media presence by removing information from it rather than considering the ways that one could be proactive with their social media use. In all cases, though, these individuals had to develop practices and strategies that worked for their unique situations to represent themselves in new professional settings online.

Each of the graduate students had questions about how best to represent themselves as developing scholars and how to connect with professional communities and with individual scholars through social network sites. Jack, Esther, Becca, and later Nicole each raised questions about what kinds of information would be advantageous to share and what kinds of activity had the potential to backfire or reflect on them poorly. Jack kept adjusting his Twitter accounts out of uncertainty about how to represent himself for the different communities in which he participated on the social network site. Becca created a profile on Academia .edu and followed other scholars on the site, yet she did not post much information about herself. Esther blended her personal and professional identities through her blog, but she did not develop a strictly professional online persona. Nicole kept most of her social media posts to professional content. Given the relative novelty of using social network sites for networking and professional development over this period, many graduate students were unsure how to represent themselves in online environments. In a discussion about networking with other academics on Twitter, Jack reported that he had received conflicting advice about how much to share online as a graduate student. Given his success in connecting to other scholars as he developed his research interests, Jack's experience points to the need for additional research on graduate students' digital professional identities, how they are representing themselves in digital environments, and what kind of training or advice they receive about developing this online identity. Similarly, the experiences of all four of the graduate students suggests the need for further conversations—within the field and between graduate students and their advisors—about their digital professional identities as they refine their research interests and focus on their own professional development.

For the undergraduate students I have profiled here, they grew up using social media throughout college and in their transition to their professional lives beyond the university. While a number of these individuals considered their data and digital footprint when it came to applying to jobs, they thought of their information in more of a defensive rather than proactive way. While Alexis balanced an online presence for her professional work with more restrictive audiences and platforms for her personal information, Ronnie instead put as little information about his professional life online as possible. Their different approaches demonstrate not only the different levels of importance given to social media in their respective industries but also a range of approaches available to professionals. There is room for writing instructors to assist students in considering their online presence more strategically, as well as in demonstrating to students the importance of continually evaluating the information they share and keep online. More research on the ways that professionals in different industries use and grow social media is important as well.

CASE STUDY METHODOLOGY, CONSTRAINTS, AND FINDINGS

Case study methodology was ideal for me to study the situated literacy practices and identity representations of a small number of people in detail, which allowed me to focus on the ways they integrated social network sites into their daily literacy practices and how that use changed over time as the sites themselves changed. The individuals I studied were a self-selected group of social network site users willing to talk with me at length about their activities on social network sites; they all had accounts on multiple sites and thought deeply about their online practices on these sites before participating in this project. These represent what Sheridan et al. (2000) called "telling cases" that point to the larger issues and theories at stake in identity representation on social network sites. While the experiences of these individuals do not speak to those of every social network site user, the close study of the ways in which these writers navigate audience groups and site interfaces and integrate their activity on social network sites within their daily literacy practices speaks to the experiences of many other social network site users. I suggest that negotiating identity representations within flattened audience groups and navigating site interfaces are activities required of every social media user; successfully negotiating these rhetorical situations and constraints represent important digital literacy skills for those writing in online environments. These descriptions also suggest implications for theories of writing in digital spaces as well as considerations for future writing research connected to social media platforms, as detailed later in this chapter.

Yet the experiences of social media users in navigating flattened audience structures are not the same, based on their own identities, life experiences, and subject positions. This study was limited in terms of demographics. I selected my initial list of participants from among the graduate and undergraduate students at a large public research university in the Midwestern United States. These individuals had or were working toward a 4-year undergraduate degree, and they all had access to high-speed internet through the university. They ranged in age from 20 to 33, which was the age demographic that most frequently used social network sites at the time of my initial data collection, according to a Pew report (Smith, 2010). My participants were also limited in terms of racial and ethnic demographics, representing what were majority populations at the university: Caucasian and Asian ethnic backgrounds and a range of religious backgrounds encompassing Jewish and evangelical Christian traditions. The activities my participants engaged in on social network sites can be seen as primarily privileged, middle-class pursuits, yet these groups are not the only ones using social network sites frequently throughout social media's first decade. Cruz Medina and Octavio Pimentel's (2018) edited collection *Racial Shorthand* not only identified specific cultural practices that writers of color engage in on social media platforms but also noted that scholarship on these specific practices is often overshadowed by conversations about access and the digital divide. A Pew study pointed to the internet connectivity of youth of color, who most frequently used cell phones with data plans to connect to others online (Smith, 2011), and certain social network sites were particularly popular with these groups across the first decade of social media, leading to significant scholarship on Black Twitter as a discursive online space. André Brock (2012, 2020) has argued for the importance of Black Twitter as a driving force behind internet culture as a whole over this period, yet my study does not speak to its influence. The additional participants I interviewed in 2013 and 2016 expanded the initial scope of this study in adding more geographically and racially diverse participants, yet larger generalizations cannot be made beyond these individuals. While I did include two African American participants who both used Twitter, this research cannot draw larger conclusions about their use of the platform in the same way Brock's work does. In addition, over the first decade of social media, these platforms were also adopted by users over 50 years old, especially Facebook (Madden & Zickuhr, 2011). While the individuals I spoke with described the difficulty of communicating with different generations of their own families through social media platforms, I did not speak with older users directly. There is a distinct need, then, for more research about digital literacy practices on social media across racial, cultural, language, and age demographics.

This project was also limited by the types of data collected for analysis. As discussed in chapter 2, literate activity on social network sites is difficult to trace because it occurs in small moments distributed throughout one's daily activity. Through the data I collected, I was able to gain information on some of these moments, from discussing with participants where they tend to update social network sites, to following their updates online, to collecting records of their activity through time-use diaries. Much of this data was self-reported and, although I compared the record of their site use through the Twitter and Facebook updates each participant left as a record on the site with the information gathered through interview conversations and the time-use diaries, I did rely on my participants' accounts for a fair amount of my data collection. From descriptions I received from my participants, social network site use is also often collaborative, where two or more individuals will compose a post or a response together that will be sent from one individual's account. As Ronnie and his roommates passed links around on Twitter as they all sat around the apartment, for example, from Ronnie's description, they also engaged in these kinds of collaborative writing activities. I was unable to be present in these collaborative writing activities, however, and relied on accounts of them from my research participants. I also restricted my data collection to communication these individuals kept open to all of their followers on social network sites. Facebook, Twitter, and other sites allow users to also send private messages to each other. While my research participants frequently used these features, these were not conversations I had access to. We did, however, discuss their use in general in our interviews.

Lastly, my analysis was also shaped by the scope of this research project. By first collecting data over a period of ten months, I was able to study these writers' use of social network sites over a longer period of time, studying their reactions to site design changes in order to see how their use changed over time as their identity representations changed and they refined their use of specific platforms accordingly. The research questions I asked about the integration of social media platforms into individuals' daily lives and daily literacy practices pointed to this wider focus that followed participants over time. Because of this focus, I did not ask individuals to allow me to observe them during an individual composing session on a particular social network site, for example. My focus on the experiences of my research participants point to the important situated digital literacy practices social network site users engage in when representing themselves online and negotiating social network site interfaces. While my additional interviews in 2013 and 2016 also discussed longer time scales of social media use, we spoke more about their contemporary social media practices. In addition, I used an archive of my original participants' social media practices over that 5-year period to draw trajectories of their social media use when I interviewed them again in 2016. I had not initially thought of making this research longitudinal, and more frequent updates, in addition to more interviews with my additional participants over this 5-year period would have allowed for thicker descriptions of their experiences during that time.

SOCIAL MEDIA'S FIRST DECADE

As I reflect here on the literacy practices that the writers I discussed here engaged in over this first decade of social media, I also want to take a step back and reflect on some changes in social media platforms themselves that occurred over this first decade. Writing this section in 2021 can feel quite far removed from the launch of Myspace and Facebook, but through hindsight, social media researchers can now more carefully consider the ways the changes have occurred over the past decade. While many of these changes and adjustments happened slowly, 2016 feels like a punctuation mark in considering social media use and its consequences. Many of the ways social media platforms were considered—and, in fact, the ways they thought about themselves—changed after November 8, 2016. Here, then, I want to suggest a few gradual changes that have implications for digital literacy practices on social media.

1. **SNS sites developed from small start-ups and were bought out by larger conglomerates.** David Kirkpatrick (2010) noted how early large amounts of venture capital were infused into social media platforms, but social media companies were, in fact, started as small companies and side projects in dorm rooms and lofts. Consolidation and greater corporate control happened for social media platforms in two ways: by buying up smaller companies and by exerting more control on the site design and infrastructure.

   Adam Banks (2006) and Dara Byrne (2007) have discussed BlackPlanet as an important online space for Black internet users, and Ellison and boyd (2007) included it among early iterations of social network sites. At the start of my research study in 2010, there were a number of small and niche social media platforms for different needs, purposes, and communities. While BlackPlanet, Friendster, and Myspace were all fading as social network sites, the writers I spoke to for this project still used a wide variety of different platforms: Facebook and Twitter, obviously, but also last.fm, Ning, Cyworld, Ravelry, Google+, Foursquare, Vine, 12seconds, TwitPic, and others. Even within Facebook and Twitter, as noted in chapter 4, these individuals used different third-party applications and plug-ins to send virtual gifts and otherwise customize their social media experience. As Facebook and Twitter became larger companies, they were able to purchase competitors and either integrate their site services into their own (like Instagram and Periscope) or shut them down (like Vine). Audience movement to these larger platforms also compounded the problem. These strategies put control into the hands of fewer people and also made it harder for smaller upstarts to compete, either in terms of capital or in terms of user base.

   As these platforms consolidated their power, they also gave users less control over the composition and design of their personal profile pages on the service. While Myspace allowed users to feature different media players and use different backgrounds (often composed through custom CSS), Facebook and subsequent social media platforms privileged a uniform look and allowed fewer and fewer design choices from users. The result was less cultural production and creative control by users.

The individuals I studied in this project put a significant amount of thought into their social network site profiles, using their digital literacy skills to carefully select photos, list favorite books and movies, and represent themselves as students, academics, music lovers, and craft artists. The social network site profile, as Kristin Arola (2010, 2017) noted, harkens back to the genre of the personal webpage but dictates available fields for information and levels of customization. While some individuals were able to customize their profiles to fit their needs, like Ronnie, the ability to customize and design these profiles was limited and contracted over the course of this study, particularly on Facebook. The profile information writers contributed to their pages was only stabilized for a short time, and each of my research participants had to constantly adjust to changes in design and to reevaluate one's information on each profile.

The decreased ability to customize a profile combined with the introduction of news-feed features that compile users' information made interactions with others in one's network the primary means for identity representation on social network sites. While social media profile pages started out as mini-websites, by the end of the decade, they had become just an amalgamation of old status updates and uploads with a short description allowed for a biography statement. Social media profiles moved from a more static identity to one that was created in the moment, changing through every update posted and every tweet sent. For most of these individuals, by 2016, their profile pages were rarely viewed by others; the news feed or timeline was where this identity work happened.

2. Genres and practices formed and codified themselves.

As social media users took to these platforms to communicate information with different audiences, they created new genres through which to share and organize information. RT and hashtag functions were innovated by Twitter users themselves rather than Twitter's creator and improved the functionality of the service (Brock, 2012). Different types of new media texts flourished on social media platforms: selfies, filters, reaction gifs, food pics, memes, and others. Terms were created: friending, vague booking, catfishing, Instagram boyfriend, selfie, subtweet, FOMO, and so on. During my initial data-collection phase, I found my research participants to be frequently engaged in practices that by the end of the decade had names, and sometimes had the functions of the genre built into the platform itself. For example, both Ronnie and Jack enacted what became codified Instagram genres (such as nicely composed shots of plated food) before Instagram existed.

A few months after Ronnie first pulled his April Fools' Day prank and created his girlfriend's profile through fake Facebook and Twitter profiles, the movie *Catfish* had its wide release in theaters, coining a term for creating involved and fake personas online in an attempt to fool others. As I noted in chapter 3, this practice of creating fake accounts reached its inevitable end during the 2016 presidential election through Russian disinformation campaigns. Engaging in catfish practices, Russian agents in the Kremlin-backed Internet Research Agency impersonated Americans on both sides of the political aisle to torment division and spread misinformation on social media platforms, going as far as to plan competing rallies in the same cities that people actually attended in person. Weaponized fake profiles have since come to be known by another term, "sock puppets"—and are now part of many internet users' awareness in considering online political discourse.

3. **Audience issues were adjusted and norms and practices changed.**
    As noted in chapter 3, one of the primary challenges faced by social media users over the course of this study was how to manage flattened structures for audience. While each of the individuals I studied made different choices to manage context collapse, and had different skills through which to manage it, each of them was concerned at different points of this study about the information they were sharing with different audiences and how to share that information with different audiences. Over the course of this study, social media platforms developed different solutions to the audience problem. Google+, for example, developed circles that allowed individuals to place users into different and overlapping groups. But Google+ never developed a user base and was discontinued in 2019. Facebook had groups features that were clunky but usable, and some of my participants made use of those features. Toward the end of the first decade of social media and since, however, services have developed that allow for small-group conversations and also private groups: GroupMe, WhatsApp, Facebook groups, and other small-group messaging services. In their public presentations in 2019, Facebook proposed also moving from whole friend list updates to more group interactions, indicating that Facebook is going to be updating their own services in this area as well. They also launched a large television campaign in 2019 to promote groups, especially groups with strangers around common interests. This move toward small groups changes social media platforms from services organized around connections individuals already have with others through various offline professional and social networks and back toward older online services organized around interests that were common with older technologies, like discussion boards and Usenet groups.

4. **The twin problems of time and persistence were confronted and adjusted.**
    Some of the largest challenges faced by social media users throughout the first decade of social media were the issues of time and persistence. While social media platforms encouraged users to post in-the-moment and ephemeral content, the content persisted forever, available on company servers, able to be searched and found by others, and circulated long after the occasion for the post had passed. This situation caused a number of the participants in this research study to delete posts that received fewer interactions (Sandra), to clean Facebook wall posts (Alexis and Stephanie), and to delete content altogether (all participants).

This challenge is one for which individuals have found their own solutions, as this study demonstrates. But social media platforms at the end of this first decade and beyond have built in technological solutions for these issues as well. Snapchat, for example, was developed to solve both audience and persistence problems; the service allows users to share content with individual users and also allows the content to expire after a short time, after the posts are viewed in some cases and after 24 hours in others. While other platforms allowed users to adjust the audience of their posts, Snapchat was the first to make it the default and defining feature through which its platform operated. Instagram and later Facebook adapted Snapchat's "stories" feature, allowing users to send information to their friends and followers that only persisted on the site for 24 hours. This feature solves the rhetorical problem of data persistence and allows individuals to have greater control over permanent versus temporary messages. In 2021, Instagram and Facebook users could decide whether they would like to share a post that appeared in the news feed and was permanently archived on their profile page or share a story that appears in a different area of the platform and was available for only 24 hours. These innovations solve a composing problem for social media users and demonstrates the ways that innovations on a new service arise from specific rhetorical problems and then are adapted by users to solve rhetorical problems.

5. **Algorithms began to shape user experience.**
    In chapter 4, I discussed the ways that Becca noticed Facebook's recommendation algorithm, and she discussed the assumptions and message behind that algorithm. While Facebook and other social media platforms have long relied on different algorithms for recommendations and other information, algorithmic sorting grew to have a larger role in social media users' experiences over the course of the first decade. Facebook added a preference algorithm to its news feed in 2011; previously, it sorted posts from a user's friends in chronological order, moving chronological updates to the "ticker" on the right side. While users could toggle between these two options initially, Facebook later discontinued that option.
    The Facebook news feed algorithm is frequently being adjusted and has come under constant criticism, from news outlets, scholars, and others for the ways that it shapes user experience and privileges certain kinds of content. Safiya Noble (2018) has critiqued information-sorting algorithms and search-engine algorithms for their racial bias, as noted earlier in this text. Activist Eli Pariser also coined the term "filter bubble," referring to Google's algorithmic sorting (Parramore, 2010), but the term came to be used for the Facebook news feed and other tools that sort information into partisan categories, creating an information ecosystem that confirms the reader's beliefs. Twitter switched to an algorithmic timeline much later, in 2015, and Instagram followed in 2016. By the end of the first decade of social media, the three most popular social media platforms in the United States used algorithmic

news feeds. The consequences of these algorithms were just beginning to be discussed at the end of social media's first decade. The *Wall Street Journal* created a tool called Red Feed/Blue Feed in 2016 that pulled content on top news issues from known partisan Facebook accounts to demonstrate how users on different sides of the political spectrum were viewing and experiencing that information. Much of this conversation about the consequences of algorithmic news feeds and their influence on social media users came at the end of the first decade and continue to be discussed as their influence continues throughout these platforms.

6. **Social media went corporate.**

As I noted above, social media over the course of the first decade has become more corporatized. From the microcelebrities that Alice Marwick (2013) studied, to Instagram influencers, to every company with a page on Facebook and a Twitter account, many of the large social media platforms have become places for commerce and corporate branding rather than their initial use as places for young people to hang out (Itō et al., 2010). The overall shift in social media platforms from creative and ad hoc spaces to professional and corporate ones happened over the course of the decade as well. As services become more established and more users join, corporations move in and younger users find new spaces that are not populated with their parents and grandparents. While it is reasonable to predict that new users will always find a new tool or new space in which to connect, it is an open question as to whether new social media platforms will continue to be developed or will persist. Starting a service is now more challenging when these companies have to compete with the user bases of more established services. Over this first decade, social media moved from messy places of online connection to corporate interfaces for monetization. Now that these services are an established part of an online media ecosystem, their path forward is an open question.

7. **Social media influenced politics and public discourse.**

Social media platforms, as Marwick (2013), Banks (2006), and Brock (2020) have discussed, developed from the genre of personal homepages and other similar integrated places for interaction, like BlackPlanet and MiGente, which emphasized personal identity representation. While the Arab Spring and the Occupy movement both demonstrated the potential for organizing and protest on the services, this potential had significantly evolved over the course of the decade. As Brock (2020) argued, identity representation is always political. Over the course of the first decade of social media, however, these platforms have been spaces for political and public discourse that have transcended digital spaces to impact civic discourse and historical events.

As noted in the introduction, the #BlackLivesMatter movement gained momentum through social media and played a significant role in both public discourse and public protests in Ferguson, Missouri, in 2014 (Freelon et al., 2016; Maraj, 2020; Richardson & Ragland, 2018). At the same time, social media platforms also fueled the rise of the alt-right and allowed the development of swarming and harassment practices and disinformation campaigns (Massanari, 2017; Trice & Potts, 2018), which also had an arguable influence on global and domestic politics. This project contains a small account of how one individual, Sam, used Twitter to share content from campus protests for racial justice and was successful in having this content amplified by prominent activists. This series of protest demonstrations occurred in October 2016, at the very end of the first decade of social media. Louis Maraj (2020) has also examined more extensive campus protests and identified important digital literacy practices, specifically the use of hashtags, as instrumental for the #BlackLivesMatter movement and for critique in digital spaces. The worldwide protests for racial justice in the summer of 2020 that were prompted by the police murder of George Floyd in Minneapolis demonstrate the increased importance of social media platforms for protest, resistance, critique, and social justice movements in social media's second decade.

WHAT'S NEXT?

Social Media in Its Second Decade

While some of the changes that I detailed in the previous section have settled some of the concerns of social media users across these plat-forms' first decade, in many ways the problems of social media have become problems that we all live with. Part of living lives, writing, and sharing information through digital spaces used for work, creativity, and social connection means learning to navigate online audiences, man-age data, and negotiate personal and professional identities and con-nections. For those writers who have used social media platforms over the past decade, they have developed individual literacy practices and strategies to navigate these issues and to adjust with platform and policy changes. These literacy practices will be essential for all social media users moving forward as well.

Although I cannot make predictions here in this project about the second decade of social media, the end of its first decade also points to new challenges. The #BlackLivesMatter protests in 2020 demon-strated the continued power of mobile cameras and digital platforms in documenting and reporting police violence and brutality as well as activism. As noted at the start of this chapter, scholarly critiques of social media platforms and their connected surveillance apparatus (Beck & Hutchinson, 2020; Benjamin, 2019; Noble, 2018) point to the contin-ued need for scholars in a range of disciplines to continue to study the ways that social media platforms reinforce structural racism, perpetuate racial hierarchies, and reinforce white hegemonic value systems.

The #GamerGate situation of 2014 demonstrated how a coordinated network of online actors could organize across platforms to wage sustained harassment campaigns (Massanari, 2017; Trice & Potts, 2018), networks that continued to work effectively to promote the presidential candidacy of Donald Trump as well as various political causes and conspiracy theories in the years since (McKew, 2018). The news headlines of 2019 reflected a national and global political culture trying to come to terms with the consequences of social media platforms, their networks, and their governance, including frequent debates about de-platforming, online extremism, privacy issues, free speech, surveillance, political advertisements, and coordinated disinformation campaigns by state and nonstate actors. In 2020 and 2021, information about the global COVID-19 pandemic also reflects concerns of medical disinformation and conspiracy theories shared on social platforms. These issues are concerns for writing studies scholars as well, as we try to understand how information circulates online, how writers effectively communicate for different online audiences, and as we teach students to find information, evaluate it, use it to make their own arguments, and represent themselves and others in a variety of forms.

Researching Social Media

As discussed in chapter 1, situated literate activity on social network sites is difficult to trace, occurring in quick moments integrated within a writer's daily experience. Viewing and analyzing the textual record of that activity on social media platforms provides only a partial picture, as the texts individuals share are part of larger chains of literate activity. In this project, I integrated that study of the digital texts written by each research participant with frequent interviews, time-use diaries, and digital profile tours recorded with video screen capture software, as detailed in chapter 2. This combination of methods allowed me to consider individuals' literacy practices on social network sites from multiple perspectives and as integrated with each participant's other online and offline activities.

These research methods, I suggest, point to approaches that can be productive for other writing researchers studying writing in digital environments. The screen capture software in particular could be used not only for the profile tours I conducted, but also for capturing an individual writer's daily use of social network sites. In order to study how an individual reads updates on Facebook, for example, a researcher could record a writer reading through the news feed and commenting on friends' updates. Time-use diaries could also be used in combination with these methods to trace how often and for what reasons a writer interacts with others on social network sites.

In order to examine how individuals write in digital environments, the specific combination of methods I used in these qualitative case studies can be productive in researching writing practices that are otherwise difficult to trace. The data I gathered through this research project presented a richer picture of these writers' social media use than I would have seen through a study of only the online texts and images these writers used to represent themselves, or through only one in-depth interview about their social network site activity. Given the ways that activity on social network sites traverse online/offline boundaries as well as boundaries between sites, understanding the ways that individuals' rich literate activity is distributed between different sites and integrated within their daily literacy practices requires these kinds of combinations of multiple methods.

The ethical issues I considered in designing my study methodology and the negotiations I engaged in with my research participants, as detailed in chapter 2, point to important issues for researchers investigating writing in digital environments. This project suggests that researchers should carefully consider how participants are represented in qualitative studies of online activity, how participants might be identified, and what kind of access the researcher should have to each writer's online information. These considerations should not only be part of a dialogue between researchers and the writers involved, but should also be continually reevaluated, as the online environments individuals engage in change frequently, and individuals' writing practices and identity representations also often change over time. While some online activity can be considered public and might not require informed consent from writers in order to study that writing, I argue that many kinds of online writing are not considered public by their writers as a simple on/off privacy switch. As this study suggests, writers take a great deal of interest in and have a great deal of concern about their online identities, and I argue that writing researchers should do their best to ensure writers have control over their information and representations.

Writing researchers should also consider the data they collect from social media platforms within context. In collecting data on public hashtags, for example, researchers now need to consider and evaluate whether those hashtags are being weaponized as part of an online harassment or disinformation campaign and what conclusions they can draw from those hashtags in light of these situations. In designing research studies, drawing boundaries around research cases, identifying and recruiting participants, and representing their work and experiences in our research, I argue that it is important to see the issues of privacy, consent, and representation as networked. The literacy practices that individuals engage in on social media platforms exist in liminal public/private spaces that are both ephemeral and persistent. While individuals often treat social media as a place for spontaneous interactions, the ways that this data persists can make publishing this data difficult. When we connect with research participants on social media, we should see these participants as part of larger networks, some of which we have access to and some of which we do not. Seeing these research settings as networked reminds us to consider the risks participants take in becoming co-researchers and to consider the ways that their social media activity is situated within particular contexts.[1]

Social Media and Teaching

As Deborah Brandt (2001) has argued, literacy has always been a resource that individuals seek to attain for particular ends. Literacy sponsors, whether school, state, economic, church, military, or family-based, have assisted individuals in achieving these literacies, shaped them, and even withheld them, and they also "gain advantage by it in some way" (p. 19). Corporate sponsors of literacy have always existed, in sponsoring writing contests, manufacturing writing tools, and supporting employees in attaining certain kinds of literacy skills. Viewing social media platforms as corporate literacy sponsors extends this idea but also brings up different implications for writers and their work. Social media users keep the sites going, not through their monetary subscriptions to these services but through their data, which these sites then monetize and sell to advertisers. These writers, then, are the products that social network sites sell.

In the 20th-anniversary issue of *Computers and Composition*, Heidi McKee (2011) pointed to important policy issues that will influence the future of writing and the teaching of writing. Among these is the issue of corporate data mining; described by Google as "interest-based ads" and by Facebook as "instant personalization," these companies collect information from their users, sell that information to advertisers, and then provide targeted ads for users on these sites (McKee, 2011, p. 280). In chapter 4, I described the ways in which the individuals I studied were concerned about Facebook's use of their information. Ronnie and Beth in particular took action on their concerns, with Ronnie adding fake information to Facebook and Beth deactivating her account entirely.

Although I describe how many of the individuals I studied subverted the design of the social network sites they were using for their own purposes, these practices do not interrupt Facebook's business model, and using social network sites like Facebook means that one pays for the service with one's personal data.

Scholars like McKee, Estee Beck, Les Hutchinson, and Chris Gilliard study the implications of digital technologies and surveillance on our work as rhetoricians, scholars, and teachers. Surveillance and privacy are issues that go beyond just social media platforms to include a wide variety of other digital platforms that writing teachers might use, including blogs, course-management systems, and grading systems. While this project did not discuss social media pedagogies in depth, as I noted in chapter 4, any use of social media platforms and similar services in the classroom should be accompanied by considerations of the ethics and consequences of asking students to share their data with different social media platforms, the visibility of that information, and its circulation during and beyond the course. Keeping the issues of audience, data management, and professional identity representation in mind while using and/or teaching social media in the classroom will help writing teachers develop reflective practices as well.

As noted earlier in this chapter, while identity representation is always political, social media platforms have also moved from spaces for personal identity representation to locations for civic discourse and activism. The #BlackLivesMatter movement demonstrates the role that social media has played in documenting and protesting racial injustice through complex assemblages of apps, cameras, mobile devices, and networked communication technologies. There is a continued need for academic research on these topics, the ways that digital literacy practices related to activist movements are present in our writing classrooms, and how to guide students in developing the critical digital literacy skills they will need to communicate effective messages in both online and offline spaces in order to be heard and to effect change.

I end this book on a tentative note, realizing that by the time it has made its way off of the presses (physical and digital) and into your hands as a reader—months or years after this date—social media platforms will have inevitably changed, and writers will have also confronted new challenges in writing and sharing information in digital spaces. While I can only guess at these changes, my hope is that this project provided a look at some of the concerns writers faced in social media's first decade, and that this description will help us understand how the first decade of social media influenced writing practices in the decades beyond.

NOTES

INTRODUCTION: STUDYING THE FIRST DECADE OF SOCIAL MEDIA

1. #GamerGate was a harassment movement targeting videogame developers Zoe Quinn and Briann Wu, as well as feminist media critic Anita Sarkeesian, essentially over who had a right to define video game culture. See Massanari (2017).

2. See Banks (2006) and Brock (2020) for analysis of BlackPlanet as a formative early social media space and one that served as an important online space for African American rhetoric, community building, and online culture.

CHAPTER 1: DIGITAL LITERACIES ON SOCIAL MEDIA PLATFORMS

1. All participant names are pseudonyms.

CHAPTER 2: STUDYING SOCIAL MEDIA PLATFORMS

1. While I argue here that the first decade of social media began in 2004, the research for this project began in 2010 for reasons of individual circumstance and practicality. I began my doctoral program in writing studies at the University of Illinois in 2006. I conducted a few initial pilot studies using similar research methods in 2007 and 2008, but this project began in earnest with my dissertation research in 2010, the year described in the introduction of this text as the year social media platforms reached mainstream usage and cultural consciousness in the United States. Scholars in internet studies more broadly have conducted a great deal of research on each social media platform as it developed, but social network sites only began to be discussed in the literature as a specific type of digital space around 2007 and 2008 with some of danah boyd's early research, work that was foundational to the development of this research project as well.

2. In 2015, Google began displaying tweets in Google search results. The search does not go back beyond the limits of Twitter's API—roughly 3,000 tweets for each Twitter user.

3. Sam is nonbinary and uses they/them pronouns.

4. A "finsta" is shorthand for "fake Instagram" account, a private Instagram account where users share less filtered and censored photos with a group of close friends.

CHAPTER 3: NEGOTIATING AUDIENCE ACROSS PLATFORMS

1. I am using a pseudonym for Ronnie's sister's Twitter handle in reproducing this tweet.

CHAPTER 4: MANAGING DATA AND INTERFACES

1. danah boyd (2008) chronicled user responses to the Facebook news feed in 2006 and analyzed its corresponding privacy concerns.

2. Selective Tweets was shelved in 2018 when changes to Facebook's API no longer allowed third-party applications to post to a user's Facebook page (Young, 2018).

3. Before Facebook established Pages for organizations and businesses, users could create "fan pages" that were more static than personal user profiles and used a nonreciprocal favoriting practice to "Like" a page rather than the reciprocal friending practice required of individual user profiles. While these pages were sometimes run by the organizations or businesses themselves, sometimes they were created by fans of a particular business, organization, service, or place.

4. All of the Twitter handles listed here for Ronnie's friends are pseudonyms.

5. "Friends of friends" is no longer a privacy setting option on Facebook.

6. Allowing users to have more than one Instagram account per device was, in fact, a conscious choice on Instagram's part that also allowed the platform to artificially increase their user numbers.

CHAPTER 6: BEYOND SOCIAL MEDIA'S FIRST DECADE

1. A more extensive consideration of social media research ethics, particularly involving public data, can be found in my article co-written with Devon Ralston in *Computers and Composition* (Buck & Ralston, 2021).

REFERENCES

Abelmann, N. (2009). The intimate university: Korean-American students and the problems of segregation. Duke University Press.

Adkins, T. (2017). Social spill: A case-based analysis of social media research. In D. Walls & S. Vie (Eds.), *Social writing/social media: Publics, presentations, and pedagogies* (pp. 53–68). WAC Clearinghouse/University Press of Colorado.

Akrich, Madeline, & Latour, Bruno. (1992). A summary of a convenient vocabulary for the semiotics of human and nonhuman assemblies. In W. Bijker & J. Law (Eds.). *Shaping technology/ building society* (pp. 259–264). MIT Press.

Alexander, K. P., & Hahner, L. A. (2017). The intimate screen: Revisualizing understandings of down syndrome through digital activism on Instagram. In D. Walls & S. Vie (Eds.), *Social writing/social media: Publics, presentations, and pedagogies* (pp. 225–243). WAC Clearinghouse/University Press of Colorado.

Amidon, T. R., Hutchinson, L., Herrington, T. K., & Reyman, J. (2019). Copyright, content, & control: Student authorship across educational technology platforms. *Kairos: A Journal of Rhetoric, Technology, and Pedagogy*. 24(1). https://kairos.technorhetoric.net/24.1 /topoi/amidon-et-al/index.html

Anson, C. (2017). Intellectual, argumentative, and information affordances of public forums: Potential contributions to academic learning. In D. Walls & S. Vie (Eds.), *Social writing/social media: Publics, presentations, and pedagogies* (pp. 309–330). WAC Clearinghouse/University Press of Colorado.

Arola, K. L. (2010). The design of web 2.0: The rise of the template, the fall of design. *Computers and Composition*, 27(1), 4–14.

Arola, K. L. (2017). Indigenous interfaces. In D. Walls & S. Vie (Eds.), *Social writing/ social media: Publics, presentations, and pedagogies* (pp. 209–224). WAC Clearinghouse/ University Press of Colorado.

Banks, A. J. (2006). *Race, rhetoric, and technology: Searching for higher ground.* SUNY University Press.

Banks, A. J. (2011). *Digital griots: African American rhetoric in a multimedia age.* SIU Press.

Basu, T. (2020, March 6). How a ban on pro-Trump patterns unraveled the online knitting world. *MIT Technology Review.* https://www.technologyreview.com/2020/03 /06/905472/ravelry-ban-on-pro-trump-patterns-unraveled-the-online-knitting-world -censorship-free/

Bawden, D. (2008). Origins and concepts of digital literacy. In C. Lankshear & M. Knobel (Eds.), *Digital literacies: Concepts, policies and practices* (p. 323). Peter Lang.

Beck, E. (2015). The invisible digital identity: Assemblages in digital networks. *Computers and Composition*, 35, 125–140.

Beck, E. (2017). Sustaining critical literacies in the digital information age: The rhetoric of sharing, prosumerism, and digital algorithmic surveillance. In D. Walls & S. Vie (Eds.), *Social writing/social media: Publics, presentations, and pedagogies* (pp. 37–52). WAC Clearinghouse/University Press of Colorado.

Beck, E., & Hutchinson Campos, L. (2020). Introduction. In E. Beck & L. Hutchinson Campos (Eds.), *Privacy matters: Conversations about surveillance within and beyond the classroom* (pp. 3–14). Utah State University Press.

Benjamin, R. (2019). *Race after technology: Abolitionist tools for the new Jim Code.* Polity.

Berry, P. W., Hawisher, G. E., & Selfe, C. L. (2012). *Transnational literate lives in digital times*. Computers and Composition Digital Press/Utah State University Press. http://ccdigitalpress.org/transnational

Bilton, N. (2010, May 12). Price of Facebook privacy? Start clicking. *The New York Times*. https://www.nytimes.com/2010/05/13/technology/personaltech/13basics.html

Bowdon, M. A. (2014). Tweeting an ethos: Emergency messaging, social media, and teaching technical communication. *Technical Communication Quarterly, 23*(1), 35–54.

boyd, d. (2008). Facebook's privacy trainwreck: Exposure, invasion, and social convergence. *Convergence: The International Journal of Research Into New Media Technologies, 14*(1), 13–20.

boyd, d. (2011). White flight in networked publics?: How race and class shaped American teen engagement with MySpace and Facebook. In L. Nakamura & P. A. Chow-White (Eds.), *Race after the internet* (pp. 203–222). Routledge.

boyd, d. (2014). *It's complicated: The social lives of networked teens* (1st ed.). Yale University Press.

boyd, d., & Hargittai, E. (2010). Facebook privacy settings: Who cares? *First Monday, 15*(8). https://firstmonday.org/ojs/index.php/fm/article/view/3086

boyd, d. m., & Ellison, N. B. (2007). Social network sites: Definition, history, and scholarship. *Journal of Computer-Mediated Communication, 13*(1), 210–230.

Boyd, P. (2013). Online discussion boards as identity workspaces: Building professional identities in online writing classes. *The Journal of Interactive Technology and Pedagogy, 4*. https://jitp.commons.gc.cuny.edu/online-discussion-boards-as-identity-workspaces-building-professional-identities-in-online-writing-classes/

Brandt, D. (2001). *Literacy in American lives*. Cambridge University Press.

Brock, A. (2012). From the blackhand side: Twitter as a cultural conversation. *Journal of Broadcasting & Electronic Media, 56*(4), 529–549. https://doi.org/10.1080/08838151.2012.732147

Brock, A. (2020). *Distributed blackness*. New York University Press.

Brooke, C. (2009). *Lingua fracta: Toward a rhetoric of new media*. Hampton Press.

Brown, N. M. (2019). Methodological cyborg as black feminist technology: Constructing the social self using computational digital autoethnography and social media. *Cultural Studies ↔ Critical Methodologies, 19*(1), 55–67. https://doi.org/10.1177/1532708617750178

Buck, A. M., & Ralston, D. F. (2021). I didn't sign up for your research study: The ethics of using "public" data. *Computers and Composition, 61*, https://doi.org/10.1016//j.compcom.2021.102655.

Buck, E. H. (2015). Facebook, Instagram, and Twitter: Oh my! *Kairos: A Journal of Rhetoric, Technology, and Pedagogy, 19*(3). http://technorhetoric.net/19.3/praxis/buck/

Bullinger, C., & Vie, S. (2017). After a decade of social media: Abstainers and ex-users. In D. Walls & S. Vie (Eds.), *Social writing/social media: Publics, presentations, and pedagogies* (pp. 69–88). WAC Clearinghouse/University Press of Colorado.

Butler, J. (1990). *Gender trouble* (2nd ed.). Routledge. https://doi.org/10.4324/9780203902752

Byrd, A. (2020). "Like coming home": African Americans tinkering and playing toward a computer code bootcamp. *College Composition and Communication, 71*(3), 426–452.

Byrne, D. N. (2007). Public discourse, community concerns, and civic engagement: Exploring Black social networking traditions on BlackPlanet.com. *Journal of Computer-Mediated Communication, 13*(1), 319–340.

Cagle, L. E. (2019). Surveilling strangers: The disciplinary biopower of digital genre assemblages. *Computers and Composition, 52*, 67–78.

Casanave, C. P. (2002). *Writing games: Multicultural case studies of academic literacy practices in higher education*. Routledge.

Castells, M. (2000). *The rise of the network society*. John Wiley & Sons.

Cazden, C., Cope, B., Fairclough, N., Gee, J., Kalantzis, M., Kress, G., . . . & Nakata, M. (1996). A pedagogy of multiliteracies: Designing social futures. *Harvard educational review, 66*(1), 60–92.

Cedillo, C. (2020). The perils of the public professoriate: On surveillance, social media, and identity-avoidant frameworks. In E. Beck & L. Hutchinson (Eds.), *Privacy matters: Conversations about surveillance within and beyond the classroom* (pp. 131–149). University Press of Colorado.

Coad, D. (2013). Developing critical literacy and critical thinking through Facebook. *PraxisWiki: Kairos: A Journal of Rhetoric, Technology, and Pedagogy, 18*(1). http://kairos.technorhetoric.net/praxis/tikiindex.php?page=Developing_Critical_Literacy_and_Critical_Thinking_through_Facebook

Coad, D. T. (2017). "That's my face to the whole field!": Graduate students' professional identity-building through Twitter at a writing studies conference. *Computers and Composition, 45*, 51–66.

Coad, D. T. (2019). *Teaching rhetorical strategies through social media: A qualitative study of FYC instructors and students* [Doctoral dissertation, University of California, Davis].

Cohen, J. E. (2012). *Configuring the networked self: Law, code, and the play of everyday practice.* Yale University Press.

Cohn, J., Fahim, N., & Peterson, J. (2020). In E. Beck & L. Hutchinson (Eds.), *Privacy matters: Conversations about surveillance within and beyond the classroom* (pp. 36–52). University Press of Colorado.

Cooper, M. M. (1986). The ecology of writing. *College English, 48*(4), 364–375.

Dadas, C. (2016). Messy methods: Queer methodological approaches to researching social media. *Computers and Composition, 40*, 60–72.

Dadas, C. (2017). Hashtag activism: The promise and risk of "attention." In D. Walls & S. Vie (Eds.), *Social writing/social media: Publics, presentations, and pedagogies* (pp. 17–36). WAC Clearinghouse/University Press of Colorado.

Debatin, B., Lovejoy, J. P., Horn, A.-K., & Hughes, B. N. (2009). Facebook and online privacy: Attitudes, behaviors, and unintended consequences. *Journal of Computer-Mediated Communication, 15*(1), 83–108. https://doi.org/10.1111/j.1083-6101.2009.01494.x

DeLuca, K. M. (2015). Can we block these political thingys? I just want to get f*cking recipes: Women, rhetoric, and politics on Pinterest. *Kairos: A Journal of Rhetoric, Technology, and Pedagogy, 19*(3). http://kairos.technorhetoric.net/19.3/topoi/deluca/index.html

Dieterle, B., Edwards, D., & Martin, P. "Dan." (2019). Confronting digital aggression with an ethics of circulation. In J. Reyman & E. Sparby (Eds.), *Digital ethics: Rhetoric and responsibility in online aggression* (pp. 197–213). Routledge. https://doi.org/10.4324/9780429266140-12

Dubisar, A. M., & Palmeri, J. (2010). Palin/Pathos/Peter Griffin: Political video remix and composition pedagogy. *Computers and Composition, 27*(2), 77–93. https://doi.org/10.1016/j.compcom.2010.03.004

Duthely, R. (2018). Hip-hop rhetoric and multimodal digital writing. In J. Alexander & J. Rhodes, J. (Eds.). *The Routledge handbook of digital writing and rhetoric,* Routledge. https://doi.org/10.4324/9781315518497-33

Dyson, A. H., & Genishi, C. (2005). *On the case.* Teachers College Press.

Edwards, D. W. (2020a). Deep circulation. In E. Beck & L. Hutchinson (Eds.), *Privacy matters: Conversations about surveillance within and beyond the classroom* (pp. 75–92). University Press of Colorado.

Edwards, D. W. (2020b). Digital rhetoric on a damaged planet: Storying digital damage as inventive response to the Anthropocene. *Rhetoric Review, 39*(1), 59-72.

Edwards, D., & Gelms, B. (2018). Vol. 6.3: Special issue on the rhetoric of platforms. *Present Tense: A Journal of Rhetoric in Society, 6*(3). http://www.presenttensejournal.org/editorial/vol-6-3-special-issue-on-the-rhetoric-of-platforms/

Eliot, M., & Turns, J. (2011). Constructing professional portfolios: Sense-making and professional identity development for engineering undergraduates. *Journal of Engineering Education, 100*(4), 630–654.

Ellison, N. B., & Boyd, D. M. (2013). Sociality through social network sites. In W. H. Dutton (Ed.), *The Oxford handbook of internet studies*. https://www.oxfordhandbooks.com/view/10.1093/oxfordhb/9780199589074.001.0001/oxfordhb-9780199589074-e-8

Ellison, N. B., Vitak, J., Gray, R., & Lampe, C. (2014). Cultivating social resources on social network sites: Facebook relationship maintenance behaviors and their role in social capital processes. *Journal of Computer-Mediated Communication, 19*(4), 855–870.

Faris, M. (2018). How to be gay with locative media: The rhetorical work of Grindr as a platform. *Present Tense: A Journal of Rhetoric in Society, 6*(3). http://www.presenttensejournal.org/volume-6/how-to-be-gay-with-locative-media-the-rhetorical-work-of-grindr-as-a-platform/

Faris, M. J. (2017). Contextualizing students' media ideologies and practices: An empirical study of social media use in a writing class. In D. Walls & S. Vie (Eds.), *Social writing/social media: Publics, presentations, and pedagogies* (pp. 283–307). WAC Clearinghouse/University Press of Colorado.

Federal Trade Commission. (2011, November 29). *Facebook settles FTC Charges that it deceived consumers by failing to keep privacy promises*. Federal Trade Commission. https://www.ftc.gov/news-events/press-releases/2011/11/facebook-settles-ftc-charges-it-deceived-consumers-failing-keep

Franzke, A. S., Bechmann, A., Zimmer, M., Ess, C., & Association of Internet Researchers. (2020). *Internet research: Ethical guidelines 3.0*. https://aoir.org/reports/ethics3.pdf

Freelon, D., McIlwain, C. D., & Clark, M. (2016). *Beyond the hashtags: #Ferguson, #Blacklivesmatter, and the online struggle for offline justice* (SSRN Scholarly Paper ID 2747066). Social Science Research Network. https://doi.org/10.2139/ssrn.2747066

Frost, E. A. (2011). Why teachers must learn: Student innovation as a driving factor in the future of the web. *Computers and Composition, 28*(4), 269–275.

Gallagher, J. R. (2017). Writing for algorithmic audiences. *Computers and Composition, 45*, 25–35. https://doi.org/10.1016/j.compcom.2017.06.002

Gallagher, J. R. (2018). Considering the comments: Theorizing online audiences as emergent processes. *Computers and Composition, 48*, 34–48.

Gallagher, J. R. (2019). A framework for internet case study methodology in writing studies. *Computers and Composition, 54*.

Gallagher, J. R. (2020). *Update culture and the afterlife of digital writing*. Utah State University Press.

Gilliard, C., & Culik, H. (2016, May 24). *Digital redlining, access, and privacy*. Common Sense Education. https://www.commonsense.org/education/articles/digital-redlining-access-and-privacy

Gilster, P. (1997). *Digital literacy*. Wiley.

Glaser, A. (2019, July 24). Don't be too impressed with the FTC's $5 billion fine of Facebook. *Slate*. https://slate.com/technology/2019/07/facebook-ftc-settlement-5-billion-fine.html

Goffman, E. (1959). *The presentation of self in everyday life* (1st ed.). Anchor.

Goode, J. (2010). The digital identity divide: How technology knowledge impacts college students. *New Media & Society, 12*(3), 497–513.

Goodling, L. B. (2015). MOAR digital activism, please. *Kairos: A Journal of Rhetoric, Technology, and Pedagogy, 19*(3). http://kairos.technorhetoric.net/19.3/topoi/goodling/index.html

Grabill, J. (2010). *Revisualizing composition: Mapping the writing lives of first-year college students*. WIDE Research Center. http://wide.msu.edu/special/writinglives/

Greenhow, C., & Robelia, B. (2009). Old communication, new literacies: Social network sites as social learning resources. *Journal of Computer-Mediated Communication, 14*(4), 1130–1161.

Greenwood, S., Perrin, A., & Duggan, M. (2016, November 11). *Social media update 2016*. Pew Research Center. http://www.pewinternet.org/2016/11/11/social-media-update-2016

Gries, L. (2015). *Still life with rhetoric: A new materialist approach for visual rhetorics.* Utah State University Press.

Gries, L., & Brooke, C. G. (Eds.). (2018). *Circulation, writing, and rhetoric.* Utah State University Press.

Grossman, L. (2010, December 15). Mark Zuckerberg: Person of the year. *Time.* http://www.time.com/time/specials/packages/article/0,28804,2036683_2037183_2037185,00.html

Haas Dyson, A., & Genishi, C. (2005). *On the case: Approaches to language and literacy research.* Teachers College Press.

Hart-Davidson, B. (2007). Studying the mediated action of composing with time-use diaries. In H. McKee & D. N. DeVoss (Eds.), *Digital writing research: Technologies, methodologies, and ethical issues* (pp. 153–170). Hampton.

Hawisher, G. E., & Selfe, C. L. (2000). Introduction: Testing the claims. In *Global literacies and the world-wide web* (pp. 1–18). Psychology Press.

Hayes, T. J. (2017). #MyNYPD: Transforming Twitter into a public place for protest. *Computers and Composition, 43,* 118–134.

Hayles, N. K. (1999). *How we became posthuman: Virtual bodies in cybernetics, literature, and informatics.* University of Chicago Press.

Holland, D. C., Lachicotte, W. S., Jr., Skinner, D., & Cain, C. (1998). *Identity and agency in cultural worlds.* Harvard University Press.

Horner, B. (2013). Ideologies of literacy, "academic literacies," and composition studies. *Literacy in Composition Studies, 1*(1), 1–9.

Hutchinson, L. (2017). Writing to have no face: The orientation of anonymity in Twitter. In D. Walls & S. Vie (Eds.), *Social writing/social media: Publics, presentations, and pedagogies* (pp. 179–207). WAC Clearinghouse/University Press of Colorado.

Hutchinson, L. (2018). Wielding power and doxing data: How personal information regulates and controls our online selves. In J. Alexander & J. Rhodes (Eds.), *The Routledge handbook of digital writing and rhetoric* (pp. 303–316). Routledge.

Hutchinson, L., & Novotny, M. (2018). Teaching a critical digital literacy of wearables: A feminist surveillance as care pedagogy. *Computers and Composition, 50,* 105–120.

Hutchinson, L., & Novotny, M. (2019, January 17). Rhetorics of data: Collection, consent, & critical digital literacies [Special issue]. *Computers and Composition.* https://call-for-papers.sas.upenn.edu/cfp/2019/01/17/rhetorics-of-data-collection-consent-critical-digital-literacies

Hutchinson Campos, L., & Novotny, M. (2021). Introduction to the special issue: Rhetorics of data. *Computers and Composition, 61,* 102658. https://doi.org/10.1016/j.compcom.2021.102658

Ibarra, H., & Petriglieri, J. L. (2010). Identity work and play. *Journal of Organizational Change Management, 23*(1), 10–25. https://doi.org/10.1108/09534811011017180

Itō, M. (2010). *Hanging out, messing around, and geeking out: Kids living and learning with new media.* MIT Press.

Ivanič, R. (1998). *Writing and identity.* John Benjamins.

Johnson-Eilola, J. (2005). *Datacloud: Toward a new theory of online work.* Hampton Press.

Kirkpatrick, D. (2010). *The Facebook effect.* Simon & Schuster.

Korn, J. U. (2016). Black women exercisers, Asian women artists, white women daters, and Latina lesbians: Cultural constructions of race and gender within intersectionality-based Facebook groups. In S. U. Noble & B. M. Tynes (Eds.), *The intersectional internet: Race, sex, class, and culture online* (pp. 115–128). Peter Lang.

Kress, G. (2003). *Literacy in the new media age.* Routledge.

Kynard, C. (2013). Literacy/literacies studies and the still-dominant white center. *Literacy in Composition Studies, 1*(1), 63–65.

Lagman, E. (2015). Moving labor: Transnational migrant workers and affective literacies of care. *Literacy in Composition Studies, 3*(3), 1–24.

Lam, W. S. E., & Rosario-Ramos, E. (2009). Multilingual literacies in transnational digitally mediated contexts: An exploratory study of immigrant teens in the United States. *Language and Education, 23*(2), 171–190.

Lange, P. G. (2007). Publicly private and privately public: Social networking on YouTube. *Journal of Computer-Mediated Communication, 13*(1), 361–380.

Lanier, Jaron. (2010). *You are not a gadget: A manifesto.* New York: Knopf.

Lankshear, C., & Knobel, M. (2008). *Digital literacies: Concepts, policies and practices.* Peter Lang.

Latour, B. (1999). *Pandora's hope: Essays on the reality of science studies.* Harvard University Press.

Lave, J., & Wenger, E. (1991). *Situated learning: Legitimate peripheral participation.* Cambridge University Press.

Lee, Y., & Hirvela, A. (2010). Technology and "self-sponsored" writing: A case study of a Korean-American adolescent. *Computers and Composition, 27*(2), 94–111.

Lemke, J. L. (2008). Identity, development and desire: Critical questions. In C. R. Caldas-Coulthard & R. Iedema (Eds.), *Identity trouble: Critical discourse and contested identities* (pp. 17–42). Springer.

Lenhart, A., Purcell, K., Smith, A., & Zickuhr, K. (2010). *Social media and young adults.* Pew Research Center. http://www.pewinternet.org/Reports/2010/Social-Media-and-Young-Adults.aspx

Leon, K., & Pigg, S. (2011). Graduate students professionalizing in digital time/space: A view from "down below." *Computers and Composition, 28*(1), 3–13.

Livingstone, S. (2008). Taking risky opportunities in youthful content creation: Teenagers' use of social networking sites for intimacy, privacy and self-expression. *New Media & Society, 10*(3), 393–411.

Lunsford, A., & Ede, L. (1984). Audience addressed/audience invoked: The role of audience in composition theory and pedagogy. *College Composition and Communication, 35*(2), 155–171.

Lunsford, A., Fishman, J., & Liew, W. (2013). College writing, identification, and the production of intellectual property: Voices from the Stanford study of writing. *College English, 75*(5), 470–492.

Madden, M. (2012). *Privacy management on social media sites.* Pew Research Center. https://www.pewinternet.org/2012/02/24/privacy-management-on-social-media-sites/

Madden, M., & Smith, A. (2010). *Reputation management and social media.* Pew Research Center. https://www.pewinternet.org/2010/05/26/reputation-management-and-social-media/

Madden, M., & Zickuhr, K. (2011). *65% of online adults use social networking sites.* Pew Research Center. http://www.pewinternet.org/Reports/2011/Social-Networking-Sites/Report.aspx?view=all

Maraj, L. M. (2020). *Black or right: Anti/racist campus rhetorics.* University Press of Colorado.

Maranto, G., & Barton, M. (2010). Paradox and promise: MySpace, Facebook, and the sociopolitics of social networking in the writing classroom. *Computers and Composition, 27*(1), 36–47.

Marwick, A. E. (2008). To catch a predator? The MySpace moral panic. *First Monday, 13*(6).

Marwick, A. E. (2013). *Status update: Celebrity, publicity, and branding in the social media age.* Yale University Press.

Marwick, A. E., & boyd, d. (2011). I tweet honestly, I tweet passionately: Twitter users, context collapse, and the imagined audience. *New Media & Society, 13*(1), 114–133.

Marwick, A. E., & boyd, d. (2014). Networked privacy: How teenagers negotiate context in social media. *New Media & Society, 16*(7), 1051–1067.

Massanari, A. (2017). #Gamergate and The Fappening: How Reddit's algorithm, governance, and culture support toxic technocultures. *New Media & Society, 19*(3), 329–346.

Mayer-Schönberger, V. (2011). *Delete: The virtue of forgetting in the digital age.* Princeton UP.

McKee, H. A. (2011). Policy matters now and in the future: Net neutrality, corporate data mining, and government surveillance. *Computers and Composition, 28*(4), 276–291.

McKee, H. A., & Porter, J. E. (2009). *The ethics of internet research: A rhetorical, case-based process*. Peter Lang.

McKew, M. (2018, October 3). Brett Kavanaugh and the information terrorists trying to reshape America. *Wired.* https://www.wired.com/story/information-terrorists-trying-to-reshape-america/

McNely, B. J. (2010). Exploring a sustainable and public information ecology. *Proceedings of the 28th ACM International Conference on Design of Communication,* 103–108.

McNely, B. J. (2015). Instagram, geocaching, and the when of rhetorical literacies. *Kairos: A Journal of Rhetoric, Technology, and Pedagogy, 19*(3). http://kairos.technorhetoric.net/19.3/topoi/mcnely/index.html

Medina, C., & Pimentel, O. (Eds.). (2018). *Racial shorthand: Coded discrimination contested in social media.* Computers and Composition Digital Press/Utah State University Press. https://ccdigitalpress.org/shorthand

Melanson, M. (2010, November 16). Facebook confirms bug disabled user accounts, fix in progress. *ReadWriteWeb.* Retrieved from http://www.readwriteweb.com/archives/female_facebook_users_take_to_twitter_complain_of.php

Mina, L. W. (2017). Social media in the FYC class: The new digital divide. In *Social writing/social media: Publics, presentations, and pedagogies* (pp. 263–282). WAC Clearinghouse/University Press of Colorado.

Nakamura, L. (2002). *Cybertypes: Race, ethnicity, and identity on the internet.* Routledge.

Nakamura, L. (2008). *Digitizing race: Visual cultures of the internet.* University of Minnesota Press.

Nakamura, L., & Chow-White, P. (Eds.). (2013). *Race after the internet.* Routledge.

Nicotra, J. (2016). Disgust, distributed: Virtual public shaming as epideictic assemblage. *Enculturation: A Journal of Rhetoric, Writing, and Culture.* http://enculturation.net/disgust-distributed

Noble, S. U. (2018). *Algorithms of oppression: How search engines reinforce racism.* NYU Press.

Odell, J. (2019). *How to do nothing: Resisting the attention economy.* Melville House.

Ong, W. J. (1975). The writer's audience is always a fiction. *PMLA, 90*(1), 9–21.

O'Reilly, T. (2005, September 30). *What is Web 2.0.* O'Reilly Media. https://www.oreilly.com/pub/a/web2/archive/what-is-web-20.html

Oudshoorn, N. E. J., & Pinch, T. (2003). *How users matter: The co-construction of users and technologies.* https://research.utwente.nl/en/publications/how-users-matter-the-co-construction-of-users-and-technologies

Paasonen, S. (2002). Gender, identity, and (the limits of) play on the internet. In M. Consalvo & S. Paasonen (Eds.), *Women & everyday uses of the internet: Agency & identity* (pp. 21–43). Peter Lang.

Parramore, L. (2010, October 10). The Filter Bubble. *The Atlantic.* https://www.theatlantic.com/daily-dish/archive/2010/10/the-filter-bubble/181427/

Penney, J., & Dadas, C. (2014). (Re)Tweeting in the service of protest: Digital composition and circulation in the Occupy Wall Street movement. *New Media & Society, 16*(1), 74–90.

Pew Research Center. (2016). *Social media update 2016.* Pew Research Center. http://www.pewinternet.org/2016/11/11/social-media-update-2016/

Pigg, S. (2014). Emplacing mobile composing habits: A study of academic writing in networked social spaces. *College Composition and Communication, 66*(2), 250–275.

Pigg, S. (2016). Researching social media literacies as emergent practice: Changes in Twitter use after year two of a longitudinal case study. In P. Thomas & P. Takayoshi (Eds.), *Literacy in practice: Writing in private, public, and working lives* (pp. 17–31). Routledge.

Pigg, S., Grabill, J. T., Brunk-Chavez, B., Moore, J. L., Rosinski, P., & Curran, P. G. (2014). Ubiquitous writing, technologies, and the social practice of literacies of coordination. *Written Communication, 31*(1), 91–117.

Porter, J. E. (2007). Forward. In H. McKee & D. DeVoss (Eds.), *Digital writing research: Technologies, methodologies, and ethical issues* (pp. ix–xix). Hampton Press.

Potts, L. (2013). *Social media in disaster response: How experience architects can build for participation.* Routledge.

Potts, L. (2015). Can't stop the fandom: Writing participation in the Firefly 'verse. *Kairos: A Journal of Rhetoric, Technology, and Pedagogy, 19*(3). http://kairos.technorhetoric.net /19.3/topoi/potts/index.html

Powell, A. H. (2007). Access(ing), habits, attitudes, and engagements: Re-thinking access as practice. *Computers and Composition, 24*(1), 16–35.

Prior, P. (1998). *Writing/disciplinarity: A sociohistoric account of literate activity in the academy* (1st ed.). Routledge.

Prior, P., & Hengst, J. (2010). *Exploring semiotic remediation as discourse practice.* Springer.

Prior, P., & Shipka, J. (2003). Chronotopic lamination: Tracing the contours of literate activity. In C. Bazerman & D. R. Russell (Eds.), *Writing selves/writing societies: Research from activity perspectives.* https://wac.colostate.edu/docs/books/selves_societies/prior /prior.pdf

Rainie, L., & Duggan, M. (2015). *Privacy and information sharing.* Pew Research Center. https://www.pewinternet.org/2016/01/14/privacy-and-information-sharing/

Raynes-Goldie, K. (2010). Aliases, creeping, and wall cleaning: Understanding privacy in the age of Facebook. *First Monday, 15*(1). https://doi.org/10.5210/fm.v15i1.2775

Reilly, C. A. (2020). Critical digital literacies and online surveillance. In E. Beck & L. Hutchinson (Eds.), *Privacy matters: Conversations about surveillance within and beyond the classroom* (pp. 17–35). University Press of Colorado.

Rettberg, J. W. (2014). *Seeing ourselves through technology: How we use selfies, blogs and wearable devices to see and shape ourselves.* Springer.

Reyman, J. (2013). User data on the social web: Authorship, agency, and appropriation. *College English, 75*(5), 513–533.

Reyman, J. (2017). The rhetorical agency of algorithms. In A. Hess & A. Davisson (Eds.), *Theorizing digital rhetoric* (pp. 112–125). Routledge.

Rheingold, H. (1993). *The virtual community: Homesteading on the electronic frontier.* MIT Press.

Richardson, E., & Ragland, A. (2018). #StayWoke: The language and literacies of the #BlackLivesMatter movement. *Community Literacy Journal, 12*(2) 27–56.

Ridolfo, J., & DeVoss, D. N. (2009). Composing for recomposition: Rhetorical velocity and delivery. *Kairos: A Journal of Rhetoric, Technology, and Pedagogy, 13*(2). https://kairos .technorhetoric.net/13.2/topoi/ridolfo_devoss/index.html

Robins, K. (2005). Identity. In T. Bennett, L. Grossberg & M. Morris (Eds.), *New keywords: A revised vocabulary of culture and society* (pp. 172–175). Wiley-Blackwell.

Ronson, J. (2015). *So you've been publicly shamed.* Riverhead Books.

Roozen, K. (2009). From journals to journalism: Tracing trajectories of literate development. *College Composition and Communication, 60*(3), 541–572.

Roozen, K. (2010). Tracing trajectories of practice: Repurposing in one student's developing disciplinary writing processes. *Written communication, 27*(3), 318–354.

Roozen, K., & Erickson, J. (2017). *Expanding literate landscapes: Persons, practices, and sociohistoric perspectives of disciplinary development.* Computers and Composition Digital Press/ Utah State University Press. https://ccdigitalpress.org/expanding

Sawyer, L. (2017). *"Don't try and play me out!": The performances and possibilities of digital Black womanhood* [Doctoral dissertation, Syracuse University]. https://surface.syr.edu/etd /785

Selber, S. (2004). *Multiliteracies for a digital age.* Southern Illinois University Press.

Selfe, C. L. (1999). *Technology and literacy in the 21st century: The importance of paying attention* (1st ed.). Southern Illinois University Press.

Selfe, C. L., & Hawisher, G. E. (2004). *Literate lives in the information age: Narratives of literacy from the United States* (1st ed.). Lawrence Erlbaum Associates.

Shepherd, R. P. (2015). FB in FYC: Facebook use among first-year composition students. *Computers and Composition, 35,* 86–107.

Shepherd, R. P. (2016). Men, women, and Web 2.0 writing: Gender difference in Facebook composing. *Computers and Composition, 39,* 14–26.

Sheridan, D., Street, B. V., & Bloome, D. (2000). *Writing ourselves: Mass-observation and literacy practices.* Hampton Press.

Sheridan, M. P. (2009). *Girls, feminism, and grassroots literacies: Activism in the GirlZone.* SUNY Press.

Sherman, A., & Frier, S. (2016, September 26). *Disney is working with an adviser on potential Twitter bid.* Bloomberg. https://www.bloomberg.com/news/articles/2016-09-26/disney-said-to-be-working-with-adviser-on-potential-twitter-bid

Shirky, C. (2008). *Here comes everybody: The power of organizing without organizations.* Penguin.

Smith, A. (2010, December 9) *Who tweets?* Pew Research Center. http://pewresearch.org/pubs/1821/twitter-users-profile-exclusiveexamination

Smith, Aaron. (2011, July 11). *Smart phone adoption and use.* Pew Research Center. http://pewinternet.org/Reports/2011/Smartphones.aspx

Smitherman, G. (1986). *Talkin and testifyin: The language of black America* (Vol. 51). Wayne State University Press.

Snyder, I. (2002). *Silicon literacies: Communication, innovation and education in the electronic age.* Psychology Press.

Stake, R. E. (1995). *The art of case study research.* SAGE.

Statista. (n.d.). *Facebook users worldwide 2021.* Statista. Retrieved June 9, 2021, from https://www.statista.com/statistics/264810/number-of-monthly-active-facebook-users-worldwide/

Statista. (2018). *Number of monthly active Twitter users.* Statista. www.statista.com/statistics/282087/number-of-monthly-active-twitter-users/

Steele, C. K. (2016). Signifyin', bitching, and blogging: Black women and resistance discourse online. In S. U. Noble & B. M. Tynes (Eds.), *The intersectional internet: Race, sex, class, and culture online* (pp. 73–93). Peter Lang Publishing.

Steele, C. K. (2018). Black bloggers and their varied publics: The everyday politics of black discourse online. *Television & New Media, 19*(2), 112–127.

Street, B. (2013). Symposium comments. *Literacy in Composition Studies, 1*(1), 38–41.

Street, B. V. (1984). *Literacy in theory and practice.* Cambridge University Press.

Street, B. V. (1995). *Social literacies: Critical approaches to literacy in development, ethnography and education.* Routledge.

Takayoshi, P. (2018). Writing in social worlds: An argument for researching composing processes. *College Composition and Communication, 69*(4), 550–580.

Thomas, P., & Takayoshi, P. (2016). Methodological matters and the invisibility of literacy. In *Literacy in practice: Writing in private, public, and working lives* (pp. 1–14). Routledge.

Tiidenberg, K. (2018). *Selfies: Why we love (and hate) them.* Emerald Group Publishing.

Trice, M., & Potts, L. (2018). Building dark patterns into platforms: How GamerGate perturbed Twitter's user experience. *Present Tense: A Journal of Rhetoric in Society, 6*(3). http://www.presenttensejournal.org/volume-6/building-dark-patterns-into-platforms-how-gamergate-perturbed-twitters-user-experience/

Tufekci, Z. (2017). *Twitter and tear gas: The power and fragility of networked protest.* Yale University Press.

Tufekci, Z. (2018, April 6). Why Zuckerberg's 14-year apology tour hasn't fixed Facebook. *Wired.* https://www.wired.com/story/why-zuckerberg-15-year-apology-tour-hasnt-fixed-facebook/

Turkle, S. (1995). *Life on the screen: Identity in the age of the internet.* Simon & Schuster.

Turkle, S. (2011). *Alone together: Why we expect more from technology and less from each other.* Basic Books.

Tynes, B., Schuschke, J., & Noble, S. U. (2016). Digital intersectionality theory and the #BlackLivesMatter movement. In S. U. Noble & B. M. Tynes (Eds.), *The intersectional internet: Race, sex, class, and culture online* (pp. 21–40). Peter Lang Publishing.

van Dijck, J. (2013). *The culture of connectivity: A critical history of social media.* Oxford University Press.

van Dijck, J., & Poell, T. (2016). Understanding the promises and premises of online health platforms. *Big Data & Society, 3*(1). https://doi.org/10.1177/2053951716654173

Vee, A. (2017). *Coding literacy: How computer programming is changing writing.* MIT Press.

Vie, S. (2008). Digital divide 2.0: "Generation M" and online social networking sites in the composition classroom. *Computers and Composition, 25*(1), 9–23.

Vie, S. (2015). What's going on?: Challenges and opportunities for social media in the writing classroom. *The Journal of Faculty Development, 29*(2), 35–44.

Vie, S. (2018). Social media as multimodal composing: Networked rhetorics and writing in a digital age. In J. Alexander & J. Rhodes (Eds.), *The Routledge handbook of digital writing and rhetoric* (pp. 115–123). Routledge.

Vieira, K. (2013). On the social consequences of literacy. *Literacy in Composition Studies, 1*(1), 26–32.

Walls, D. (2017). Visualizing boutique data in egocentric networks. In *Social writing/social media: Publics, presentations, and pedagogies* (pp. 145–160). WAC Clearinghouse/University Press of Colorado.

West, L. (2017, January 3). I've left Twitter. It is unusable for anyone but trolls, robots and dictators. *The Guardian.* https://www.theguardian.com/commentisfree/2017/jan/03/ive-left-twitter-unusable-anyone-but-trolls-robots-dictators-lindy-west

West, S., & Pope, A. (2018). Corporate kairos and the impossibility of the anonymous, ephemeral messaging dream. *Present Tense: A Journal of Rhetoric in Society, 6*(3). http://www.presenttensejournal.org/volume-6/corporate-kairos-and-the-impossibility-of-the-anonymous-ephemeral-messaging-dream/

Williams, B. (2009). *Shimmering literacies: Popular culture and reading and writing online* (First printing edition). Peter Lang Inc., International Academic Publishers.

Williams, B. T. (2017). Having a feel for what works: Polymedia, emotion, and literacy practices with mobile technologies. In D. Walls & S. Vie (Eds.), *Social writing/social media: Publics, presentations, and pedagogies* (p. 17). WAC Clearinghouse/University Press of Colorado.

Wolff, W. I. (2015). Baby, we were born to tweet: Springsteen fans, the writing practices of in situ tweeting, and the research possibilities for Twitter. *Kairos: A Journal of Rhetoric, Technology, and Pedagogy, 19*(3). http://kairos.technorhetoric.net/19.3/topoi/wolff/index.html

Wolff, W. I. (2018). Programmed method: Developing a toolset for capturing and analyzing tweets. *Kairos: A Journal of Rhetoric, Technology, and Pedagogy, PraxisWiki, 22*(2). http://praxis.technorhetoric.net/tiki-index.php?page=PraxisWiki%3A_%3ATwitter+Archives

Wysocki, A. F., & Johnson-Eilola, J. (1999). Blinded by theletter: Why are we using literacy as a metaphor for everything else? In G. E. Hawisher & C. L. Selfe (Eds.), *Passions pedagogies and 21st century technologies* (pp. 349–368). Utah State University Press.

Young, A. (2018, August 12). *RIP selective tweets: 27th Jan 2009–1st Aug 2018.* Medium. https://insomanic.me.uk/rip-selective-tweets-27th-jan-2009-1st-aug-2018-2babc22aad57

Young, V. A. (2009). "Nah, we straight": An argument against code switching. *Jac,* 49–76.

Zephoria. (2016). *Top 15 valuable Facebook statistics.* Zephoria. https://zephoria.com/top-15-valuable-facebook-statistics/

INDEX

Page numbers followed by *n* indicate an endnote.

Abelmann, Nancy, 98
Academia.edu, 60, 61, 65, 75, 152, 160, 165, 179
Accidental Billionaires, The, (Mezrich), 3
activism, 10, 12, 16, 48, 82, 188, 192
activists, 16, 67, 83–84, 90, 188
affordances, of social media, 30–33, 52 74–75; participants' use of, 103–104, 108–112, 133, 139, 147, 167, 174, 176
algorithmic audiences. *See* audience
algorithms, 14, 17, 41–42, 74, 128–131, 135, 137, 186–187
Alone Together (Turkle), 172–173
alt-right, 188
Amidon, Tim. R., 146
Android, 117
Anson, Chris, 108
antiprogram, 132
Apple, 64–65
Arab Spring, 7, 12, 187
archive, digital, 23, 100, 170, 186
Archive of Our Own, 9
Arola, Kristin, 14–15, 23, 37, 44, 184
Asian Avenue, 3
assemblage, 9, 12–13, 19, 22, 38–41, 113, 117–133, 148, 174, 177, 192
Association of Internet Researchers, 55
audience, algorithmic audiences, 30; audience addressed, 33–34; audience invoked, 33–34; intended/unintended audience, 44–45, 58, 116–118, 133, 137, 180; managing audience groups, 5–8, 18–20, 72–112, 148, 176–177; professional audiences, 20, 45–46, 147, 149–171, 178–179; research on, 30–36, 188–192; strategies for, 36–40, 45–46, 134–135, 174–175; trends on social media, 184–186

Banks, Adam, 26, 29; *Race, Rhetoric, and Technology,* 13, 183, 187
Barton, David, 24
Bawden, David, 26, 28
Beck, Estee, 14, 113, 192; *Privacy Matters,* 14, 40, 113

Benjamin, Ruha, 14, 173
Berry, Patrick, 27, 30, 51, 112, 125
Besnier, Nico, 28
Blackboxing, 41, 129
#BlackLivesMatter, 7, 12, 16, 187–188, 192
BlackPlanet, 3, 10, 183, 187
Black Twitter, 15, 181
blog, 9–11, 16, 55, 61, 64–67, 75–76, 79, 96, 125, 136–137, 143–148, 154, 175, 179, 192
blogger, 4, 33–34, 60, 63, 80–82, 93, 109, 149, 156, 162, 172, 176
Blogger (platform), 61, 64
bots, 3–4
boyd, danah, 8–10, 19, 33–34, 37, 39–40, 60, 94, 134, 149, 183; *It's Complicated,* 15, 166
Boyd, Patricia, 152
Brandt, Deborah, 28, 51, 191
#bringbackourgirls, 16
Brock, André, 13, 15, 29, 34, 44, 110, 151, 173, 181, 187
Brooke, Collin, 28, 175
Brown, Nicole, 48
Bruckman, Amy, 57
Buck, Elizabeth, 17
Bullinger, Cory, 17
Butler, Judith, 43
Byrd, Antonio, 52
Byrne, Dara, 183

Cagle, Lauren, 38, 120
Cain, Carole, 43
Cambridge Analytica, 4, 14, 115–117
Carr, Nicholas, 4
Casanave, Christine, 151
case study methodology, 19, 49, 56, 180–182
Castells, Manuel, 42
catfish (internet practice), 107, 184
Catfish (film), 4, 106, 184
Cedillo, Christina, 151, 173
chronotopic laminations, 119
circulation, 35–37, 49, 99, 103, 111, 114, 118, 142, 192; deep circulation, 118
Club Penguin, 67

Coad, David, 17, 109
Cohen, Julie, 148
Cohn, Jenae, 146
conceptual objects, 133
Conover, Adam, 88
context collapse, 19, 32–35, 37, 73, 79, 84, 89, 100, 157, 162, 185
Cooper, Marilyn, 27
COVID-19, 189
critical digital literacies. See literacy
crowdsourcing, 11–12
Culik, Hugh, 146
Cyworld, 60, 62, 91–93, 124–125, 137–138, 175, 177, 183

Dadas, Caroline, 16, 47, 54
data collection, by platforms, 13–15, 40, 142, 146
data scraping, 48, 71
dataveillance, 173
deep circulation. See circulation
defensive strategies, 32, 37, 41–42, 46, 101–104, 133–145, 152, 160–163, 179
Delete (Mayer-Schonberger), 72
delivery, 35, 103
desktop computer, 21, 39, 41, 62, 65, 121, 125–126
DeVoss, Danielle, 35, 103, 176; Digital Writing Research, 47–48
Digg, 11, 61, 143
digital detox, 172
digital literacy. See literacy
digital multitasking, 119
digital writing, 6, 16, 47–48
Digital Writing Research (McKee & DeVoss), 47–48
discussion board, 152, 185
disinformation, 4, 7, 12, 115, 184, 188–190
Disney, 5
Dubisar, Abby, 110–111
Duthely, Regina, 6

e-reader, 118
eBay, 8
Ede, Lisa, 33, 74–75
Edwards, Dustin, 9, 15, 38, 118
Electronic Privacy Information Center to the Federal Trade Commission, 4, 114
Ellison, Nicole B., 8–10, 60, 94, 149, 183
environment selecting and structuring practices (ESSPs), 125–126
Erickson, Joe, 30, 50–51
Ethics of Internet Research, The (McKee & Porter), 54–55, 57–58
Etsy, 65

Facebook, algorithms, 129, 135, 186–187; audience management on, 33–37, 82–92, 97–109, 161–165, 169, 175–178; company of, 3–5, 7–11, 114–118, 129–133, 138–139, 185, 191–192; data privacy and, 4, 39, 118–146, 178; Facebook Connect, 114; Facebook Groups, 16, 121, 135, 140, 145; news feed, 10, 23, 40, 94, 114, 135, 186; posts, 38, 50–52, 122; profiles, 57–58, 60–69, 111, 133, 163, 172, 184; wall, 39, 135
Facebook Effect, The (Kirkpatrick), 3, 39, 183
Fairey, Shepard, 36
Faris, Michael, 17
FarmVille, 8
Ferguson protests, 7, 12, 187
filter bubble, 186
filters, 184
finsta, 67nn4–68, 140–141
Flickr, 8, 10, 11, 61, 63–64, 76, 91, 97, 143
Floyd, George, 188
following (internet practice), 6, 9, 56, 75, 156–157, 162, 165, 181
#FOMO, 172, 184
Forbes, Cassidy & Jessica, 93
Foursquare, 183
friending (internet practice), 6, 9, 37, 56–57, 94, 138, 184
Friendster, 3, 10–11, 66, 106, 149, 183
Frost, Erin, 17

Gaia Online, 67
Gallagher, John, 34–35, 75, 177
#GamerGate, 4n11, 12, 48, 189
Gee, James, 24
Gelms, Bridget, 9, 15, 38
gender, 17, 27, 43–44, 106, 113, 150–151, 170–171, 175
Genishi, Celia, 56
genre, 11, 21, 28, 31–32, 38, 80, 107–111, 158, 167, 174, 184
Gilliard, Chris, 146, 192
Gilster, Paul, 26
Goodreads, 9, 91
Goode, Joanna, 166
Google, 58–59, 63–64, 129, 160, 165, 186, 191; Google+, 183, 185; Google Docs, 146
Grabill, Jeff, 6
Gries, Laurie, 36
Grindr, 15
Grossman, Lev, 11
GroupMe, 52, 61, 89, 185
Groupon, 8

Haas, Christina, 28
Haas Dyson, Anne, 56
Hamilton, Mary, 24
Haraway, Donna, 43
Hart-Davidson, Bill, 6, 69–70
Hargittai, Eszter, 39
hashtag, 23, 50, 74, 109–111, 188, 190;
    hashtagging, 17, 29; on Instagram,
    49–50; on Twitter, 16, 72, 78–81, 88, 90,
    107, 122, 128, 160, 176, 184. *See also* tag
Haugen, Frances, 4
Hawisher, Gail E., 25, 27–28, 30
Hengst, Julie, 22, 51
Hirvela, Alan, 124
Holland, Dorothy, 43
Horner, Bruce, 24, 26
How to Do Nothing (Odell), 172–173
Hutchinson / Hutchinson Campos, Les,
    29–30, 38, 83, 132, 192; *Privacy Matters*,
    14, 40, 113

Ibarra, Herminia, 152
Identity, digital identity, 33–34, 40, 44, 103,
    131–132, 144, 179–180, 182; identity rep-
    resentation, 4–5, 12–16, 20, 37, 40, 56,
    68, 70, 73, 75–77, 95, 118, 135–139, 187,
    190, 192; identity tourism, 106; invis-
    ible digital identity, 14, 146; networked
    online identity, 44; professional iden-
    tity, 42, 45–46, 76, 80, 83, 147, 146–171;
    race and, 16, 28–29, 33–34, 43–44,
    151; theories of, 43–45, 106–107, 118,
    146–148, 172–174
influencers, 149, 187
Instagram, 5, 11, 37, 60–68, 149, 177,
    183–184, 186–187; audience and, 23, 77,
    101, 137–138, 140–141, 177; photos on,
    6, 87–90, 97, 101, 109, 119–121; research
    of, 48, 49–52
interfaces, 14–15, 27–28, 39, 47–48, 92, 114,
    116–123, 133, 141, 154, 175, 178–182
Internet Research Agency, 108, 185
inward-facing information, 134, 141–146
iPhone, 61, 63, 105, 117, 120, 126
It's Complicated (boyd), 15, 166
Ivanič, Roz, 24, 44–45

Johnson-Eilola, Johndan, 25, 133
Jones, Leslie, 4
Joost, Henry, 4, 106

Kaepernick, Colin, 90
KaKaoTalk, 125
Korea, 62, 91–93, 124–125, 177
King, Shawn, 90

Kirkpatrick, David, *Facebook Effect*, 3, 39,
    183
Knobel, Michele, 14, 25–26, 28
Korn, Jenny, 16
Kress, Gunther R., 25
Kynard, Carmen, 28

Lachicotte, William, 43
Lagman, Eileen, 28, 52
lala, 64, 91
Lam, Wan Shun Eva, 124
Lange, Patricia, 110–111
Lanier, Jaron, *You Are Not a Gadget*, 4,
    172–173
Lankshear, Colin, 14, 25–26, 28
laptop, 39, 41, 50, 61–66, 105, 118, 121, 175
Laquintano, Tim, 28
last.fm, 21, 60, 69, 91, 122, 130, 132, 175, 183
Lave, Jean, 151
Lee, Youngjoo, 124
Lemke, Jay, 42–43, 150–151
Leon, Kendall, 50–51, 70, 119
LibraryThing, 61
Life on the Screen (Turkle), 43–44, 106, 118
likes & liking (internet practice), 6, 57, 90,
    100, 104, 113, 129
LinkedIn, 5, 11, 61–67, 69, 75, 135, 152–154,
    160–165, 170, 175
Literacy, 6, 24–32, 43; critical literacy, 27,
    29–30, 192; digital literacy, 7–8, 18–23,
    25–32, 174–175, 178, 180–184, 188,
    192; functional literacy, 27; literacy
    ecologies, 27–30; literacy events, 22, 28,
    52–53; literacy practices, 5, 8, 10, 13,
    16–32, 40–42, 47–53, 70–71, 73, 113–114,
    175, 177, 188–192; literacy sponsor,
    61–65, 191; literate activity, 8, 18, 20–23,
    28, 30–31, 49–53, 119, 175, 189–190;
    New Literacy Studies, 24–25, 28; rhetor-
    ical literacy, 27, 31, 49; situated digital
    literacy practices, 21–22, 32, 52–53, 60,
    74, 122, 173–175, 182
LiveJournal, 10, 63–64
LookBook
Lunsford, Andrea, 6, 33, 74–75

Manjoo, Farhad, 93
Maraj, Louis, 17, 28–29, 110, 188
Markham, Annette, 54
Marwick, Alice, 19, 33–34, 40, 134, 136;
    Status Update, 10–11, 15, 20, 98, 149,
    169, 172, 187
Mayer-Schonberger, Viktor, *Delete*, 72
McKee, Heidi, 13–14, 47, 191–192; *Digital
    Writing Research*, 47–48; *Ethics of Internet*

Research, 54–55, 57–58
McNely, Brian, 16, 48–50
medial interfaces, 175
Medina, Cruz, 181
Meta. *See* Facebook and Instagram
Mezrich, Ben, *Accidental Billionaires,* 3
microcelebrities, 16, 149, 172, 187
MiGente, 3, 10, 187
Mina, Lilian, 17
Miranda, Lin-Manuel, 89
Muller, Robert, 4
multimodality, 29, 60, 146–47
Myspace, 3, 10–11, 15, 61, 63–66, 72, 76, 149, 183

Nakamura, Lisa, 44, 106, 118
Napster, 63
network society, 42
New Literacy Studies, 24–25, 28. *See also* literacy
New London Group, 27
news feed, 9–10, 14, 17, 74, 92, 129, 137, 184, 186–187. *See also* Facebook news feed, Twitter news feed
Nicotra, Jodie, 13, 38
Ning, 61, 183
NLS. *See* New Literacy Studies
Noble, Safiya, 14, 129, 173, 186
Novotny, Maria, 29–30

Obama, Barack & Michelle, 36, 129
Occupy movement, 187
Odell, Jenny, *How to Do Nothing,* 172–173
Ong, Walter, 33
O'Reilly, Tim, 11
Orkut, 64–65
Oudshoorn, Nelly, 132
outward-facing information, 133–134, 146

Palmeri, Jason, 110–111
Pariser, Eli, 186
Periscope, 183
Perry, Tyler, 129
Petriglieri, Jennifer L., 152
Pew Internet and American Life Project, 5, 18, 139
Picasa, 64
Pigg, Stacey, 17, 50–51, 70, 119, 127
Pimentel, Octavio, 181
Pinch, Trevor, 132
Pinterest, 5, 67–68, 91, 104, 135
platform studies, 9
Poell, Tomas, 9
politics, 3–12, 53, 83, 90, 101, 151, 177, 185–192

Porter, James, 47, *Ethics of Internet Research,* 54–55, 57–58
Potts, Liza, 16
Powell, Annette Harris, 29
Prior, Paul, 22, 50–51, 119, 125, 151,
privacy, 3–5, 14–15, 113–118, 146–148, 172, 174–178, 190–192; networked privacy, 40, 71, 134–137; privacy settings, 37–42, 53–56, 74, 101–107, 138–145, 161–170
Privacy Matters (Beck & Hutchinson Campos), 14, 40, 113
proactive strategies, 36–37, 41, 45, 75, 91, 118, 127, 166, 178
profile picture, 37, 70, 94–95, 99, 105, 138, 161–163, 169
PureVolume, 61, 76

queer theory, 54
Quinn, Zoe, 4n1

race, 26, 28–30, 43–44, 129–130, 151, 170–171, 174
Ragland, Alice, 16
Race, Rhetoric, and Technology (Banks), 13, 183, 187
Ravelry, 9, 60, 64–65, 93–97, 109, 175, 183
Raynes-Goldie, Kate, 39, 134
Reddit, 9, 109
Reilly, Colleen, 146
Reyman, Jessica, 14, 113, 117–118, 133
Representation. *See* identity representation
Rheingold, Howard, 96
rhetorical literacy. *See* literacy
rhetorical velocity, 7, 32, 35, 73, 90, 99–100, 103, 111, 176
Richardson, Elaine, 16
Ridolfo, Jim, 35, 103, 176
Robins, Kevin, 42
Rohingya, 4
Ronson, Jon, 36, 72–73; *So You've Been Publicly Shamed,* 73, 173
Roozen, Kevin, 30, 50–51
Rosario-Ramos, Enid, 124

Sacco, Justine, 72–73
Sarkeesian, Anita, 4n1
Sawyer, LaToya, 16, 51
Schrage, Elliot, 115
Schulman, Ariel, 106
Schumer, Charles, 4, 114
Selber, Stuart, 27, 30
Selective Tweets, 122n2
self-censorship, 101, 103, 134–138
Selfe, Cynthia L., 13, 25–28, 30
selfie, 67, 77, 109, 184

Shallows, The (Carr), 4
Shepherd, Ryan, 17
Sheridan, Dorothy, 52, 180
Sheridan, Mary, 52
Shimmering Literacies (Williams), 16
Shipka, Jody, 50, 119, 125
Silicon Valley, 10, 149, 172
SixDegrees, 3, 10
Skinner, Debra, 43
Skype, 60, 66
Smith, Will, 129
Snap, 5. *See also* Snapchat
Snapchat, 5–6, 23, 52, 67, 186. *See also*
    Snap
Snyder, Stacy, 72–73
So You've Been Publicly Shamed (Ronson),
    73, 173
Social media. *See* names of individual
    platforms
social media platform, definition of, 6–7,
    9–20; future of, 188–191. *See also* names
    of individual platforms
Social Network, The (Sorkin), 3–4
social network site, definition of, 8–10, 60;
    study of, 13–18, 189–192. *See also* names
    of individual platforms
sock puppet, 185
Sorkin, Aaron, *The Social Network*, 3–4
Spotify, 66, 91
Springsteen, Bruce, 16, 48
Stanford Study of Writing, 6
Status Update (Marwick), 10–11, 15, 20, 98,
    149, 169, 172, 187
strangershots, 38
Steele, Catherine Knight, 16, 33, 44
Street, Brian, 22–28

tag, internet practice, 40, 99–103, 113, 135,
    152–154, 170, 176; untag, 99–100, 103,
    135, 152. *See also* hashtags
Takayoshi, Pamela, 16–17, 24, 30
Thomas, Patrick, 24, 30
TikTok, 23, 52
time-use diary, 69–70, 189–190
Trump, Donald, 4, 108, 189
Tufekci, Zeynep, 115–116
Tumblr, 18, 61, 64, 75–76, 110–111, 136, 175
Turing test, 107
Turkle, Sherry, *Alone Together*, 172–173; *Life
    on the Screen*, 43–44, 106, 118

Tweet. *See* Twitter
12seconds, 120–121, 183
TwitPic, 120–121, 130, 177, 183
Twitter, activism and, 4, 12, 48; audience
    on, 33–34, 36–37, 72, 75–87, 90–92, 96,
    104–111, 164, 170, 176–177; company,
    3–5, 10, 133, 186–188; data management
    and, 119–128, 130, 135–139, 144–147;
    news feed, 6, 23, 83, 119; participant
    accounts, 21, 60–69, 175; professional
    communities on, 151–162, 179; research
    on, 15–18, 48, 55, 57–58, 181–184
Twitterific, 63, 126

United States, 11–12, 60–62, 91, 125, 174,
    180, 186
Usenet groups, 11, 185
user-generated content, 8–9, 11, 61

van Dijck, José, 6, 8–15
Vee, Annette, 25–29
Vie, Stephanie, 7, 16–17
Vieira, Kate, 24, 28
Vimeo, 64
Vine, 121, 183
viral/virality, 35, 90, 110

Walls, Douglas, 16, 50
Watson, Emma, 89
Wayne, Lil, 129
Weebly, 168
Wenger, Etienne, 151
West, Lindy, 4–5
WhatsApp, 11, 52, 125, 185
web design, 23, 61
Williams, Bronwyn, 16; *Shimmering Litera-
    cies*, 16
Wolff, William, 16, 48
WordPress, 9, 62, 64, 67, 168
Wu, Brianna, 4n1
Wysocki, Anne. F., 25

#yesallwomen, 16
Yiannopolos, Milo, 4
YikYak, 15, 52, 64
You Are Not a Gadget, (Lanier), 4, 172–173
YouTube, 5, 8–10, 16, 61–64, 88, 91, 110

Zuckerberg, Mark, 3–4, 11, 115–116
Zynga, 66